D0947778

Sense of the Possible

Sense of the Possible

An Introduction to Theology and Imagination

L. Callid Keefe-Perry

FOREWORD BY
Heather Walton

CASCADE *Books* · Eugene, Oregon

SENSE OF THE POSSIBLE
An Introduction to Theology and Imagination

Cascade Books
An Imprint of Wipf and Stock Publishers
199 W. 8th Ave., Suite 3
Eugene, OR 97401

www.wipfandstock.com

PAPERBACK ISBN: 978-1-4982-8037-2
HARDCOVER ISBN: 978-1-4982-8039-6
EBOOK ISBN: 978-1-4982-8038-9

Cataloguing-in-Publication data:

Names: Keefe-Perry, L. Callid, author. | Walton, Heather, foreword.

Title: Sense of the possible : an introduction to theology and imagination / by L. Callid Keefe-Perry ; foreword by Heather Walton.

Description: Eugene, OR: Cascade Books, 2023 | Includes bibliographical references and index.

Identifiers: ISBN 978-1-4982-8037-2 (paperback) | ISBN 978-1-4982-8039-6 (hardcover) | ISBN 978-1-4982-8038-9 (ebook)

Subjects: LCSH: Imagination–Religious aspects–Christianity | Christian life

Classification: BR115.I6 K10 2023 (print) | BR115.I6 K10 (ebook)

03/10/23

For Melanie—

who first led me through Kaufman's little book and also insisted that I maintain a deep enough spiritual life to be able to do something faithful with it on the other side.

Contents

List of Illustrations

Foreword

THIS BOOK SPEAKS IN clear, concise, and engaging tones. It displays an educator's concern to communicate complex ideas and make them usable in practice. It frames its message respectfully and does not lecture or rebuke. Yet at heart it is a prophetic work. It issues a strong call and an urgent challenge:

> Beloved in Christ. Companions on the way. It's time to move now! Loosen the ties that hold you in place and set out on the journey.
>
> As you go forward do not rely on what your eyes can see or what your ears can hear. For eyes have not seen, ears have not heard what God has prepared for you.
>
> Remember the songs of Zion and sing them on the road. But be ready to speak in strange tongues too—as the time demands and as the Spirit gives you voice.
>
> When darkness falls keep walking. Feel the earth beneath your feet, the sacred presences that surround you and hold each other's hands. Walk by faith and not by sight . . . Imagine!
>
> It is time to move now!

Can imagining be urgent? Surely in these strange and difficult times other things should claim our time and energies. Serious things. Such as peace and reconciliation, climate justice, combatting racism, and renewing the life of our anxious and uncertain churches. Clearly these things matter. However, this book is written for people of faith, out of the conviction that the constraints of customary practices, established identities, and conventional expectations may be restraining us from responding to the crucial challenges of our day. What the poet William Blake called our "mind-forg'd manacles" hold us fast. Perhaps these bindings should be pictured not as rusty chains we would be glad to shake off but rather those strong ties that seem most precious to us. Our shackles may be formed from the very things that help us feel securely anchored in contemporary contexts of deep anxiety concerning the future.

However painful it may be, Callid Keefe-Perry urges us to employ the critical resources of imagination to free ourselves from the comforts of bondage. They tie us to the world as it is and prevent us conceiving its transformation. Clearly imagining in this liberative sense must be understood as far more than dreaming as we sleep or wishing while we are awake. Nor, Keefe-Perry argues, is it to be principally identified with the efforts of artistic creators to produce new perspectives through their skillful manipulation of words and images. This book painstakingly works to unpick our assumptions about what imagining might be. Through introducing us to ancient wisdom and contemporary knowledge concerning this peculiar human faculty we are brought to understand imagining as a familiar and common process of individual and shared visioning. Rooted in everyday life, it reaches beyond this to provoke new ventures in faith, sustain vistas of hope, and ground us in relations of love. In circumstances of constraint in which conventional reason remains bounded, it is imagination that takes flight and sustains a "sense of the possible." Imagination enables us to take risky steps forward into the future.

Eyes have not seen or ears heard.

As Keefe-Perry continually reminds us, imagination is that which opens us to the *future—possible* by enabling us to engage with things that both our physical senses and "common sense" struggle to comprehend. This does not mean that imagining is either an innocent or benign faculty. The current ordering of the world might itself be understood as an imaginative construction that has concretized over time into the powerful social imaginaries that now regulate communal life. Imagining is also active in the formation of the destructive conspiracy theories that fuel contemporary culture wars. By its nature resistant to regulation and correction we must always recognize that imagination is an ambiguous quality. As Keefe-Perry writes, "both our liberation and domination are tied to our ability to imagine."

With this in mind, readers are introduced to the good reasons philosophers and theologians have advanced as to why imagination should be treated with great caution. But these warnings of potential danger are balanced by an appreciation of the ways in which contemporary theologians have valued imagination as a place of encounter; a space in which "deep calls to deep" and the Spirit groans with our spirits as new births are brought forth. In this frame, imagination and hope are closely intertwined as they reach together beyond what sense can reveal. We can quantify our current crises through devastating measurements; how much the average global temperature has risen, how many children live in poverty, what percentage of the world's wildlife has been lost. However, it is the imagination of our hearts that recalibrates these grim realities and allows us to discern within them a divine imperative that calls for our response.

Sadly, as we know, this challenge may go unheeded. Keefe-Perry draws on biblical images which speak of a people whose eyes do not see and whose ears do not hear and reminds us that "the healing of the people requires that they understand with their hearts," a task they are not ready to do "because their hearts have 'grown dull.'" Clearly these prophetic metaphors do not refer to any physical or sensory impairment: "some other issue was preventing them from understanding." We are afflicted by a deadening numbness so severe that hearts can lose all hope of healing. Where vision fails the people perish. But when imagination is renewed new and healing ways of perceiving can become possible. Ones that bring past insights, present concerns, and future possibilities into powerful conjunction.

Sing the old songs but learn to speak in strange tongues too.

When the ancient philosophers considered the nature of imagination, they frequently characterized it as a faculty closely linked to remembering. Similarly, David Hume, the enlightenment thinker, spoke of a wonderful stock of resources previously generated by internal and external senses that imagination was then able to combine with creative variety. Contemporary theorists are less likely to circumscribe imagination in this way. They recognize that disruptive *new* imaginings sometimes take place, provoking decisive breaks with what has gone before and generating new paradigms. The "converting" force of a new vision often strikes us to the ground at first. New concepts, symbols, and practices must be devised through which to express it. But while we seek to comprehend what radical departures from previous ways of being might be called for, we must also be attentive to the memories, stories, and "redemption songs" that can sustain people through change. Though imagination can lead us far from the securities of home, we are still likely to dedicate our babies and consecrate new habitations with the words of an old blessing.

The necessity of honoring an inheritance while still being responsive to the inbreaking of the new poses particular challenges for faith communities in which traditions enjoy a sacred status. Keefe-Perry explores the intense theological disruption takes place when new visions (often born from the insights of marginalized people) raise challenges not easily assimilated or accommodated. One of the lovely qualities of this book is that it fully recognizes that "big" visions have local consequences in the everyday practices of worship, pedagogy, and pastoral care. There are griefs as well as gains to be experienced when old loves confront new longings:

> I think that part of "spiritual maturity" and "religious leadership" has to do with discerning how to walk the path between continuity and change, between tradition and imagined transformation. At any level—from congregational Sunday school to national accrediting organizations—there is imaginative work to be done that can lead to greater faithful flourishing.

You do not walk alone.

The concern to revise life together expressed above is a constant refrain throughout this work. Whether it be at international or local level the desire to nurture flourishing community is the inspiration behind every page we read. At a number of points Keefe-Perry specifically addresses what might be our biggest imaginative challenge of all.

Through many centuries of development, Western culture has contrived a powerful image of individual human autonomy, guided by reason, and has predicated this upon a firm separation of "the human" from the natural order of our living planet. The novelist and climate activist Amitav Ghosh has persuasively written about the madness, or what he calls the "great derangement," of this perspective. He argues that the illusion (or delusion) of discreetness is one reason why we are failing to respond to the urgent signs of environmental collapse. We are quite simply unable to make the connections that need to be made.

It is in this context that the understanding of imagination as bridge making becomes vital. Keefe-Perry presents this as taking place on many levels. First of all, there is the continually traversed bridge between our internal worlds and the external world as visions construct the "reality" that we both receive and transform. Then there are the bridges of empathy, solidarity, and loving care that imagination spans between ourselves and others. We are schooled to celebrate these in our faith and practice, but more is needed. The sacredness of our connection to planetary vitality and the myriad living presences with which we are enfolded must be reimagined. While indigenous peoples of many cultures have retained a sensibility of the deep connections with an intimate mystery that sustains us, Western modernity continues to fantasize about human mastery. Finally, there is the need to rekindle wonder at the ways in which God overcomes all separations through the person and work of Christ. Keefe Perry writes, "imagination . . . is the means to bridge our internal realities to those of others," recognizing the parallel that "Christ is also a bridge between Creation and God." Imagination can illuminate for us the saving truth that God is all, is in all, and works through all things for good.

In the darkness walk in this light.

Feel the earth beneath your feet, the sacred presences that surround you and hold each other's hands. Walk by faith and not by sight . . . Imagine!

Heather Walton

Professor of Theology and Creative Practice
School of Critical Studies
University of Glasgow

Introduction

IF YOU DO A quick internet or library search for topics related to "imagination and theology" or "Christianity and imagination," a couple of things become apparent rather quickly. One trend is that the space between blog posts and technical academic writing is sparsely inhabited. There are not that many books written for nonspecialists who are interested in this topic. What already exists as formal "philosophy of imagination" and "theology of imagination" can get dense *fast* and there hasn't been much work done to help make this material more accessible.

Another notable trend is that discussion of "the imagination and religion" often becomes a conversation about "the arts and religion," with these topics nestled next to each other as if they only come as a pair. What about the imagination itself? What about the intersection of imagination, faith, and *science*? Is art the only place imagination emerges? What role does the imagination play in my everyday life of faith?

This book is written in light of those questions and these trends. It is meant to serve as an introduction to what has been written about imagination and theology in a way that is more accessible than many of the books it references. It attempts to focus on the imagination and its role in Christian faith and practice in a way that doesn't assume the reader has a PhD in theology.

On Style

To help you correctly set your expectations for this book, I thought I'd be clear at the outset with my intentions. One of the reasons I wanted to write this book was that there would be an accessible entry point into the world of academic thinking about imagination and Christianity. This means at least two things to me.

First, it means trying to convey some key ideas about imagination as they pertain to Christianity in an approachable way. This is largely what is behind my decision to write in a more conversational tone than you would usually find in academic books and journal articles. I write in the first person when it seems appropriate, and I sometimes write about *you*, the person reading this book. Second, working toward accessibility means providing broad exposure to the theologians and philosophers who have written explicitly about the topic. For those interested, I hope this book can serve as a signpost to books and articles in which longer, more nuanced exploration of theology and imagination is done. There's also quite a bit about "theological imaginaries," or how the ways we imagine God to be in the world shapes our perception of the world.

If you are looking for heaps of cutting-edge ideas about theology and imagination, you won't find them here. Some of my own constructive thinking about practices and theological imaginaries is present, but mostly I've tried to be a close and generous reader of the work of others, collecting it here for easy access. This book isn't a grand constructive proposal for a unified theology of imagination but a window into some of the significant voices and trends in what has been written thus far. Given the above, this volume is perhaps best considered as a guidebook: you'll hear my voice as the guide throughout, but I'm primarily interested in pointing out the scenery to you.

Of course, the above doesn't mean I've somehow managed to eliminate my own perspectives and theological commitments. For example, throughout the book, I consistently make the argument that I think imagination is something that should be considered more seriously by people of faith, including theologians. I am entirely biased in this regard and don't pretend otherwise. However, the nature of this book as an "introduction to the discussion" means that it doesn't cohere as a single argument: it contains multiple viewpoints from other thinkers that often conflict with one another. Rather than try to resolve tensions between authors, I tend to leave it as it is, inviting you to recognize that multiple paths are available before us.

A book written for the purposes noted above is well-served by some attempts to make the text easily digestible. In terms of citation, that means I do quite a bit of paraphrasing. If I use quotations from people that are technical or particularly jargony, you should know I've included them because it is the language that gets talked about or cited a bunch. That is, I want you to know how people talk about this stuff, even if it is challenging. Block quotes are included when particular phrasing seems important or when an author's style is especially relevant. I've attempted to strike a balance between wanting you to read the actual voices of people writing about imagination and wanting to write this book in a way so that it is easier to read. I've also worked to avoid rabbit hole footnotes that explore side themes without forwarding the main idea. Those few that remain survived my editorial attempts at removal and are things that seem too important not to at least mention.

The chapters have been written assuming some folks will skip around, so feel free to bop about. I do think that reading all the way through might give you a more nuanced experience, but if reading about methodology or doctrine isn't what you're looking for, then by all means, get to the imagination stuff that feels compelling to you. When I reference something that came up in a previous chapter, I note that so you can flip back to find it if you're interested and missed it.

On Audience

First and foremost, this book is for Christians who have little to do with the academy but want to peek in a bit and see what has been said about imagination and faith by people who think and write about that for a living. One of the reasons I was excited to be asked to write this book for Cascade is because one of their goals is to produce books that make academic study accessible to a broader audience. What that means for *this* book is that I was able to write in a way that would be hopefully more accessible, spending more time on explanations of things that might get skipped over in texts written mostly for other academics.

I envision a broad cross section of folks who might have interests in imagination and faith. In fact, I wrote the discussion questions at the end of each chapter hoping that some church small group leaders, pastors, or adult religious education directors out there might find them useful for the church as a whole. Drop me a line if you're one of those folks hoping to use this for your community. Having written much of this during the first waves of COVID-19, I am vividly aware that Zooming into churches is viable: I'd love to be able to support you in your explorations!

Second, this book serves as a survey of the theology and imagination conversation for those interested in getting a sense of the scope of this discussion in the academy. This might mean you're an undergraduate reading this for a class or a seminary student looking to see if you want to dig into some of the more advanced work I reference. I have tried to contextualize all the thinkers I use at length in this book, writing a bit about their background and other things going on in their time and place so that you can get a sense of where they're coming from. I've tried to balance (a) not presuming too much background knowledge on the reader's behalf with (b) not wanting to come off as condescending or overly simplistic. Hopefully, I've come up with a good mix.

Finally, for those who already know they are interested in diving deeper into research on imagination and theology, I hope that the text has some occasionally useful reflections and that how I've oriented the ideas here helps you to see some new constellations in familiar stars. While it would be foolish to say that everything about imagination and Christian theology is referenced in this book, I have intentionally labored to make sure this book is a solid introduction to this material. I've captured many of the different ways this conversation has developed, so between the "Related Readings" sections and the authors I've cited, you'll have a pretty useful sense of where in the bibliography you might want to turn next. I've opted to provide a thorough index for ease of use, thinking that some of you might end up using this book as a quick reference text to brush up on an author or idea.

As I was writing, I tried to keep these three audiences in mind. What I included and how I decided to present it was shaped from the beginning of this project by the idea that I wanted to create a book that would be both comprehensive and relatively easy to read. To that end, I want to thank all the students at both Boston University and Boston College who saw early versions of many of these thoughts. I appreciate all the folks who were part of thinking along with me in early drafts. I'm also incredibly grateful to those who helped me polish and tighten the text in the summer of 2022: Caesar Baldelomar, Holly Baldwin, de'Angelo Dia, Robert Dove McClellan, Zachary Moon, Bob Schmitt, Christian Stanzione, and Kimbol Soques. These audiences and these readers have all helped me to think about what should be referenced in this book and how much attention should be paid to different ideas and authors. Many thanks.

On Curation

Before launching, I thought it might be helpful to share a little about the book's logic in terms of how it is organized and how I selected what content would be discussed. In broad strokes, my vision for curation in this book was primarily twofold: be comprehensive and be expansive.

In this context, I've taken comprehensiveness to mean that the book should spend some substantial time wrestling with the authors and ideas that have been the most significant in the work of *other* authors. For example, in addition to Paul Ricœur being someone who wrote and thought about imagination himself, it is also the case that many scholars refer to his work in their own explorations of that material. As such, there is some lengthy consideration of Ricœur in *this* book: he has had an outsized impact on academic discussions about imagination and theology, so he has a significant presence here.

However, I've also understood comprehensive to mean that the book shouldn't just reference the "big names" and skip over those whose work isn't cited as much. For example, some excellent dissertations and articles written on imagination and theology have not yet found their way into published books. There are also recent volumes published in the last few years and have not yet had time to garner the kind of prestige that can come with decades of presence. If I found a thinker that substantially added something unique to the conversation, I've tried to include them here, whether they are a long-established scholar or not. This is, in part, what I mean by "expansive."

Within the existing books that have a chapter or section dedicated to "the history of imagination and theology," there are some common trends. Usually, a timeline is created that runs something like "Plato to Aristotle to Aquinas to Hume to Kant and Coleridge." Those are the regular players, which gets us to the early 1800s. Going forward from that point to the present, there is somewhat less consistency about who shows up, but some of the frequently appearing folks after that are George MacDonald, Jean-Paul Sartre, William Lynch, Ray Hart, Gordon Kaufman, Paul Ricœur, Amos Wilder, Mary Warnock, David Tracy, John McIntyre, Garrett Green, Richard Kearney, Charles Taylor, and Trevor Hart. Ludwig Feuerbach also shows up a fair bit as well, but many folks are afraid of him. I, however, have invited him to our party just the same. In fact, *all* the folks I just mentioned show up in this book. And . . . as I worked, I became increasingly convinced that there were other thinkers whose work belonged on that list. If you're interested, I created a timeline that you can find in the back of the book, starting on page 223, where you can see who the major players are and when they wrote.

Having "expansiveness" be a guide to my curation has also meant asking questions about what perspectives were left out when the same lineages are published repeatedly. So, into that more common lineage of imagination and theology scholarship, this book has also braided in two additional lines of thought. Specifically, I have opted to include thinkers writing from within some version of liberation theology and those who work with ideas about "imaginaries" and the sociological imagination. In addition to those names above, you'll also hear from Cornelius Castoriadis, Rubem Alves, Mary Daly, Peter Phan, Ada Maria Isasi-Diaz, Kwok Pui-lan, Emilie Townes, and Willie James Jennings. While those scholars don't always talk about imagination the same way as the folk in the first list do, I think they forward scholarship about imagination and theology in critical ways. I include them here precisely because I think they expand the conversation, even if they don't cite Plato, Kant, or Charles Taylor. Perhaps also *because* they do not.

OK. What didn't make the cut and why?

Five major areas of work live adjacent to much of the literature I've considered but have no significant presence in this book. At various points, I thought they might all have a place in here, but by the time I finished wrestling with the chapters, none of them had a spot in this volume. I do, though, feel like you should know what is out there if your interests are piqued. Because I want this book to serve as an expansive overview of theology and imagination, naming the gaps seems useful.

The first significant area that doesn't show up much here is theology from Christian Orthodox traditions. There are a few spots in chapter 4 and chapter 8 where perspectives from Eastern and Russian Orthodox traditions are considered regarding imagination and prayer, but I've hesitated to include more for two reasons. First, the context of Orthodox theology is largely foreign to me and far enough from my research areas that I fear I would not be a faithful interpreter of the tradition. Second, as far as I have been able to tell, the standard Orthodox position is staunchly opposed to the idea that imagination can be usefully and fruitfully included as any part of Christian prayer and formation for the masses. For example, Father Seraphim Rose wrote that "imagination came into use only after the fall of Adam and Eve," is "one of the lowest functions of the soul" and a "favorite playground of the devil," who uses "human imagination in order to deceive and mislead even well-meaning people."[1] While some very holy Orthodox men might be able to faithfully use imagination piously, for the rest of us, the general advice from Orthodox theologians is to steer clear of imagination. While that position is worth noting for a fuller understanding of how imagination is considered theologically, it is a position largely at odds with much of the rest of this book, so it does not often appear here.

The second area not significantly present is contemporary philosophical scholarship on imagination. In focusing on theologies of imagination, this book must secondarily explore some philosophies of imagination. That is unavoidable. A robust discussion is happening in the realm of contemporary philosophy that, while fascinating, is too far from my purposes here to be included. If folks are interested in that, I'd encourage you to turn your attention to the work being done at the Science and Philosophy of Imagination conferences at the University of Bristol in the UK. I'd also highly

---

1. Rose, *Letters*, 12–13.

recommend the *Routledge Handbook of the Philosophy of Imagination*, edited by Amy Kind. It is a treasure trove of recent work.

The third major area I have largely opted to exclude from the rest of the book is the fascinating scholarship about imagination coming out of social science and neurology. For example, the research coming out of The Imagination Institute at the University of Pennsylvania in Philadelphia is exciting, with new measures, insights, and research trajectories developing yearly. Their work is interdisciplinary, with material in education, psychology, and spirituality. There's much value in their work, especially for pastors or community leaders trying to think about how imagination might shape the lives of people of faith. However, in a book focused on imagination and *theology* in particular, including lots of science research was too much.

The fourth notable exclusion is imagination and theology scholarship from other religious traditions. I know of scholarship on religion and imagination in the context of Judaism, Hinduism, Islam, and Buddhism. I don't know how deep those conversations go, but I will note a few pieces in the event others may wish to pursue these avenues.

Medieval Jewish rabbi and scholar Maimonides claimed that prophecy is "the most perfect development of the imaginative faculty."[2] Hindu scholar Sthaneshwar Timalsina argues that "contrary to Western traditions, Indian traditions give centrality to imagination."[3] W. C. Chittick says that the teachings of the Sufi Muhyiddīn Ibn 'Arabi suggest that "the Islamic concept of imagination (*khayál*) . . . is interconnected with every main idea of Islamic thought."[4] In *Buddhist Meditation*, Kamalaśīla claims that "in normal life, you are imagining everything . . . from what you might have for dinner, to what it might be like to meet someone, to how that person themselves might feel. . . . You even imagine yourself—indeed, you do that more than anything else."[5] To what extent these glimpses are indicative of extended scholarship, I'm not clear, but, at the very least, it should be noted that there are many more things to explore about religion and imagination than those that have made it into this book. This text explores *Christian* theological perspectives on imagination.

The fifth and final area of scholarship that is closely related but largely absent is work on theology and the arts. Since so much writing on imagination and theology *does* engage the arts (and you might have been

---

2. Hartman, "On the Jewish Imagination," 202.

3. Timalsina, "Imagining Reality," 50.

4. Chittick. *Sufi Path of Knowledge*, 6.

5. Kamalaśīla, *Buddhist Meditation*, 206.

expecting me to do it as well), I think I should be explicit about my decision *not* to do that and why.

Let me start by saying that there isn't really anything wrong with people sliding quickly from discussions about imagination and theology into the merits and benefits of art for theological reflection. It isn't inherently a problem *per se* to yoke imagination and artistic practice. But . . . it does open the door more widely to at least two things I think *are* problematic: what I call the "elite view problem" and the "Western canon problem."

Having a discussion of "imagination and theology" shift to "theology and the arts" creates conditions in which it is easier to make the "elite view" mistake. I'll talk more about it in the first chapter, but in brief, when imagination is too closely hitched to artistic practice, it is more likely that people will gloss over the fact that imagination is part of much of *all* human experience, not just the narrow realm of what we call "art." I refer to this as the "elite view" problem of imagination because it boxes imagination into far too small of an area of relevance.

Thinking that imagination is mostly just a concern for "creative people" or "artists" misses the point I want to make. Even if expanded to "people who like or appreciate art," I think the art-related approach is too narrow. I'll develop this idea more later, but since it is a central theme throughout the entire book, I'll be clear about it up front: our imaginations are *always* employed whenever we are thinking about the world around us, how we might act in it in the future, and what it means that God is active in our lives. Imagination is part of the process of perception and interpretation. Always. Regardless of whether or not art is involved.

A related problem happens when "theology and imagination" slides into "theology and the arts" and then *that* slides into theological reflection on beauty or aesthetics. Again, it isn't a problem to consider what can be said about beauty from a theological perspective; it is just that this is not the same as staying focused on imagination itself, which I think deserves its own broad discussion. Amazing books about theology, art, and beauty are already out there. This book isn't one of them. The arts will appear periodically in the following chapters, but they are not my focus. Imagination is.

The second reason why I don't focus on "The Arts" as a category—especially with the important capitalization!—is because that area of research has a history of connotation with "fine art," which, in turn, has an undue weighting towards Eurocentrism. This is the "Western canon problem." There are an increasing number of "theology and popular culture" books that don't fall into this category, but they generally only talk about the dailiness of the imagination in terms of music, film, or television, which is a problem for me because of the "elite view" problem noted above. Outside of the pop culture engagements with imagination and theology, the texts that have formed the core of the field of Christian "theology and the arts" are *very* Eurocentric. This is beginning to change somewhat, but the fact is that if you look at the books that have been written about theology and the arts, they are primarily written about "classical" works of European origin.

There isn't anything particularly wrong with focusing on European or European-American art in general. However, because I think that exploring the imagination can be part of *expanding* how we think about God in the world, I don't want to focus on areas of scholarship that have historically marginalized significant portions of the church. Especially since the existing philosophy and Christian theology written about imagination is *itself* primarily male and Eurocentric, I am wary of doubling down on that count.

If you are looking for excellent work that engages more directly with artistic and creative output, I strongly encourage a book series called the "Routledge Studies in Theology, Imagination and the Arts." The editors there have done a consistently excellent job putting together volumes at the cutting edge of scholarship with aesthetics, artists, and Christian theology. Turning to that series will put you directly into some of the best work there is on that intersection.

In addition to that series, I'd also encourage you to pick up *Imagination in an Age of Crisis: Soundings from the Arts and Theology*, a multiauthor volume grounded in a (mostly) Australian context and edited by Jason Goroncy and Rod Pattenden. In a single book, you get a lot of excellent work in art and theology. In the realm of online resources, I suggest you consider Transpsitions.co.uk, ArtAndTheology.net, and JournalARTS.org. Those will also get you connected to the art and theology conversation.

On Structure

The book is set up in three parts. Part I includes chapters 1 through 3 and provides some of the historical and conceptual background on which the rest of the book rests. Part II is chapters 4 through 6 and is where the most-cited writers on imagination and theology are discussed. Imagination is considered in terms of interpretation, theological method, doctrine, and how societies view religion. Part III is chapters 7 through 9, which both consider the ways in which people have explored specific Christian practices and their connection to imagination.

Chapter 1 does three things. First it looks at some of the scriptural contexts in which imagination is discussed, including a consideration of the ways in which what we mean by "imagination" has likely changed over the centuries. Then, in a whirlwind tour of philosophical history, I give a very brief accounting of the development of major, oft-cited writing about imagination in the West, starting with Plato in 347 BCE and ending in the present, which is currently 2022. The chapter closes with a short "working definition" of imagination and seven further clarifications. The definition is used (and nuanced) throughout the rest of the book.

Chapter 2 has some significant exploration of what exactly hermeneutics and apocalypse are and why I think these terms are a useful way to discuss imagination for theological purposes. I talk about why I generally dislike conversations about "types" of imagination and why discussions about a "continuum of imagination" might be preferable. This chapter helps to flesh out a bit more about what imagination is and what it does.

Chapter 3 is a dive into two related issues. First is a consideration, especially prevalent in the Victorian era, that Christians ought to be wary of consuming things that were too imaginative lest their imaginations run wild and lead them into temptation. Why are some traditions fearful of the imagination and what is behind that? Second is the "so is all of this religion stuff just make believe?" issue, in which Feuerbach plays a leading role. The idea of a "hermeneutics of suspicion" is considered, pointing the way to a substantial exploration of Paul Ricœur's work.

Chapter 4 is the beginning of Part II, where the scholars of theology and imagination start to take center stage. After a significant discussion of Ricœur's philosophical ideas about suspicion and affirmation, the theology of Garrett Green is considered. Green is one of the most prolific scholars who has written about theology and imagination and so is worked with at length. The chapter closes with a consideration of the work of Ada Maria Isasi-Diaz, whose own work is resonant with some of Green's conclusions, but for varied reasons than his.

Chapter 5 takes up one of the other most prolific imagination theologians, Gordon Kaufman. The first half of the chapter explores Kaufman's work, with an emphasis on his early scholarship. The second half of that chapter is all about the people who thought Kaufman was wrong and ought to be viewed quite skeptically. This chapter is mostly about *how* it is that theology should be done and explores themes pertaining to the challenges of balancing the calls of tradition and innovation.

Chapter 6 explores the writers that have produced doctrinal theologies that specifically engage with the imagination in a substantial way. Where the previous chapter was about the connection between imagination and *how* theology is done, this one is about *what* theology is produced. Topic explored the doctrines of revelation, God, Holy Spirit, anthropology (Christian views on humanity), and eschatology (Christian views of the end times). In each of these areas there have been scholars who have suggested that imagination might be an important concept to consider.

Chapter 7 is the beginning of Part II and looks at the idea of imagined worlds or "imaginaries." The chapter begins with an exploration of social imaginaries in the philosophical work of Cornelius Castoriadis and Charles Taylor, before looking at how the concept has come into theological work. Specific attention is given to the ways in which colonization and race shape Christian imagination about how the world—and God—works. Scholars explored include Mary Daly, Emilie Townes, Kwok Pui-lan, and Willie James Jennings. The chapter ends with an exploration of how it is that social imaginaries might be shifted, suggesting that there is a connection between Christian imaginaries and Christian practices.

Chapters 8 and 9 explore how practices and imagination are connected. Each of the practices explored has been written about by one or more scholars who have argued that a specific consideration of imagination would benefit our understanding and use of the practice. Chapter 8 considers prayer, reading Scripture, preaching, worship, and participating in sacraments. Chapter 9 explores religious education, spiritual formation, and theological education.

The book closes with a brief epilogue and a timeline of the major scholars considered.

Part I: Theological and Philosophical Contexts

1

What Is Imagination and Why
Should Christians Care?

THIS BOOK BEGINS ALREADY backed into a corner. It is written for Christians eager to consider how the imagination relates to their faith, but it also recognizes that "the imagination" is not talked about much in Scripture or theological writing. Why, then, is this topic something worth considering? That is precisely where we will begin.

We'll start looking at how imagination shows up in the Bible, both in terms of the actual word "imagination" in Greek and Hebrew and its implication. We'll then look at how people think about imagination now differently from how it was considered in the times when the Bible was written. After a section exploring Scripture, we'll turn to philosophy, doing a fast pass through the history of philosophies of imagination from Plato until the present. This chapter is a kind of crash course in "Imagination 101," getting some of the foundations set so that the more nuanced pieces of theology can be built on top in the coming chapters. To start, though, we'll look at why all that Bible and philosophy content might be worth reflecting on from a Christian perspective.

Why Bother?

Perhaps you came to this book already convinced that the imagination could play a beneficial role in a faithful life and theological reflection. Perhaps not. In either case, the question of relevance remains: why *exactly* is this important to think about for a Christian? I'll get more nuanced about my answers to that question throughout the book, but there are at least two clear responses that I want to offer to start us out. One short, one not so much.

First: the short one.

I think that as people of faith, we must recognize how important our imagination is. I think we ought to be concerned about how we value and make room for it—or not—in our churches and communities. I passionately believe that imagination is implicated "in our ability both to internalize collective habits of thought *and* to free ourselves from them."[1] Without attention to both of these facets of imagination, I fear we are not getting as full of a sense of things as we could. Both our liberation and domination are tied to our ability to imagine.

Though imagination and creativity are not the same, there is a close linkage between imaginative reflection and creative practice. Significant social science research suggests—in the United States at least—that since the 1990s, we are steadily getting less creative, generation by generation.[2] I think that as Christians, we ought to care that our children might be less able to imagine the world as different than how it is. I want my daughter to know that she can be an active participant in the transformation of social structures, not just a passive recipient of the world as it pushes her around. I think that more attention to the imagination can help with that. As a Christian theologian, I believe that a particularly Christian perspective on *why* imagination might help with that attention can be helpful.

OK. Now the second one.

In much of the literature that asks how religion or spirituality intersects with creativity, imagination, and art, there is often a kind of overly simplistic accounting that is done. Religion and spirituality that uses the arts and communicates in creative, imaginative, and aesthetic ways is good and in touch with life-giving parts of the tradition. Theological thinking that uses "regular" means of communication—academic prose, traditional sermon styles, no attempts to engage visual media, etc.—is bad or outmoded.

I myself have been guilty of this kind of reductive assessment in the past, so I understand its appeal. What I've come to believe, however, is that while there is ample reason to be excited about the consideration of imagination in religious reflection, the reality of the situation is more complex than a simple division of "theology with imagination" and "theology without imagination."

Another way of thinking about this is to say that the phrase "a lack of imagination" doesn't hold up under scrutiny. I believe that what people mean when they talk about "a lack of imagination" is that things aren't changing the way they want. Consider this passage from an interview with Rodger Nishioka, a Presbyterian religious education scholar.

1. Fettes, "Senses and Sensibilities," 114–29.
2. Kim, "Creativity Crisis," 285–95.

One of the ordination questions we ask of people in my Presbyterian tradition is, "Will you serve the people with energy, intelligence, imagination, and love?" I'm so grateful that the writers of that liturgy put the word "imagination" in there, because frankly, I'm a little worried these days that we lack a theological imagination. I think over and over again that one of the things that makes us created in the image of God, uniquely as beings on the face of the earth, is that God instills in humankind the ability to imagine—that is, the ability to move beyond whatever the concrete limitations are of our lives and to think thoughts that take us into distant places that we may never have dreamed before. That's an imagination. And a theological imagination is one that is attentive to how God is at work in the world.[3]

I'm all for the direction I think Nishioka is headed. However, I think it is a mistake to say that today we "lack a theological imagination."

I think it is more accurate to say that the patterns of current dominant theological imagination are not ones I like as much as what might come next. The current state of things theological is the result of dominant theological imaginations, not the *absence* of imagination.

The way that we currently discuss God is always already a function of our imagination. It isn't that the options are "imagination" and "no imagination." It is that patterns of imagination wrestle with one another for our attention, and we form habits and practices that maintain or disrupt ways of imagining. Living in a world with "no imagination" is actually living in a world where the imaginations of those in power generate the dominant stories, symbols, and hopes of the age. When we miss this idea, it is at least partially a result of the overly narrow "elite view" of imagination that associated it too closely with the arts and not enough with the everyday.

Imagination is not any more good or bad than intelligence. We can use intellect to determine how to make both neighborhood health centers *and* napalm. So too with what we can imagine. Theology and literature scholar Janine Langan says it well:

> Free to play with the givens, to reject or distort input, at the interface between our senses and our selves, our imagination has a terrible power over our inner life, over the decisions we make. . . . Educating the imagination is thus of primordial importance.[4]

3. The interview itself can be seen here: Yale Youth Ministry Institute, "Imagination – Dr. Rodger Nishioka," 00:19–1:23.

4. Langan, "Christian Imagination," 65.

How we educate ourselves about imagination should be connected to our theological commitments and our interpretations of the symbols and stories that form the soil from which our faith grows.

I wrote this book because I think Christians can have particular perspectives on imagination. More to the point, given that Scripture seems mostly *anti*-imagination, I think some work needs to be done to explain how it is that there can be any redeeming perspective on the topic. So that is how we'll start: first, we'll look at how Scripture seems to want to dismiss the importance of imagination. Then we'll consider some of how we might be able to find another possible, faithful way of seeing things.

Imagination in Scripture

A thorough search of the NRSV Bible will reveal only four canonical references to the imagination, with another three found in the Apocrypha.[5] The references themselves are not generally positive. For example, Ezekiel is told to "prophesy against the prophets of Israel" because they "prophesy out of their own imagination."[6] We also get a firm reminder from Paul that "we ought not to think" our concept of God can ever be captured as "an image formed by the art and imagination of mortals."[7] In both of these examples, the idea is that imagination itself is a falsehood, the origin of falsehoods, or, if not outrightly false, at least not as accurate as we might want it to be. In all these cases, imagination is not something that should be referenced if one is hoping to be faithful. I refer to these conceptions of imagination as "photocopier models."

With photocopiers, even if there was an authentic original at some point, attempting to reproduce the truth results in blurry copies that are not trustworthy. A photocopy of a photocopy of a photocopy is not an especially clear document, especially if the photocopier is broken. In this case, the "brokenness" might be sin, and it might be causing the resulting copies to have smudges and distortions that were not in the original. This model says we ought not to trust the imagination when discussing things that are God-related because whatever it is that the imagination produces will not adequately capture the truth of how things are.

If you stop there, just searching for instances of the word "imagination" in a contemporary translation of the Bible, that is the end of the road. However, as with many ideas in Scripture, things are not quite so simple.

5. Prov 18:11; Ezek 13:2, 17; Acts 17:29; 2 Esd 6:5; 16:54, 63.

6. Ezek 13:2.

7. Acts 17:29.

One issue is that different denominations prefer different translations of the Bible, and in some translations, there are words translated as "imagination" that most scholars now agree shouldn't be understood that way.

For example, imagination shows up more in the King James Version because in addition to *millibbām, bemaskito*, and *enthumésis*, six different Hebrew and Greek words in the Bible texts were translated as imagination. These words include *yetser*/יֵצֶר (Gen 6:5; 8:21; Deut 31:21, *sheriruth*/ שְׁרִירוּת (Deut 29:19; Jer 3:17; 7:24; 9:14; 11:8; 13:10; 16:12; 18:12; 23:17), *machashebeth*/מַחֲשָׁבָה (Prov 6:18; Lam 3:6); *dianoia*/διάνοια (Luke 1:51); *logismos*/λογισμός (2 Cor 10:5); and *dialogismos*/διαλογισμός (Rom 1:21). In earlier translations, none of these terms have positive associations in terms of faithfulness.[8]

As an illustration, consider that the NRSV translates Gen 6:5 as "The Lord saw that the wickedness of humankind was great in the earth, and that every inclination of the thoughts of their hearts was only evil continually." That same passage in the King James translation is rendered as "And GOD saw that the wickedness of man was great in the earth, and that every imagination of the thoughts of his heart was only evil continually." This is a relatively minor change but given that almost all the places that imagination shows up in the King James it is considered negatively, this impression has remained very present for some segments of Christian culture.

A related issue we have to contend with is that how people thought the human mind worked thousands of years ago is notably different from contemporary views of psychology or neuroscience. Perhaps the most significant thing to know is about the Hebrew word לֵב/*lebh*, or "heart": within the Israelite view of the human being, the heart was the home of both cognitive *and* emotional responses.[9] Feeling and thinking were *both* seated in the heart. That's why the phrase "every inclination of the thoughts of their hearts" makes sense in the context of the Israelite worldview. Similarly, in Ezek 13:2, there is a critique of false prophets who prophesy "out of their own imagination," and the word used is *millibbām*/מִלִּבָּם. Taken literally, this means "out of their own heart," but because we know that the heart was where the mind and intellect also resided for Hebrew speakers of that time, we have to think about the term differently.

When I see "heart" in Scripture, I internally think of it as "heart (and mind)." One of the things that this suggests is that whenever we read about the heart in the Bible, especially if the speaker was Jewish, something more

---

8. McIntyre, *Faith, Theology, and Imagination*, 5.

9. For example, Prov 3:3; 6:21; and 7:3 all refer to the heart as the center of thinking and reason and Prov 15:15 and 30 have emotions there as well.

than just emotion is going on. Consider Jesus' description of why he uses parables in Matt 13:12–17.

> The reason I speak to them in parables is that "seeing they do not perceive, and hearing they do not listen, nor do they understand." With them indeed is fulfilled the prophecy of Isaiah that says:
>
> "You will indeed listen, but never understand, and you will indeed look, but never perceive. For this people's heart has grown dull, and their ears are hard of hearing, and they have shut their eyes; so that they might not look with their eyes, and listen with their ears, and understand with their heart and turn—and I would heal them."
>
> But blessed are your eyes, for they see, and your ears, for they hear. Truly I tell you, many prophets and righteous people longed to see what you see, but did not see it, and to hear what you hear, but did not hear it.

The healing of the people requires that they "understand with their heart," a task they are not ready to do, at least partly because their hearts have "grown dull." Something other than just sensory perception is going on here. It isn't that "many prophets and righteous people" had physically diminished eyes and ears. Some other issue was preventing them from perceiving what was happening. They were caught in a space in between: their hearts had grown too dull to receive the truth of the moment, but they were still not yet able to *imagine* what Jesus was coming to preach.

Once we know that it is very likely Jews would have spoken as though the heart and mind were both involved in thinking and feeling, several other passages seem as if they might apply to what we would today call "the imagination." To be clear, that word only shows up where I mentioned it above, but there are passages that seem to presume the presence of an imaginative capacity. Consider, for example, the story of the prophet Nathan and King David in 2 Sam 12.[10]

In that passage, Nathan is headed to David to speak to the king about his abuse of power. David had killed Uriah the Hittite and taken his wife for his own. Nathan, as prophet, feels compelled to address the issue. Rather than lead with an argument about what a king's duty ought to be, how clear the commandments are, and the ethical problems with murder and adultery, Nathan takes a different approach. He tells a story about a rich man

---

10. I'm indebted to Garrett Green for his reflection on the imagination in this passage.

who steals from a poor man. Nathan was apparently a rather good story-teller because we read that after hearing the story, "David's anger was greatly kindled," and he said that "as the Lord lives, the man who has done this deserves to die" (2 Sam 12:5). At this point, Nathan executes one doozy of a switcheroo ending, exclaiming to David, "*You* are that man!" This revelation and Nathan's follow-up prophesying apparently work well because rather than defend himself or have Nathan killed, David admits that he has sinned (2 Sam 12:13). Nathan was able to get David to see something about himself that was true by first telling a story that was not.

Whenever we are asked to understand something metaphorically, we are inherently being told to hold the knowledge in a way that transcends the literal and requires us to presume something that is not the case *as if* it were. For example, when Jesus commands that "you shall love your neighbor as yourself" (Matt 22:39) or to "rejoice with those who rejoice" and "weep with those who weep" (Rom 12:15), we're being asked to be empathetic, that is, to imagine that we are somehow more like someone else than we usually per-ceive. Similarly, when we read that "faith is the assurance of things hoped for, the conviction of things not seen" (Heb 11:1), it is clear that our faith isn't just about perception but our ability to hold onto an understanding of the way the world is without having any firm evidence that this is the case.

We understand that there is a metaphorical comparison going on when God is called a potter and faithful people clay (Isa 64:8) or when Jesus says that he is "the vine" and the disciples "the branches" (John 15:5). We are not supposed to take those lines to communicate that somehow God is actually a person into ceramics or that Jesus can become a plant. We recognize that this metaphorical language is being used to express that some qualities of potter-ness and vine-ness are also qualities of God and Jesus. This capacity for symbolic thought entails recognizing that even in considering some-thing that is not strictly true on a literal level (Jesus is not, in fact, a plant), there can nonetheless be truth in it.

Outside of some science fiction plot, it is physically impossible that I am also my neighbor. However, though impossible, something is com-municated when I think about what it means to love my neighbor as if the neighbor was me. Though "imagination" is not discussed much in Scripture, there are many places where the nature of Scripture requires that we read with something more than just a literal eye.

Looking at any object, person, or circumstance "as if" it was some-thing else requires an act of imagination. So does considering any object or experience "as if" it carried some inherent significance or meaningfulness. Imagining has something to do with how we understand the complexities of human behavior and communication. What that "something" is will be explored as we look at some definitions and models for imagination.

A Western History of Imagination

I'll discuss this at greater length in chapter 3, but for now, it is worth noting that much of philosophical writing on imagination relates to its relationship to knowing and knowledge. These models are not the only ones I'll be using in this book but given their importance and how often they are referenced, they are a good starting point for comparison. What follows is a "greatest hits" review of imagination through Western philosophical scholarship. I'll touch on the "must-know" pieces often referred to by theologians, but in no way should this be taken as a comprehensive survey of the material. This is the ten-thousand-foot view. To get some sense of the contours of the history being covered here, you might be served by flipping to the back of the book and looking at the "Bibliography Timeline" appendix on page 223.

First, it is important to know that in the West, it was not until the Enlightenment that we find anything that could be called a fully worked out theory of imagination. Before that period, the only way imagination explicitly showed up was in brief passages and asides in other arguments. Though we can sensibly talk about how imagination was viewed, there was no sustained philosophy, only a patchwork. That being said, we can explore quite a few patches. In the earliest sustained Western consideration of imagination, the Greek philosopher Plato (428–348 BCE) did not have very positive things to say. Plato affirmed *reason* as the primary tool by which humanity came to know the truth. Imagination could produce, at best, a cheap copy or knockoff of truth. He discussed imagination directly in his arguments that artists are functionally imitators since they try to represent things that are not what they appear to be.

As Plato had it, when someone enjoys perceiving art, they are "seduced into valuing imitations instead of reality."[11] There is a firm separation between "belief" (*doxa*) and "knowledge" (*epistêmê*) that parallels the difference between imitation and reality. This is evident in the Greek word *dokein*, which can mean "to suppose" and "to imagine," as well as "to seem; to pretend; to believe so."[12] In Plato's thought, knowledge is knowledge of what is *real*. Belief and imagination are concerned with imitations and things that only *seem* real.[13]

11. Thayer, "Plato on the Morality of Imagination," 594–618.
12. Strong's 1380 δοκέω / *dokeo* (Strong, "G1380").
13. Thayer, "Plato on the Morality of Imagination," 594–618.

When people of faith are worried about the "damage" that imagination and the arts can do, they are often unwittingly rehearsing a Platonic argument: we need to concern ourselves with the real and the truly Good, not just "make things up" and "imagine" them. I see this especially in churches that regularly proclaim that it is important to "speak where the Bible speaks, and be silent where the Bible is silent," frequently emphasizing 1 Peter 4:11 and 2 Timothy 2:15.

This line of argument presupposes that somewhere—e.g., higher Platonic levels of existence, the Mind of God, or in Scripture—there is a complete, fixed, finished, and accessible Truth and that we do it a disservice when we imagine things that don't live up to its Goodness or Beauty. In this imitation model, if I were to say, "imagine you are safe at home eating your favorite meal," while you were, in fact, on a boat, you would pull on your prior history and sensory experience, calling them to mind, cognitively attempting to be *mentally* present to a situation which *physically* is not actually the case. In terms of details, nuance, and complexity, your imagination of that experience would inherently be lesser than the experience itself.

This is the photocopier model again: our imagination is attempting to imitate a version of home when home is not present. Imagination viewed this way has been looked at suspiciously for millennia. At best, it results in pleasant daydreaming. At worst, it can be destructive self-delusion. But that's not the only way to think about it. As William James aptly put it, "there are imaginations, not 'The Imagination.'"[14]

Following Plato, we have the Greek philosopher Aristotle (384–322 BCE), who saw imagination slightly differently. He wrote about it in a limited fashion in *De Anima*.[15] For him, imagination was a distinct human capacity, to be distinguished from perception and mind. Imagination is a faculty in humans (and most other animals) that makes, stores, and retrieves images. He believed that all thought requires images held in the imagination. This is important because while perception itself is never false, the *recall* of images from imagination might be. In Aristotle, imagination is the warehouse of images, not the source of creativity or newness. In fact, any "newness" is a problem when what you are looking for is archival records. If something is new it means it is now false because what was *supposed* to be stored in the imagination was perfect copies of perceptions.[16]

The first Christian theological commentary on imagination comes from the North African theologian and philosopher Augustine (354–430

14. James, *Principles of Psychology*, 137.
15. Aristotle, *De Anima*, 3.3.
16. Shields, "Aristotle's Psychology."

CE). Augustine's thinking drew on Plato indirectly through the Neoplatonic Greek philosopher Porphyry.[17] While not lengthy, it nonetheless is significant and has lasting repercussions. Specifically, Augustine considered imagination in his *De Genesi ad Litteram*, book 12. It is not a prolonged discussion and comes up as part of a conversation about the Christian afterlife and what kind of perception people will have in their resurrection bodies.

As Augustine framed it, humans have three kinds of sight, each operating via a different human capacity: the eyes, the spirit of man (*spiritus hominis*), and the mind. It is with the spirit of man that we can "think up the sky, the earth and all we can see in them, even if we are sitting in darkness and not actually seeing anything with the eyes of the body. . . . Nevertheless, we are looking at bodily likenesses in the mind."[18] Like Aristotle, the *spiritus* stores the images. What does this have to do with resurrection bodies? Well, earlier Augustine clarified the difference between the physical "*animale corpus*" humans have on earth with the "*corpus spiritale*" we'll get in heaven. This suggests that the vision associated with the *spiritus* will be with us even after death. This leads to an interesting connection for the imagination.

Augustine believed that when the soul leaves the body, it is carried to "*spirital*" regions where it will receive reward or punishment. For the theology of afterlife being considered it is important that these possible rewards or punishments not be seen as false. They are real, but a kind of realness lacking any physical form. These afterlife consequences will be "true joy or sorrow experienced in the imagination, just as the joy and terror we experience in dreams or nightmares are due to the same faculty but are very real."[19] The corollary to this is that the afterlife is a reality, but "one that belongs to the realm of the imagination rather than to that of the body."[20] The eternal nature of the imagination as part of the spiritual body meant that great attention had to be paid to make sure what it was storing was right.

Augustine used the word "*phantasia*" to refer to an image retrieved from memory and "*phantasmata*" to refer to the product resulting from the combination or alteration of mental images that are edits or distortions of stored images of perception. Philosopher Marianne Djuth pointedly notes the consequences of this perspective.

> This creative function of the imagination is viewed with suspicion by Augustine. He seems to regard phantasmata as potentially deceptive, a contaminant of the heart, the root of idolatry,

17. Watson, "Imagination," 54–65.
18. Watson, "Imagination," 63.
19. Watson, "Imagination," 63.
20. Watson, "Imagination," 63.

heresy, and diabolical contrivance, and capable of generating false images of Christ's life and death.[21]

We see in Augustine some of the earliest documented Christian suspicions of imagination. Admittedly, his concept of imagination is not exactly how the term is used today, but a negative connection was made, nonetheless. Centuries later, when the Italian theologian and philosopher Thomas Aquinas (1224–74) used Augustine's three types of vision in his own theological work, some of this suspicion also came through.

In Aquinas, the "*phantasia*" or "*imaginatio*" is once again the image warehouse and can combine or distort. As Aquinas put it, "there is a certain operation of the soul in man which, by dividing and composing, forms different images of things, even images of things which are not received through the senses."[22] As with Augustine before him, Aquinas is suspicious of this "operation of the soul," writing that "Demons are known to work on men's imagination, until everything is other than it is."[23] This theme will also reemerge later, with the imagination being seen as the weak point through which evil can get in.

The "sensation warehouse" model of imagination was the dominant perspective on imagination for centuries after Aquinas. It wasn't until the Scottish philosopher David Hume (1711–76) that there was a widely spread opinion that differed significantly. It is not particularly surprising that Hume's ideas are different from Aquinas' in that five hundred years is a long time for any idea to remain unchanged. However, it *is* noteworthy that Hume points to some of the very same ideas as Aquinas but has a radically different assessment of them.

> Nothing is more free than the imagination of man; and though it cannot exceed the original stock of ideas furnished by the internal and external senses, it has unlimited power of mixing, compounding, separating and dividing these ideas in all the varieties of fiction and vision.[24]

In Hume, as before, we see that the imagination is the faculty by which we can "envisage things in absence." However, it is in Hume, for the first time, that there is a claim that imagination is a part of the act of perception and interpretation not just when accessing the image warehouse, but *even as we*

21. Djuth, "Veiled and Unveiled Beauty," 88.
22. Aquinas, *Summa Theologica* 1.84.6; as cited in Watson, "Imagination," 63.
23. Aquinas, *Summa Theologica* 1.84.6; as cited in Watson, "Imagination," 63.
24. Hume, *Enquiry Concerning Human Understanding*, 5.2.

are seeing. Furthermore, Hume argued that human genius resulted from a highly skilled imagination.[25]

I think the difference between Hume and what came before him has to be considered in the context of the fact that part of Hume's work was some intense philosophical interrogation of religion: he was not worried about false images of Christ's life or imaginative demon gateways. Nonetheless, it is notable how praiseworthy he is of imagination given the history before him. Indeed, Hume and his contemporary Immanuel Kant (1724–1804) are the major turning point in perspectives. Kant, a Prussian philosopher, radically changed how scholars viewed the imagination.[26]

In 1781's *Critique of Pure Reason*, Kant called imagination "a hidden art in the depths of the soul," a "faculty of representing in intuition an object that is not itself present."[27] Whereas Plato's concept of imagination had it as a possible obstacle to knowledge, Kant argued that imagination was *essential* to knowing. Philosophers Mark Johnson and Desiree Berendsen interpret Kant to suggest that his work establishes four aspects of imagination: the reproductive, productive, schematic, and creative.[28]

The "reproductive aspect" of imagination connects perception and reason. This is imagination as a warehouse of perception. When the power of imagination is functioning reproductively, it is based on previous experience. That is, it pulls from past images (including all senses, not just sight) and brings them to mind. Memory is imagination working this way when I remember what I had for breakfast yesterday and can accurately recall the sensations of the small sad bowl of oatmeal that started my day.

The "productive aspect" of imagination operates to produce interpretations that connect incoming perceptions and memory. When it functions productively, the imagination is able to produce images and connections for new experiences even if we have *not* experienced them before. Before I was a father myself, I could imagine what being a father might be like. I could also imagine eating alligator, though I've never done that. This aspect of imagination allows us to think categorically, perceiving possible objects and events as objects and events of a certain kind: though I hadn't ever had the experience of fatherhood before, I knew I wanted to label it as "good" and desirable and could project that into my imagined future. I've also heard that

25. Warnock, *Imagination*, 129.

26. I'm indebted in this section to the very lucid and concise work that Samantha Matherne has done in detailing Kant's approach. For more details see her entry on "Kant's Theory of the Imagination" in the *Routledge Handbook of the Imagination*, 55–68.

27. Kant, *Critique of Pure Reason*, 180–81.

28. Berendsen, "Imagination and Art." See also Johnson, *Body in the Mind*, 139–66.

WHAT IS IMAGINATION AND WHY SHOULD CHRISTIANS CARE?   15

alligator tastes like chicken and can use that to imagine eating it though I've never had that experience before. What we imagine shapes what we want in the future. Imagination also allows us to recognize that certain experiences in the present, while not materially real, have a bodily impact.

When we watch a large movie screen and experience a quickened pulse as a monster arrives, we might jump even though we know we are safe. Imagination connects reason to imagined futures *and* to experiences of artistic and creative expression in the present. For Kant, this aspect of imagination was a human capacity within the mind which functioned as a kind of bridge between sensory input data and understanding.[29] By thinking categorically, we are able to automatically sort images into similar groups, providing the tagging needed to mix, match, and combine images for later production of new imagined images. I imagined fatherhood would feel like some other experiences tagged #good, and that alligator will be like #poultry.

Imagination's "schematic aspect" is how we make connections between perceptions and thought. This function of imagination allows connection between things that are not at all similar, for example, between abstract concepts and material objects. This capacity enables us to make, use, and understand symbols. Nothing about a small loop of metal inherently means anything particular about marriage, but when worn on the left ring finger in the USA, a meaning emerges. We can see that specific type of metal loop as a symbol of something larger than itself. This aspect of the imagination functions like a dynamic switchboard or database where perceptions, symbols, and memory are associated. When these "entries" begin to be cross-listed with emotional states, it is the "creative aspect" of imagination that is operative.

The creative aspect of the imagination is the capacity of the other aspects of imagination to be united with emotion. This aspect results in a particular meaning or significance being attached to the object, concept, or experience being considered. In this aspect, imagination is "reason with feeling."[30]

> Imagination, in its creative aspect, helps one see ordinary objects as significant in a new way. The interpretative function of imagination, which is its normal function, may be heightened so that what is present to us takes on a new meaning. This power

29. Horstmann, *Kant's Power of Imagination*, 28–31.
30. Berendsen, "Imagination and Art," 220.

is identical with the power of representation, of forming images
of things, in order to think about them in their absence.[31]

Taken together, Kant's aspects of imagination draw on prior sense experience and imagining to allow people to understand the whole of an object or event when only a portion of it is perceivable. We see only one side of a cab but can imagine that the car has another side and isn't just a cardboard cutout of a car.

For something to be able to be known, reason and experience need to be connected. For it to have meaning and significance, the joining of reason and experience must be united with emotion. Imagination is a connective capacity, the public square where the perception of senses and understanding meet. Because imagination serves as this connection point, Kant argued that imagination has a central role in all human evaluations of morality, aesthetics, and reason. Pushing even further than Hume, Kant argued that imagination is one of the sources that produce human understandings of truth.

As philosopher Richard Kearney puts it, "Kant rescued imagination from its servile role as an intermediary faculty between our sensible and intelligible experience, declaring it to be the primary and indispensable precondition of all knowledge."[32] Imagination pulls together various fragments of perceptual experience from the past and combines them with current sensory input to produce knowledge in the present. The idea in Kant is that it is through the transcendental work of the imagination that our experience of the world is made available to us.

If it weren't for the imagination's capacity to stitch things together, our experience of the world would be a barrage of sense data without meaning, just an onslaught of perception without comprehension or context. As Kant understood it, imagination is like a restaurant's head chef, directing the flow of raw materials, considering what they should become, what else they should be combined with, what the final product should look like, and how to serve it to produce a specific experience or association. Imagination brings internal order to experience, allowing it to have meaning for us.

Kant's distinction between the "reproductive" and "productive" aspects of imagination is significant for nearly all philosophy of imagination that followed him. Contrary to the perspectives of Augustine and Aquinas, Kant was far more optimistic about images made by productive imagination. Like Hume, Kant thought genius, including artistic genius, was a function of imagination. In his *Critique of the Power of Judgment*, Kant

---

31. Berendsen, "Imagination and Art," 220.
32. Kearney, *Wake of Imagination*, 156–57.

argues that when imagination is used as part of cognitive processes, it is bounded and constrained by the need to result in understanding. However, when the imagination is used for aesthetic purposes, the imagination is capable of bringing into being "unsought" and "extensive" material.[33] He claimed that imagination can create "as it were another nature, out of the material the real one gives us."[34] The imagination can bring to life new ideas and understanding. This perspective hugely impacted the scholarship that followed, including the work of his contemporary, the German philosopher Friedrich Schelling (1775–1854). Under the mentorship of the German novelist and scholar Johann Wolfgang von Goethe, Schelling's early work expanded on Kant's philosophy. However, as Schelling's own vision grew, his work pushed beyond Kant.

Schelling took Kant's perspective further than Kant himself did, working to address what he saw as inconsistencies in Kant's thinking.[35] For example, he thought Kant was mistaken in identifying knowledge itself as transcendental when knowledge was produced by humans. Instead, Schelling considered *nature* as transcendent: the created order (humans included) has been created in such a way that it leads to more life and the "human consciousness capable of knowing nature."[36] Relatedly, Schelling suggested that the concrete elements of Creation work together to express a continually unfolding idea: "the evolving world of nature gives concrete expression to God's imagination."[37] Knowledge was a phenomenon of nature, not separate from it.

In 1805 Schelling published *The Philosophy of Art*, expanding his ideas about knowledge into the explicit realm of imagination and creativity. For Schelling, the tensions between human subjectivity and the world are resolved in art. Imagination takes what seems like a duality (my sense of myself vs. everything that isn't me) and fuses them together or "resolves the duality" into a symbol.[38] As part of this, Schelling recognized three levels of imaginative capacity in people.

First, there is the "passive imagination" (*ursprüngliche Anschauung*) which receives and records perception from the senses. Second, there is an "active imagination" (*Einbildungskraft*) which sorts and organizes the perceived sensations to create some internal understanding of the whole

33. Kant, *Critique of the Power of Judgment*, 185.

34. Kant, *Critique of the Power of Judgment*, 185.

35. Gare, "From Kant to Schelling."

36. Gare, "From Kant to Schelling," 29.

37. Bednar, *Faith as Imagination*, 168.

38. Bednar, *Faith as Imagination*, 168.

context. Finally, there is an "artistic imagination" (*Kunstvermögen*) through which an individual's personal expression is brought out of themselves and into the world. When a person's inner life is expressed outwardly, all three types of imagination have been integrated, perceived dualities between self and world diminish, and self-reflexivity is high.[39]

Interestingly, Schelling reflects somewhat on the term "*Einbildung-skraft*" itself, noting that it has an etymological meaning of "the power of building into one."[40] For Schelling, the pinnacle of possibility for imagination is precisely its ability to unify dualities in tension through sensible means. This concept of imagination makes for a form of knowledge that is embodied as well. That is, while "intellectual intuition affords a knowledge of being gained solely through reason apart from all sensibility," imagination and aesthetic intuition provide "a vision of the world of ideas by means of the senses."[41] This is relevant because he was pushing back against the idea of the imagination as a faculty of just image-making. In arguing that imagination had this "power of building into one," Schelling claimed that the ability to perceive (and express) a connective framework between disconnected events and concepts was not only positive but something that was God-given.

> Art is for humanity what nature is for God. Imagination frees a person from subjectivity by the creation of art whereby the self becomes objectified, real, and in relation to concrete reality. Imagination liberates the person from the confines of the self. Through acts of the creative imagination, a person becomes real. Through the mediating power of imagination, reality is attained. It is there that a person "imitates" God, or participates in the divine, most closely.[42]

We'll see themes resonant with Schelling emerge in chapter 6 when we consider doctrines of theological anthropology. The idea that the product of imaginative creativity is a close analog to God's creation shows up in several places, including in the work of the English poet and philosopher Samuel Taylor Coleridge (1772–1834).[43]

Coleridge, though not a theologian, produces a theory of imagination that is very theologically grounded. Along with Kant, his work is most cited for key understandings of imagination by contemporary theologians

39. Bednar, *Faith as Imagination*, 168.

40. Summerell, "Theory of the Imagination," 89.

41. Summerell, "Theory of the Imagination," 89.

42. Bednar, *Faith as Imagination*, 16.

43. Stockitt, *Imagination and the Playfulness of God*.

engaging with imagination. In 1807 he published the *Biographia Literaria*, which contains his most concentrated philosophical reflection on the topic. Influenced significantly by the work of both Kant and Schelling, Coleridge's basic position is that imagination manifests in two forms.

The "primary imagination" is "the living power and prime agent of all human perception, and as a repetition in the finite mind of the eternal act of creation in the infinite I AM."[44] Two things are simultaneously affirmed in this claim. First, that imagination is the faculty of perception; it is how we can perceive the world at all. Second, imagination is a trace of an infinite God's creative power in the finite human mind. Coleridge's primary imagination is the human capacity to take in perceptions of the world. We can perceive God's activity in the world through our primary imagination. By being open and receptive to perceiving God's movement in the world we are, in some small way, participating in God's work. Sharing what we perceive is sharing what God has done.

Following this, the "secondary imagination" is "an echo of the former, coexisting with the conscious will, yet still as identical with the primary in the kind of its agency, and differing only in degree, and in the mode of its operation."[45] The idea is that imaginative human output—for Coleridge this means the arts—echoes God's work in creation. Humanity cannot create *ex nihilo*, from nothing, as God did in creation. However, we can, through an echo of God's creation in us, create *new* things that have never before existed. The argument is that humanity's imaginative production is a way of derivatively participating in God's ongoing act of creation.

Taken together, the primary and secondary imagination are the "means through which we gain a telos and significance" because the "higher divine life is transposed on the lower."[46] Imagination is one means of "partaking in divine nature" (2 Pet 1:4) by willfully noticing God's work in the world and then adding to it with creative (artistic) production. As theologian Robin Stockitt puts it, Coleridge understood imagination as "God's co-worker on earth, both mirroring and sharing in the activity of the Divine."[47] You'll note similar themes throughout the book you're currently reading, as Coleridge has left a significant legacy, especially among theologians of imagination.

After Coleridge, there is a considerable time gap before work emerges that is regularly referenced in contemporary theological scholarship on imagination. The additional sources of reflection are from the twentieth

44. Coleridge, *Biographia Literaria*, 159.
45. Coleridge, *Biographia Literaria*, 159.
46. Sellars, *Reasoning Beyond Reason*, 49.
47. Stockitt, *Imagination and the Playfulness of God*, x.

and twenty-first centuries. Since these more contemporary thinkers show up significantly throughout the rest of this book, I won't go into great detail here, but I do want to note their significance in the growth of philosophies of imagination.

English philosopher Mary Warnock (1924–2019) published her book, *Imagination*, in 1975. Ever since, it has been one of the most cited volumes on the subject. Though now somewhat dated, the book's historical recounting of Western philosophies of imagination through the modern era is still solid, focusing on Hume, Kant, Schelling, Coleridge, and Wordsworth. Warnock stands in the line of Hume and Kant, arguing that imagination is part of all perception. Her work is often cited for her ideas about how imagination allows us to "see into the life of things" and is functionally a version of "seeing-as."[48] In terms of her own perspectives, Warnock largely follows Kant's aspects, though they lead her to markedly different conclusions.

> Imagination is our means of interpreting the world, and it is also
> our means of forming images in the mind. The images them-
> selves are not separate from our interpretations of the world;
> they are our way of thinking of the objects in the world.[49]

Recognizing that how we think about objects in the world is a function of our imagination led Warnock to argue that imagination should be a more significant area of reflection when considering moral and religious questions.

Warnock claims that imagination—in its broadest sense—is at the heart of all religious life. Imagination explains how meaning is made, how symbols operate, and how experiences take on significance. Because of this, she suggested that imagination is better than belief in providing a basis for reflection on religion.[50] In fact, she even goes so far as to argue that the foundations of moral conviction are built upon imagination.[51] Following this, Warnock suggested that given (a) contemporary efforts toward democratic pluralism and (b) the need for conversations in the public square that can speak across differences, that imagination is a viable secular category to be emphasized as common ground for ethical collaboration.[52] The theological implication of these themes is considered at length via consideration of

---

48. Warnock, *Imagination*, 202.
49. Warnock, *Imagination*, 194.
50. Warnock, *Dishonest to God*, 158–59.
51. Warnock, *Imagination and Time*, 160.
52. Warnock, *Dishonest to God*, 162.

Gordon Kaufman in chapter 5 of this book. It also features significantly in the work of the Irish philosopher Richard Kearney (born 1954).

Kearney's philosophical work on imagination is a mainstay of contemporary theology engaging the topic. Most frequently, this includes reference to his treatment of the history of philosophy of imagination. His book, *The Wake of Imagination*, was published in 1988, providing a more comprehensive historical account than even Warnock.[53] Beginning with biblical and Greek accounts of imagination, Kearney stretches further to the present, exploring the same thinkers as Warnock and adding substantial considerations of Kierkegaard, Nietzsche, Camus, Heidegger, Sartre, Lacan, Foucault, and Derrida. However, more than just a historian, Kearney's work in *Wake* also came with a clear argument.

Recounting the history of the imagination in the West was an essential part of his project as he intended to show that while premodern and modern views of imagination are no longer intellectually viable, postmodern views are ethically nebulous and without commitment, a "mirroring which mirrors nothing but the act of mirroring."[54] His proposal is not a nostalgic return to a bygone era but retrieves elements of past perspectives to "radically reinterpret the role of imagination as a relationship between self and other."[55] As Kearney sees it, there must be an ethical commitment to the philosophical reinvigoration of imagination. This trajectory is identifiable in nearly all his work after that as well.

Part of what makes Kearney a *de facto* citation for theologians of imagination is that he is a philosopher comfortable with reading and citing theology and has been so attentive to the importance of imagination throughout his career. A decade after *Wake* came *Poetics of Imagining*, which continued the exploration but with an even greater focus on phenomenological, hermeneutic, and postmodern philosophies.[56] After *Poetics*, Kearney returned with numerous articles, chapters, and additional books, exploring themes related to the consequences of how we imagine the world and the power of symbols to shape lives.

> Insofar as stories shape even our account of the good life and how to pursue it, we can never simply abandon the stories or traditions that have previously shaped us, even when they cease to be helpful. Instead, we must always return to (ana) those stories, even and perhaps especially after those stories have been

53. Kearney, *Wake of Imagination*.
54. Kearney, *Wake of Imagination*, 254–55.
55. Kearney, *Wake of Imagination*, 363.
56. Kearney, *Poetics of Imagining*.

called into question (critiqued, deconstructed, found wanting). And we return to these stories precisely in service of 'healing,' of becoming healthier, that is, of being better able to navigate our world in ethical, Other and self-honoring ways.[57]

Kearney's ethical commitments, routine reflection on religion, and prolific publication record contribute to his regular presence in theological work on imagination. I expect Kearney's work will remain highly cited for years to come. However, I think his name may well be joined by another.

To close this section, I feel obliged to note that I think the frontrunner for the newest addition to this list would be Kathleen Lennon and her 2015 book, *Imagination and the Imaginary*.[58] It hasn't been long enough to tell, but there is good reason to think her volume will be referenced often in the coming years. Just as Kearney deepened beyond Warnock in his consideration of psychoanalytic, phenomenological, and postmodern philosophies, so does Lennon further deepen in these areas and expand again to richly consider the philosophies of gender and social imagination. As Lennon herself writes in her conclusion:

> One of the tasks of writers, visual artists, musicians and, perhaps, political leaders is to offer us new imaginary structures. But this is also a task in which we *all* take some part, via our everyday iteration of everyday imaginaries.[59]

As Lennon sees it, philosophical considerations of imagination are also political questions. The book makes it clear that the study of imagination is a viable means of studying social structures, oppression, and justice as well.

In a catalog of philosophy that begins with Plato and runs to the present, it seemed appropriate to include work currently on the edge of being received into the field. I think Lennon's work will be beneficial to theologians wanting to think about imagination and its intersections with spiritual practices, liberation thought, and social justice. Her take on "social imaginaries" significantly supported the development of chapter 7 of this book, which takes up questions about imaginary structures and how one might change them. Before we get there, though, we have to finish *this* chapter . . .

---

57. DeRoo, "Kearney's Relevance for Psychology," 207–25.

58. Lennon, *Imagination and the Imaginary*.

59. Lennon, *Imagination and the Imaginary*, 138.

A Working Definition

While I did feel it was necessary to walk with you through the above history in some detail, I also think it can be refreshing and welcome to consider the content in a summarized and decontextualized way. Noting developments and repeated themes is easier to see when there is more detail, but zooming out for the big picture can also be useful. For this purpose, the work of philosopher Leslie Stevenson is quite helpful.

In 2003, Stevenson wrote a concise journal article, "Twelve Conceptions of Imagination."[60] In it, he covers much of the same history as we have, extracting from it his sense of the various discrete meanings. Given how succinct he is, considering his approach is an excellent way to rapidly recap what we saw develop. His twelve conceptions are below, and though the specifics of his language are slightly different in some places, all of these items should be familiar if you read the last section. As Stevenson frames it, imagination is:

1. The ability to think of something not presently perceived, but spatio-temporally real.

2. The ability to think of whatever one acknowledges as possible in the spatiotemporal world.

3. The liability to think of something that the subject believes to be real, but which is not.

4. The ability to think of things that one conceives of as fictional.

5. The ability to entertain mental images.

6. The ability to think of anything at all.

7. The nonrational operations of the mind, that is, those explicable in terms of causes rather than reasons.

8. The ability to form perceptual beliefs about public objects in space and time.

9. The ability to sensuously appreciate works of art or objects of natural beauty without classifying them under concepts or thinking of them as useful.

10. The ability to create works of art that encourage such sensuous appreciation.

11. The ability to appreciate things that are expressive or revelatory of the meaning of human life.

60. Stevenson, "Twelve Conceptions of Imagination," 238–59.

12. The ability to create works of art that express something deep about the meaning of life.[61]

While Stevenson's list is hopefully helpful as a summary of sorts, it is unwieldy as a definition, which is something we'll need going forward.

This section will establish a basic definition of imagination that I will use just so that we are starting on the same page. I'll push and prod at it a bit and complicate things for the rest of the book, but for now, having something specific to concentrate on is helpful. I'll break down some pieces of this below, but to start, here it is: *imagination is the human capacity to bring into consciousness things that are not observably present.* I'll be using this in numerous places throughout the book, so it is worth some clarification now to make sure my intent is evident. There are seven clarifications or nuances that seem important to specify in regard to this definition.

First, the "things" that are brought into consciousness could be (1) recalled concepts or perceptions of objects and situations that have been previously experienced, (2) things the imaginer has not ever encountered before, (3) concepts or perceptions of objects and situations that have not yet existed anywhere. Additionally, as David J. Bryant states, "imagining is the activity of taking something as something or of understanding things as having some sort of significance."[62] These "things" might also be (4) attributions of meaningfulness or significance. If I find a unique rock at the site of a pivotal moment in my life, I may well bring into consciousness an unobservable but profound sense of importance to that rock. In any case, imagining can call forth any of these "things" into the present within the mind of the person imagining.

Second, imagining is an action that can be willfully initiated (I can ask you to imagine me becoming a horse or to imagine if a particular pair of shoes was important to you, and you could start to do that). However, it also sometimes runs on autopilot without you intentionally meaning to imagine. If you are a parent and your teenage child isn't home, is supposed to be, and their phone is off. . . . Well . . . imagination might be active whether you want it to be or not.

Third, imagination is an *interior* activity only. When we physically bring into being things that were not present before, we are being *creative*, which is related but not synonymous with *imaginative*. Imagination is what we call the human ability to recall and create mentally and internally. Creativity is the capacity to use knowledge, experience, skills, and imagination

---

61. Stevenson, "Twelve Conceptions of Imagination," 238.

62. Bryant, "Imago Dei and Ecological Responsibility," 37.

in novel ways to produce something outside of one's self. These concepts are intimately related, but they are not identical.

Fourth, one of the common themes in the existing literature is an association between imagination and an "image." This is true in nontechnical places like a dictionary (Merriam-Webster says that imagination is "the act or power of forming a mental image of something not present to the senses or never before wholly perceived in reality") as well as very technical resources like the *Routledge Handbook of Philosophy of Imagination*. What the philosophers make clear, though, is that when they use the word "image" it is meant to "apply to the products of other sensory modalities as well, so that there is also auditory imagery and olfactory imagery, and so on, along with visual imagery."[63] I'm also in the philosopher camp and especially think that the embodied, or "somatic imagination," has a vital role in thinking about religion, faith, and spirituality.[64] Though you may think of "imagining" something as mentally recreating the *vision* of that thing in your "mind's eye," this is too narrow of a conception of imagination.

The philosopher David Abram puts it well when he says that imagination is "the way the senses themselves have of throwing themselves beyond what is immediately given, in order to make tentative contact with the other sides of things that we do not sense directly, with the hidden or invisible aspects of the sensible."[65] Going "beyond what is given" is an apt way of describing imagination: it reaches past the present state of things toward what more might come.

As I think of it, there is a parallel relationship between (a) sensory perception and what is perceivable and (b) imagination and what is possible. Imagining a thing is not the same as perceiving, believing, experiencing, or knowing that thing. But . . . it is an integral part of how we make meaning from our perceptions, beliefs, experience, and knowledge. Imagination is also a central part of how we develop expectations of the future. Imagination gives us a sense of what is possible even when we have not yet experienced it. One of the particularities to note in my definition is that "bringing things into consciousness" is an open-ended category that encompasses all the possible ways we perceive. Imagining is getting a sense of what is possible. Vision is our sense of sight and imagination is our sense of the possible.

Given the above, I wish we could swap the word "imagination" out for something else. The word "image" is clearly a part of imagination and for

---

63. Kind, "Introduction," 5.

64. Some of the most thorough work on the idea of "somatic imagination" is in Mark Fettes, "Senses and Sensibilities," 114–29.

65. Abram, *Spell of the Sensuous*, 58.

most people "image" means something visual. It is all well and good that philosophers have said that technically "image" means *all* the senses, but this is not intuitive to most folks. Doing a Google image search does not result in sounds and smells. I've thought that rather than imagination (which makes me think "image"), a better word would be sensation (which makes me think "sense"). However, talking about "The Christian Sensation" is off in a different direction entirely. Likewise, I sometimes think of imagination using the nonexistent word "experience-ation," as it captures the idea that it isn't just about the recollection of visual images but of perception of experience in general. But again, that isn't a word. So "imagination" it is.

Fifth, it is important to clarify that I firmly believe that the imagination isn't just a perception warehouse. It is that and . . . bringing into consciousness concepts or perceptions of objects and situations that have never existed anywhere can catalyze new ways of thinking, perceiving, and acting. As Maxine Greene said, imagination "is the capacity to break with the ordinary, the given, the taken-for-granted and open doors to possibility. One way of describing it is as a 'passion for possibility.'"[66] Likewise, I affirm Maria Montessori's claim that "we often forget that imagination is a force for the discovery of truth."[67] This doesn't mean imagination is *always* a force for discovering truth, but it is important to remember it *can* be that.

Sixth, in the context of Christian theological considerations of imagination, I think responsibility requires that theologians working with imagination address worries related to those of Augustine and Aquinas. Though perhaps no longer worded as a concern that "demons are known to work on men's imagination, until everything is other than it is,"[68] the fact is that there remains some suspicion of the imagination and to what degree it is a valuable part of a life of faith. To distinguish between "bad imagination" and "good imagination," some people use the category of "fancy" or "fantasy" to denote a quality of imagination that is undesirable or opposed to the "discovery of truth" as discussed above.

> Whereas imagination sunders and re-creates, fancy re-arranges experienced givens in novel patterns; thus the centaur, a conjoining of man and horse, is a fanciful image. The imagination has deep symbolizing power, while fancy can achieve only a skillful piece of photographic editing.[69]

66. Greene, "Imagination and the Healing Arts," 1.

67. Montessori, *Absorbent Mind*, 177.

68. Aquinas, *Summa Theologica*, 1.85.2.

69. Hart, *Unfinished Man and the Imagination*, 201.

The next chapter addresses this, so I won't go into great detail about it here, but I think it is a mistake to think about "fantasy" as a different type of faculty than imagination.

I don't think that imagination is solely "deep symbolizing power." It can be that for sure, but it is also thinking about centaurs. In fact, it is precisely because imagination can result in both powerful products of faith *and* dangerous delusions that it is crucial to consider imagination from a theological perspective. This is part of why I think Christians can be served by emphasizing the role of imagination in a life of faith.

Seventh, and finally, I want to recognize that human imagination operates in human bodies and social contexts. While I think there is always the possibility that an individual's imagination can craft some new vision of the world, it is also the case that the stories, symbols, and practices someone is exposed to influence what their imagination has access to as reference material in the future. Relatedly, given that imagination draws on sense experience, it is vital to recognize that there is no universally similar human experience. To be sure, we have some shared fears, hopes, and drives, but even there, the particulars of *how* they are experienced are not the same for everyone.

My identity as an able-bodied, white, educated man in the United States influences my experience of the stories I hear, the media I consume, and the symbols that have meaning to me. How I relate to those stories and perceive those experiences shapes the content and quality of what goes in my "warehouse" of imagination. Later, when I am looking through the aisles of that stockroom to see what I might want to use to imagine the future, the nature of those experiences shapes what it is I can imagine. What we can bring into consciousness is affected by what we have been exposed to previously: our experiences as particular bodies in particular contexts shape not just who we are in the present but also what more we might imagine.

Because of all of the above, I want people of faith to give more attention to the work of the imagination in our lives. I want to see better how it shapes what I believe and how I act. I want to see if there's anything I can do so that my inner life can be more informed by a vision of the world that resonates with God's peaceable reign. I've written this book to hopefully help with all that.

Questions for Reflection

1. Are you concerned at all to learn that social science data shows that people's imaginative and creative capacities are declining? Why or why not? Anything particular to church life or to people of faith?

2. What do you think about the argument that there are parts of Scripture that "presume the presence of an imaginative capacity" in people? Does it seem to you that imagination is required to read Scripture? Why or why not?

3. What do you think of the framing of the "elite view" problem of imagination? To what extent do you think that imagination is a regular part of daily life?

4. Have you ever encountered Christian ideas about the dangerousness of imagination? If so, what were the concerns being voiced? What do you think of this wariness and critique?

5. What are some of the differences you noticed between the various perspectives on imagination considered? What similarities? Was there a trend or pattern you noticed among them?

Related Readings

Brann, Eva. *The World of the Imagination: Sum and Substance*. Savage, MD: Rowman & Littlefield, 1991.

García-Rivera, Alejandro. *The Community of the Beautiful: A Theological Aesthetics*. Collegeville, MN: Liturgical, 1999.

González-Andrieu, Cecilia. *Bridge to Wonder: Art as a Gospel of Beauty*. Waco, TX: Baylor University Press, 2012.

Kearney, Richard. *The Wake of Imagination: Toward a Postmodern Culture*. London: Routledge, 1994.

Viladesau, Richard. *Theological Aesthetics: God in Imagination, Beauty, and Art*. New York: Oxford University Press, 1999.

Warnock, Mary. *Imagination and Time*. Oxford; Cambridge, MA: Blackwell, 1994.

2

Imagination and Experience

IN THE LAST CHAPTER, we discussed how Kant's reproductive and productive imagination categories became influential ways to think about the topic. We also noted that throughout the history of academic reflection on imagination in the West, there have been concerns about how imagination can be duplicitous or "fake" versions of reality. This chapter will explore how these concepts are connected and other ways of looking at the dynamics they describe. Let's first consider two major distinctions: how the imagination can operate in "fantasy-prone" and "reality-prone" ways.[1] In Kant's terms, both of these would be forms of the productive imagination. They are not about retrieving an image from the imagination warehouse but about remixing and making new images. However, they function differently.

I previously referred to the reproductive imagination as the "photocopy model" in that all it can do is reproduce images that already exist. This is similar to the idea of imagination as the warehouse of sense memory. Nothing new is "supposed" to be made, just perfect copies of past experiences: pristine folders pulled out of file cabinets stored in the archives of personal history. Now consider what would happen if that photocopier was broken and had a crack in the scanning glass. New copies would have cracks running across them, though the original does not. Something "new" is being made, but only because an error is being introduced into what is supposed to be an accurate copy. I refer to this concept as imagination working in a fantasy-prone way. This can be problematic because this kind of imagination can layer over our actual experience with an imagined mental veneer or outright falsehood. I don't have cracks in my forehead, even if it looks like I do in copies.

---

1. Loomis, "Imagination and Faith Development," 251–63.

Figure 2.1: A photo and photocopy of the author,
made with a cracked photocopier screen.

You may recall from the last chapter that Augustine referred to imagination of this sort as producing "phantasmata," which were "potentially deceptive, a contaminant of the heart, the root of idolatry, heresy, and diabolical contrivance, and capable of generating false images."[2] Similarly, consider the situation in which women are regularly portrayed in specific ways in the media and the fact that people can begin to confuse photoshopped *representations* of women for what a woman actually is or ought to be. Our imagination of what people are can be an obstacle to knowing people as *they* are. So too with our imagination of how the world works and how God works in it. What we imagine can get in the way of perceiving what is actually the case.

Conversely, another version of the productive imagination seems to be when it operates in "reality-prone" ways that envision and enable possibilities that have not been considered before. For example, we see this other aspect when Emily L. Howard, an engineer, credits her childhood days watching *Star Trek* as one of the reasons she went into science.

> I can't give all that power to a single show, but it certainly helped
> fuel my interest. . . . There were other things happening at the
> time, but at that young age to be exposed to these amazing pos-
> sibilities about the future, planted a seed very deeply in me.[3]

Something within an *imagined* world of TV fiction took root and bore fruit in Howard's actual life and work. We might consider this as willfully and

2. Djuth, "Veiled and Unveiled Beauty," 88.
3. Gaudin, "50 Years of Star Trek," para. 19.

intentionally taking images from the archives and making a collage with them, combining pieces of what we've experienced before to create a map of a place we have not yet seen. In both aspects of imagination, it is clarifying to note that there is no determinism at play. They are both "prone" toward fantasy and reality, not guaranteed to go there.

We'll talk more about it later, but it bears observing that these categories are somewhat porous and overlapping. For instance, when young girls watch negative portrayals of women and attempt to become in material actuality what is represented in a film, what kind of imagination is taking place? Exposure to fantasy can shape people in reality. This is imagination's power over our inner life. Reality can shift to become more like what would have been previously considered fantasy. The cost of shifts like this means that the question of what counts as "realistic imagination" bears more scrutiny.

Working with a very similar distinction of imagination "types," the philosopher Richard Kearney categorizes one as the "representational faculty which reproduces images of some pre-existing reality" and the other as "a creative faculty which produces images which often lay claim to an original status in their own right."[4] The technical distinctions articulated within a robust philosophy of imagination are not as vital to detail here as are some of their implications. Most important among these is the claim that insofar as "reality" refers to the present material conditions in which we are embedded, imagination has the capacity both to distract us from that reality *and* to help us envision a means of transforming that reality.

Kearney writes compellingly on the capacities of the creative imagination to point the way to substantial changes in actual, material conditions:

> The metaphors, symbols, or narratives produced by imagination
> all provide us with imaginative variations of the world, thereby
> offering us the freedom to conceive of the world in other ways
> and to undertake forms of action which might lead to its trans-
> formation. . . . The possible worlds of imagination can be made
> real by action.[5]

If imagination were just "fantasy-prone" and unable to be anything but cracks in our thinking of the world, it would be strange to consider it beneficial. However, understood as also possessing "reality-prone" characteristics, the productive imagination is part of how we can participate in the work of positive and faithful change in the world. Developing capacities of the generative

---

4. Kearney, *Wake of Imagination*, 15.

5. Kearney, *Poetics of Imagining*, 149.

reality-prone imagination allows for seeing new ways of being that have not yet come to be, discerning a sense of what more might be possible.

As Jesuit John W. O'Malley wrote, "inventiveness and innovation require intelligence, but beyond intelligence they entail imagination, that is, the mental agility to make a leap beyond the accepted paradigm to another and to see the relationship between them that has escaped others."[6] In this form, imagination carries with it the capacity to conceive and *reconceive* of possibility. Ultimately, imagination might not only enable one to conceive of new possibilities, but, brought into creative action, can birth new ways of being.[7] The seeds of these new possibilities can take root through the imagination at multiple levels.

I think of imagination as being experienced across a series of embedded continuums. First, there are the large distinctions between imagination's reproductive and productive aspects. Then, within the productive aspect, there is a continuum between the fantasy-prone and reality-prone aspects. Finally, within the reality-prone aspect, there is another continuum across which imagination functions and is experienced. Within this last continuum, I refer to the experiences as "hermeneutic" and "apocalyptic."

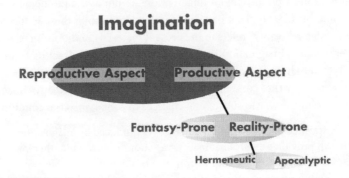

Figure 2.2: A visual representation of the imagination "types" most used in this book.

6. O'Malley, "Jesuit Schools and the Humanities," 28–29.

7. Paul Ricœur argues that the generative imagination is "connected with an ontology" and that the new possibilities seen via imaginative exploration lead to "a kind of second ontology" in which new ways of being enter the world first through the imagination and then later in substance and action. Ricœur, "Lectures," 19:13, cited in Taylor, "Ricœur's Philosophy of Imagination," 93.

Within the spectrum embedded within the reality-prone aspect of imagination, there is an experience of imagination as hermeneutic or interpretive. These imaginative processes allow us to "weep with those who weep" even when we ourselves have not lost what has caused the tears. This is reality-prone imagination in that it helps us to be empathetic and communicate complexities to others across difference. It is how we come to derive meaning from Jesus as the vine: we can hold onto descriptions of the present that are not true but reveal truth. We act and are different in the world because we can imagine what it is like as another person. This kind of imagining often feels distinctly intentional. I say that this kind of experience of imagination gives a home to hermeneutics. We become better connected to people and ideas, recognizing that empathy and interpretation both have their roots in imagination. It feels like something we *do*, like putting on glasses to help us see differently, or speaking through an interpreter so that we might be understood.

On the other side of the spectrum from hermeneutic considerations of imagination is an aspect of reality-prone imagination which I call "apocalyptic." These are experiences of an event or catalyst. These experiences of encounter or "opening" can profoundly shift how we see ourselves and our surroundings, revealing new ways of seeing and being in the world. I think about what happened to Saul on the road to Damascus and how afterward he not only experienced the world differently but experienced *himself* differently in relation to it. What he imagined to be possible had radically shifted. We'll talk about this at length in chapter 4, but this is similar to the theologian Garrett Green's claim that imagination is the "point of contact" (*Anknüpfungspunkt*) where human experience encounters revelation.[8] The experience of imagination as "apocalyptic" feels less like it is something under your control and more like something you encounter.

Just as there is an overlap between fantasy-prone and reality-prone qualities of imagination, there is a connection between hermeneutic and apocalyptic experiences of imagination. I've named them as separate because they feel different to me, but I also want to be clear that I don't think they exist as wholly separate and discrete "types." That is why I talk about them as ways we might *experience* imagination rather than as a particular kind of imagination. I think about—and name—aspects of imagination in terms of their consequences.

Let's say that God's Spirit is still at work in the world and gifts of the Spirit are still poured upon us today. But . . . let's also say that I've been told that God ceased offering gifts of the Spirit after the apostles. In this case, my

8. Green, *Imagining God*.

capacity to see God at work around me might very well be diminished. How I imagine the world to be (one *without* current gifts of the Spirit) interferes with my ability to see it as it is (one *with* current gifts of the Spirit). When imagination is doing that, it is functioning in a "fantasy-prone" way. My imagination is misleading me, making me think things are true that are not. This would also be the case if the situation was flipped around and I imagined it was possible there were gifts of the Spirit, but, in fact, God stopped handing those out thousands of years ago, or never did in the first place.

However, consider a situation where I'm encouraged to think about God's gifts being present today and that God *is* at work around me. As a result, I can better interpret God at work for myself and communicate how I see that happening to others. To some significant degree, what imagination is doing is the same in both cases; it is just that the surrounding circumstances have changed. This is an important distinction.

It isn't as if there is one "type" of imagination that is fantasy-prone and a separate one that is reality-prone. Instead, depending on how imagination is at work and the actual circumstances of the world, we *experience* it as pointing us toward different things. This will be discussed quite a bit in the book, but it is worth briefly acknowledging now: imagination can produce challenging and problematic interpretations just as well as it can reveal new and healing ways of seeing. This is one of the reasons that discernment is so important to conversations about faith and imagination. Something other than imagination needs to assess the rightness (or usefulness) of imagining. This book is mainly about imagination as a source of what *is* possible rather than as a fantasy overlay on top of things without change.[9]

Within that play of the possible, I refer to the difference between hermeneutic and apocalyptic experiences of imagining. As with the "fantasy-prone" and "reality-prone" imagination discussed before, I am not suggesting that these terms point to separate capacities or faculties that produce distinct kinds of imagination, simply that it can be helpful to name different ways in which we can experience imagination. This chapter explores these distinctions and how they can be part of the life of faith.

---

9. I should note that many atheists would claim that the entirety of the religious imagination is "fantasy-prone." This is a major thing to think through and has been an important idea to wrestle with since Ludwig Feuerbach (and then later Karl Marx). This idea will come up again in chapters 3 and 4.

Why Hermeneutics?

The hermeneutic function of imagination helps us interpret the people and events around us, shaping our views and providing interior sketches of the results of our actions. It helps us to create metaphors to explain our experiences *to* others and is part of what allows us to understand the views *of* others. It helps us to have empathy and is a vital part of our capacity to connect with other people and bring ourselves to an understanding of how they might feel even though we don't have the same perspective.

While I'm unlikely to get it exactly right, I can imagine what another person might think or feel. This is a reflective "What if . . . ?" capacity of imagination: I use it to consider what it might be like to see and feel things from another person's perspective. A related function of the imagination is when I consider the future consequences of action. What if I take a job that pays less but feels more aligned with my values? What might happen?

If imagination is the capacity to bring things that are not observably present into consciousness, then one way to think about "what may be" is to consider it an imaginative interpretation of the present. Future possibilities are definitionally not observably present, so when we consider what is *possible in the future,* we necessarily need to use something more than sense perception.

For those of us that believe there is reason to see God still at work and moving in the world, the hermeneutic function of imagination is vital and routine. The fact that interpretation, empathy, and reflection on the future are a regular part of life is amazing! Rather than think about its dailiness as a mark against its noteworthiness, I am inclined to think about how incredible it is that there are many days when our present actions are decided based on their consequences in the future. This can be as mundane as when I save up money with hopes to buy something in the future, act with kindness and empathetic mercy imagining what life as another is like, or as work to change some social issue, the impacts of which I may never live to see.

In these examples, the imagination draws on other experiences and knowledge to explore what *might* be. Imagination does not pluck possibility from the void and point toward ways of being radically and wholly disconnected from the present. Instead, it is a capacity which works with what is and has already been to surface what might yet be. This is part of why I think there is something to be gained by thinking about the hermeneutic function of imagination.

Hermeneutics is the study of interpretation, the academic investigation of how people make meaning (usually from texts). Related to theological conversations, the phrase "biblical hermeneutics" is often used, suggesting that how we interpret the Bible isn't straightforward but needs contextualization and nuance. I find that it helps me to remember that within the word "hermeneutics" there is a clue as to its nature.

The root word inside hermeneutics comes from the Greek verb *hermeneuein*, which means to "make something clear, to announce or unveil a message."[10] The *"herme-"* part of the word comes from "Hermes," the Greek god associated with messengers, travel, and language.[11] He's the one who helps to pass notes between the gods on Mount Olympus and mortals; is able to bop back and forth between hells, heavens, and the earth; and is the patron and protector of travelers, inventors, and poets. Oh, and also thieves, those who take from others for their own purposes . . .

I often envision the study of hermeneutics as an interview with Hermes about the various techniques he uses when he's transporting meaning from the texts to the minds of readers. What happens to meaning in transport? When you pick up a fresh delivery of meaning how long before it spoils? Are certain vehicles better than others? Do you ever have a hard time finding someone to sign the slip to accept the shipment? Do some goods get marked "undeliverable"? What do you do if there isn't any parking available?

Going further back, the word "hermes" itself predates the god, stemming from the Greek *herma*, the word for a "cairn, pathmarker, or boundary stone."[12] Some part of hermeneutics is about how we find our way along the roads of meaning. Boundaries can keep others out just as well as keep us within what we think of as safe. Hermeneutics asks questions about how we interpret texts, how our surroundings and assumptions influence our understanding, and how we want to proceed once we know that the path from text to meaning isn't always straight.

10. Thompson, "Hermeneutics," 360–61.

11. Harper, "Hermeneutic."

12. Grau, *Refiguring Theological Hermeneutics*, 83.

Figure 2.3: A cairn on the summit of Brown's Law
in Northumberland National Park, England.

In public domain. Photo by Geoff Holland.

If you knew—asks hermeneutics—that someone was a career criminal who had been found guilty of financial fraud, wouldn't you make sure to listen with a bit of a filter when that person was giving investment advice? Well—says hermeneutics—every person and every text has a story like that, some helpful framing and background that it would be good to know about as you take text on the page and try to make meaning out of it for your life. Learning about the contexts and backstories helps us to make more informed "filters" through which we can read and interpret.

If I headed to the Atlantic Ocean and filled up a liter container with seawater, I could boil it away until I was left with nothing but a small pile of salt weighing about thirty-five grams. I could also replicate this experiment in the Pacific and up and down the coasts of most places in the world. I would get the same result every time. The thing is, meaning does not work like salt.

Texts do not contain meaning in such a way that there is a process (boiling) that removes all the extraneous material (water) and leaves behind a consistent quantity of meaning (salt) that anyone can find. To be sure, some things reveal themselves if you know more about the context or can read the original language in which something was written. However, there is a slipperiness to meaning and interpretation that often requires the interpreter to do some imagining.

Seawater boiling breaks down as a metaphor, at least in part, because the experiment works independent of the experimenter. No matter who collects the water, who sets up the hot plate, or what ocean is used, the result is a bit of salt. The salt-finding process happens regardless of the person doing it. This is not how meaning is found in the texts we identify as Scripture. Even when it is useful, adding context and providing reason and rationality is not like adding heat: meaning is not saturated in texts like salt in water. Even if the neurological processes of sensual perception (visual, auditory, tactical, etc.) were precisely identical between all people, what we imagine them to mean could differ.

I don't want to wade far into the debates of whether or not there is inherent meaning in text, the role of authorial intent, and reader-response criticism, but I do think it is worth noting that very few contemporary scholars have a strictly "positivist" approach in which all meaning is like an ore that can be mined from the ground of text.[13] Meaning cannot be extracted like salt or silver. It is contingent—at least usually—on the circumstances in which it emerges. That being said, there are limits, and context plays a huge role.

Monthly bank statements with increasingly smaller balances likely means that less money is available. To the extent that this is a kind of numerical reasoning, it is, in fact, pretty straightforward. The *implications* of what this might mean regarding how I plan to pay bills require some contextualization and imagination, but some meaning (I don't have much money left) can be pretty clearly "pulled out" without much interpretation. This kind of clarity is not limited to numbers either.

For example, if my wife texts me, "Please get some milk on your way home," and I interpret it as "Feel free to invest our life savings in crypto-currency," she'd be well within reason to question my skills of interpretation. Why? Partly because the circumstances surrounding a text message like that are not usually ones that merit such a stretch of the imagination: there doesn't seem like there is a good reason to imagine that it needed such intense interpretation to be understood. Also, an interpretation like that should raise some serious questions about whether or not I am acting in good faith and attempting to understand the content. I might just be using the act of "interpretation" as a cover for seeing whatever I want in

---

13. In terms of good work on the nature and development of biblical hermeneutics I highly recommend both Vanhoozer's *Is There a Meaning in This Text?* and Schneiders's *The Revelatory Text.*

the text. Another way to say this is to ask whether or not my interpretation is "reasonable" given the context. Asking it this way shows one of the conundrums of thinking about the interpretive and hermeneutic function of imagination.

Viewed from one perspective, reasonableness seems an entirely appropriate category for reflection on my "interpretation." Barring some preestablished system in which we've agreed that "Please get some milk on your way home" is actually code for "Feel free to invest our life savings in cryptocurrency," it is not reasonable to interpret one as the other. Viewed another way, it seems that using "reasonableness" would have a pretty limiting effect on one of the positive things productive, reality-prone imagination should be good at: allowing for new viable, creative ideas. In fact, imaginative innovations that have had significant ramifications often were first seen as profoundly *un*reasonable and worth dismissing.

Critics were brutal when the painter Claude Monet first started to paint in a new hazy style in the 1860s. His work was considered "formless, unfinished, and ugly."[14] He is now widely regarded as a founder of the French Impressionism movement and an influence on Vincent van Gogh and Henri Matisse.

In the early 1900s, German geophysicist and meteorologist Alfred Wegener first proposed the theory of continental drift, that all the continents were once connected. He was literally laughed out of an academic conference with his work referred to as "Germanic pseudo-science." He was accused of falsifying evidence, spinning himself into "a state of auto-intoxication."[15] Today the concept of "Pangea" is universally accepted among established geologists.

Madeleine L'Engle, now widely revered as a pillar of fantasy literature, received twenty-six rejections from publishers before someone was willing to publish her most famous book. In her memoir, L'Engle remembers feeling "I was, perhaps, out of joint with time . . . my books for children were rejected for reasons which would be considered absurd today: publisher after publisher turned down *A Wrinkle in Time* because it deals overtly with the problem of evil, and it was too difficult for children."[16] One editor rejected the book saying he loved it, but "didn't quite dare do it, as it isn't really

---

14. Getty Museum Collection, "Claude Monet," para. 2.

15. Conniff, "Continental Drift."

16. L'Engle, *Circle of Quiet*, 20.

classifiable."[17] That book went on to win the Newbery Medal, the Sequoyah Book Award, and the Lewis Carroll Shelf Award.[18]

Comparable stories could be told of Galileo Galilei, Gabriel García Márquez, and Jean-Michel Basquiat, among others. It is clear, for example, that Jesus had a vision for the people of God that authorities of his time did not think was reasonable. Here's the tension as I see it: when new imaginative and innovative ideas or interpretations are put forth and fail to gain purchase with others, they are often mocked or dismissed as useless, frivolous, false, or downright detrimental. However, if people can only ever put forth things that are already acceptable, it is hard to see how exactly the imagination contributes to new ways of seeing. I've found that political science's concept of an "Overton window" is helpful in thinking about this issue.

The Overton window is a model to help understand how social norms change over time and influence politics. The idea is that if a politician is interested in remaining in office, they are limited in what policy they can support: it is safest to only pursue policies based on ideas that are widely accepted throughout society. For any given issue, there is an Overton window, and "acceptable policies" are *within* the window for that issue. Other possible policies exist which *theoretically* could be advocated for, but politicians are less inclined to support them because it would likely result in them losing the popular support they need to remain in power. To some degree, *any* movement away from the norm makes support harder to find. The window can move, widen, or shrink, but it is rare that any single individual can markedly push the window either in size or position.[19] It happens sometimes, but usually it is a slow, incremental change. I think this is similar to how the hermeneutic function of imagination works in relation to individuals and society.

Figure 2.4: An Overton window diagram with
Joshua Treviño's six degrees of acceptance.

17. L'Engle, *Circle of Quiet*, 218.

18. Martin, "Madeleine L'Engle."

19. Mackinac Center for Public Policy, "Overton Window," para. 2.

Interpretation of perception happens within the context of both a personal and societal history. Interpretations of texts and experiences in the present gain social purchase when they are digestible by others. "Digestibility," as such, is determined by a combination of individuals' personal inclinations and openness as well as social norms and mores that influence what counts as acceptable behavior or thinking. Imagination, as the capacity to bring into consciousness things that are not observably present, can bring new ideas and interpretations into being. However, for them to remain in the world outside of an individual, those new ideas and interpretations need to be brought into circulation among others.

I think often of the fact that the word hermeneutics traces itself back to the idea of a path marker or boundary stone. How we interpret the world can shape where we end up going and what paths we take. As we make trails others can follow. Sometimes the invitation into another person's imagination can be catalytic for a larger change. When Dr. Martin Luther King Jr. "had a dream" and imagined that "one day every valley shall be exalted, every hill and mountain shall be made low," and that "on the red hills of Georgia the sons of former slaves and the sons of former slave-owners will be able to sit down together at a table of brotherhood,"[20] he made a choice to interpret the current circumstances, bringing into consciousness a possible future that was not yet present. How we imagine the future is an interpretation of the present.

In this same vein, the Jesuit theologian William Lynch suggests that faith is a way we experience reality, not some separate, discrete object that we can possess.

> Faith is a way of producing images and a way of assembling the facts so they become intelligible as evidence that the world is more like the one portrayed by images of faith than not. . . . Faith is the imagination which produces images that become evidence for living life according to that faith. Fullness of life in its deepest meaning should be the result of faith.[21]

For Christians that understand the world as something created by God, the situation can be a bit more complex than interpreting a text message or a passage of Scripture. How do we "assemble the facts" of the world? How do I imagine myself living in the future? What are we all headed toward? At its most expansive, the imagination invites us to consider questions of this depth. It is at this level I think of the apocalyptic function of imagination.

20. King, "I Have a Dream."
21. Bednar, *Faith*, 136–37.

Why Apocalypse?

The apocalyptic function of imagination exists on the other side of the spectrum from a hermeneutic one. It is an encounter with imagination that is experienced as an event or catalyst that changes how you interpret things and how you understand yourself, the world, God, or your relationship to those things. As I noted before, I think about what happened to Saul on the road to Damascus and how afterward, he not only experienced the world differently but experienced *himself* differently in relation to it.

Imagination in this respect feels less like it is something under your control and more like something you encounter. It is less of "a day in the life" when "a day" is a stand-in for regularity and routine. It is more of "*the* day when everything changed." Imagination functioning in hermeneutic ways is "a day" and in apocalyptic ways is "the day." The hermeneutic function of imagination can significantly impact one's life, but it feels akin to a willful and voluntary interpretation of what we imagine a text might mean or what another person intends to communicate. The apocalyptic function of imagination feels less like there is a clear distinction between the interpreted content and the interpreter. We experience the apocalyptic function of imagination when we imagine ourselves as someone new, the world as something we did not see before, or God as being present in ways we previously had not considered.

Though this is in some ways simply the hermeneutic imagination drawing upon different ratios of "source material" for its work, experientially, there does seem to be a difference between imagining what a text means or what a person is feeling and imagining what "I" means or what God is. Owing to how this kind of imagining can have broader ripples in the experience of a person of faith, I think reflection explicitly dedicated to it is warranted.

In colloquial speech, an apocalypse is the end of the world. For example, postapocalyptic movies like *Mad Max* and *Bird Box* depict a vision of the world after such a disaster that normal society is no longer possible. Related to Christian theological conversations, "apocalyptic literature" is a term that refers to Scriptures that reflect on the ending of the world. Most commonly, this is a reference to the books of Daniel and Revelation, though there are portions of other books that are apocalyptic as well.[22] Important to note is that while popular usage has "the apocalypse" as a reference to possible *events*, a biblical apocalypse is a revelation or unveiling of some truth.

---

22. E.g., Isa 24–27; Mark 13; 2 Pet 3; et al.

The word "apocalyptic" itself comes from the Greek *apokalyptein,* meaning to "uncover, disclose, reveal."[23] In the Christian context, the first three words of the "book of Revelation" establish that it is, in Greek, the *apokalypsis* of Jesus Christ. Something about Christ and the world is revealed or unveiled in that text. That is, it isn't just a prediction of what *will happen* but an imaginative invitation to consider what *is already happening* in the present. Bible scholar Leonard Thompson, an expert on the book of Revelation, describes it well:

> Through poetic and imagistic language the seer creates a world which cannot be interpreted as simply an allegory of the sociohistorical times. Undoubtedly, the seer makes commentary upon life both inside and outside the church. . . . Such language, however, does not simply describe in code universally observable social realities of Jews, fellow Christians, and the Roman Empire; the language creates a symbolic universe which transforms and re-presents social reality in terms of its own order.[24]

Apocalyptic literature is not a fortune teller's forecast of the future, but a vision intended to hold a transformative mirror to the present.

When I think about the idea of apocalypse in a theological sense, I find myself oscillating between thinking of it as (a) an interpretable political critique of the present and (b) a literary invitation into a vision of the possible future. Bible scholar Amos Wilder points to this exact multifacetedness:

> On the one hand we take [apocalyptic texts] too literally and ignore the poetical mentality of the race and the age. On the other hand we make a mistake if we think of them as merely symbol and poetry as a modern would understand them.[25]

The notion of apocalypse isn't just about a poetic take on the present but an opportunity to see the present intertwined with what might be in such a way that current events and meanings take on new hues.

Where I've come to rest is that the invitation of apocalyptic text requires me to orient myself with it so that I cannot entirely comprehend it. Active apocalyptic interpretations are not something that I can make submit to my understanding and expertise. They are not just coded messages and with enough heat from historical fact and biblical scholarship I can burn away the excess, leaving only the "important stuff" left. Instead, they invite

---

23. Harper, "Apocalypse," para. 1.

24. Thompson, "Sociological Analysis of Tribulation," 147.

25. Wilder, "Relation of Eschatology to Ethics," 7.

me into a reinterpretation of the present and an experience of the possible. This invitation reminds me of a story.

C. S. Lewis's books of Narnia end with an allegorical description of heaven. In it, all the main characters and "everyone you had ever heard of " end up following the Christ figure of Aslan the Lion through the country-side to continuing calls of "further up and further in."[26] As they parade along, a curious thing begins to happen. The further along they go, the more intense and real things seem to feel. The situation is described as similar to the feeling of turning to view a shoreline through a window after first looking at it only through a mirror. Lewis says that the waves in the mirror were just as real, yet the waves through the window "were somehow different—deeper, more wonderful."[27] Turning from the mirror to look out on the shore directly is like the experience of those headed "further in." In Lewis's words, "the difference between the old Narnia and the new Narnia was like that. The new one was a deeper country: every rock and flower and blade of grass looked as if it meant more."[28]

Eventually the whole procession passes through golden gates and into a garden. It is there that Lucy has a realization. The garden was not just a garden but the whole of the world.

> "I see," she said. "This is still Narnia, and more real and more beautiful than the Narnia down below, just as it was more real and more beautiful than the Narnia outside the stable door! I see . . . world within world, Narnia within Narnia. . . ."
> "Yes," said Mr. Tumnus, "like an onion: except that as you continue to go in and in, each circle is larger than the last."[29]

The explicit suggestion in the book is that heaven is a perfected form of what we have known, just "more real and more beautiful."

Lucy's "I see" is apocalyptic in that it unveils the nature of what is to come both to Lucy and the reader. There are clear echoes of the biblical idea of "new heavens and a new earth,"[30] but this unveiling is also expressly lik-ened to Plato's Cave which suggests that the revelation is total or complete. Lewis has the narrator say it quite plainly in the book's last line, writing that "all their life in this world and all their adventures in Narnia had only been the cover and the title page: now at last they were beginning Chapter One of

26. Lewis, *Last Battle*, 140.
27. Lewis, *Last Battle*, 150.
28. Lewis, *Last Battle*, 150.
29. Lewis, *Last Battle*, 158.
30. E.g., Isa 65:17; Rev 21:1; 2 Pet 3:13, etc.

the Great Story."[31] There's the world you knew, and then there's the perfected world of the garden that is just like that world, but better.

I must admit that this vision leaves me slightly unsatisfied.

What if the invitation to "further up and further in," is always available? What if instead of a fixed point to which we're being led, the leading never ends? Having heard of the "deeper country" where "every rock and flower and blade of grass looked as if it meant more," can transform how we see and live in the present. This is the kind of apocalyptic vision I think the imagination can unfold when put into faithfulness's service without a firm dividing line at the garden's golden gate. Not just a "here" and "there" of reality, but an unending unveiling: what awaits is the possibility of something ever more real and more beautiful.

Earlier I briefly considered the circumstances around trailblazing artists and scientists whose imaginations and creations were eventually accepted as true or beautiful but started out being derided or dismissed. I also described the concept of the "Overton window" and how it illustrates one way of looking at social change. Now I want to bring these ideas together to help explain how I think about the function of the apocalyptic imagination. To do that, we'll start with a look at the work of Thomas Kuhn, a philosopher of science.

A Paradigm Problem

In literature about societal change, Kuhn's concept of a "paradigm shift" often surfaces. His theory was first articulated in his seminal 1962 text, *The Structure of Scientific Revolutions.*[32] At its core is the claim that each established scientific field operates within a set of conceptual assumptions (the paradigm) that provides the structure which supplies the vocabulary for describing the world as it is observed. All scientific research within the paradigm is what Kuhn refers to as "normal science" and is about trying to see how far the paradigm can be expanded to explain the world.

> The discovery of anomalous results does not lead easily to the abandonment of a paradigm; scientists are more likely to explain anomalies, initially at least, as limitations of experimental method or equipment. But it is this very dogged adherence to a paradigm that allows certain experimental results to be understood as anomalous.[33]

31. Lewis, *Last Battle*, 160.

32. Kuhn, *Structure of Scientific Revolutions.*

33. Shedinger, "Kuhnian Paradigms and Biblical Scholarship," 455.

The paradigm is the agreed-upon model on which understanding is built. As a result, scientists are purposefully on watch for research results that do not seem to match what the paradigm would predict.[34] Noting these anomalies is at the heart of the scientific process.

> Over time, anomalous results accumulate to a degree that they demand to be taken more seriously. At this point, [an innovative scientist] will question the theoretical presuppositions of the currently reigning paradigm and articulate a new paradigm that has power to explain the anomalous results in a systematic way. When this happens, the scientific community is on the verge of a paradigm change.[35]

Given enough discrepancies between predicted outcomes and what is happening, the entire system eventually comes to a tipping point, after which the prediction model has to be reassessed and potentially reformed.

The theologian Garrett Green uses this idea when he talks about the "paradigmatic imagination" as the means of taking "a leap beyond the accepted paradigm to another."[36] A similar move is also part of the work of biblical scholar Walter Brueggemann:

> The world we take as "given" is a long-established act of imagination that appeals to be and claims assent as the only legitimate occupant of the field. It follows, then, that long-imagined "givens" can indeed be challenged, and a "countergiven" is entertainable. I take this to be the point of Kuhn's "new paradigm," and I will argue it is the point of Christian proclamation that aims at conversion.[37]

Similar comparisons are made by numerous Bible and religion scholars. It does seem like a useful metaphor to explain changes. For example, I think about the origins of my own denomination of The Religious Society of Friends (Quakers) and the experience of Margaret Fell when she heard early Quaker minister George Fox preach for the first time.

> [The preaching] opened me so, that it cut me to the heart, and then I saw clearly we were all wrong. So I sat me down in my pew again, and cried bitterly: and I cried in my spirit to the

---

34. Shedinger, "Kuhnian Paradigms and Biblical Scholarship," 455.

35. Shedinger, "Kuhnian Paradigms and Biblical Scholarship," 455.

36. See Green, *Imagining God*, esp. chapters 3 and 4.

37. Brueggemann, *Texts Under Negotiation*, 13.

Lord, "We are all thieves, we are all thieves, we have taken the scriptures in words, and know nothing of them in ourselves."[38]

Though Fell already knew the Bible in a profound way *before* she was "cut to the heart," something happened in her experience of Fox's ministry such that she had to reexamine her relationship to Scripture and reorient her understanding of what she thought faithfulness was. It seems metaphorically viable, in other words, to say that Fox brought about a paradigm shift in Fell and others who joined the Quaker movement. Similar arguments could be made about the advent of historical-critical method of interpreting Scripture or Vatican II as moments of paradigm shift, among many others. But . . . I'm wary of doing so.[39]

In natural science, a new paradigm only surfaces when there are enough unexpected results in experimentation that there is evidence to suggest that something may be wrong with the predictive capacities of the model. If a new model can explain the old and the new data, it will eventually become the new paradigm. As biblical scholar Robert Shedinger puts it, in science the paradigm shift "forces itself upon scientists; it is not the result of imaginative or subversive work by scientists." In fact, "scientists use their imaginations first and foremost to save the current paradigm, not intentionally to subvert it!"[40] When a new scientific paradigm sets in, older ones are shifted out. No one is at a research university doing scientific work on alchemy, for example. However, something else is going on for biblical studies, religion, and theology.

> Because a biblical studies discipline is always marked by multiple paradigms and inter-paradigm debate, there is no linear movement from paradigm to paradigm that can be construed as advancement. . . . Whereas in science the adoption of each new paradigm constitutes a new foundation on which all scientists in a discipline agree and forms a new fundamental platform from which to move forward like rungs on a ladder, biblical scholars continue to debate which paradigm constitutes the correct foundational platform.[41]

38. Fell, as cited in Braithwaite, *Beginnings of Quakerism*, 101.

39. I'm indebted to the work of Robert Shedinger in his article "Kuhnian Paradigms and Biblical Scholarship." In that piece he put his finger on something that had been bothering me for years but had not articulated well. I commend it to anyone looking for a more robust account of the issues at stake.

40. Shedinger, "Kuhnian Paradigms and Biblical Scholarship," 463.

41. Shedinger, "Kuhnian Paradigms and Biblical Scholarship," 466.

The situation is even more complex in the arts and societal norms. For example, the concept of linear progress is not applicable to painting. While Claude Monet may be regarded as an innovator, the result of French Impressionism isn't that realistic representational painting was left behind. Nor did Jesus' birth, teaching, and sacrifice move things "forward like rungs on a ladder" so that all agreed on the new paradigm.

There is undoubtedly metaphorical power to the notion of intense imaginative innovations being paradigm shifts, but I find that thinking of them in terms of the apocalyptic function of imagination seems more fruitful. Talking about the apocalyptic function of imagination allows for an option that is less about proceeding down the one-way tracks of progress and more about hearing the story of a deeper country where every rock and flower looked as if it meant more and consequently feeling as if the present means more as well. Apocalypse invites us

> between time and the eternal, between the veiled and the unveiled, between the human and the inhuman, between order and chaos. . . . It opens up a kind of third space—a paradoxical central margin, an evocation of the human within the human, the veiled within the unveiled.[42]

There are certainly imaginative interpretations that result in major shifts in thinking, but outside of natural sciences, they rarely stop people from having other interpretations.

How people imagine and interpret faith is always in a contest with other people's visions and interpretations. When a "paradigm-shifting" interpretation emerges in theological thought, it doesn't move "forward like rungs on a ladder," it broadens or narrows the edges of the Overton window, making new ways of being seem more or less viable. The constant invitation to the deeper country of imagination includes the possibility of discovering new depth in something long known. In fact, sometimes retrieving older symbols or practices can bring new life into present circumstances.

Continuums in Imagination

The apocalyptic is the space where what is and what is possible blend, even if just for a moment. Imagination can break open our experience of the present and its sense of stability, reminding us something more might yet come. Novelist Ursula K. Le Guin said it well: "imagination, working at full strength, can shake us out of our fatal, adoring self-absorption and

42. Mills, *Approaching Apocalypse*, 20.

make us look up and see—with terror or with relief—that the world does not in fact belong to us at all."[43] How we imagine God and the world that God is inviting us into is shaped by what we have seen and sensed in the past. However, it is not limited to only that which has come before. Our imagination rests in the space of overlap, a seedbed of the future that can nourish ideas of change in the soil of the present.

I think of imagination in spatial terms as the "place" where our ideas of now and later both live. It is the overlap between how we interpret the present and how we think the future might be. Imagination is the home of interpretation. The theologian Rubem Alves describes this dynamic powerfully.

> Imagination is not an instrument of clairvoyance made for revealing the secrets of the future or of another world. It is a mirror. The impossible it reflects is the impossible that is actually lived. The secret of utopias is thus the reality from which they grow.[44]

What we find in our imagination—especially as we ask what we imagine God wants for us and the world—can be transformative. Seeds of the future are nourished in the imagination of the present.

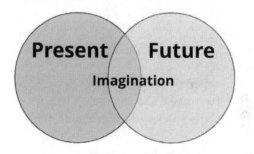

Figure 2.5: A Venn diagram of time, with imagination in the overlap.

It is precisely because this ground *is* so fertile and imagination draws from the interface of past, present, and possible to influence how we think about ourselves, others, and God that it is worth giving greater attention to the imaginative dimension of spiritual life.

As long as you remember that I think that the imagination experientially works along a continuum and not as discrete "types," then the following chart might be a useful way to sum up where we've arrived. It isn't

43. Phillips, "Fantastic Ursula K. Le Guin," para. 4.
44. Alves, *Tomorrow's Child*, 106.

exhaustive regarding all the things that can be used as the "raw materials" to mix with imagination, nor does it contain all the possible outcomes, but it gives some sense of the scale I am considering.

Function of Imagination	Input	Result
Hermeneutic	Particular existing texts, conversations, and events	Imagined meaning
Apocalyptic	Imagined meaning in the present	Imagined future, sense of self, relationships

If imagination is the capacity to bring things that are not observably present into consciousness, then the "Result" column is "what is brought into consciousness." The "Input" column contains the things that are the scaffolds or launching platforms from which the imagination takes its primary orientation. So, for example, you might hear a sermon and, as a result, may have a new sense of the meaning of some piece of Scripture. What that Scripture means has opened new imagined possibilities. In the wake of this, in wrestling with that new meaning, you might realize the newly discovered meaning thrusts the imagination out into considering the consequences of that meaning. You might realize it points to new imaginable ways of being in the world and relating to others, to oneself, and to God. This does, though, raise several questions.

Regarding the hermeneutic imagination, how can we tell if the meanings we interpretively imagine about the present are true? Relatedly, when we interpret the present and imagine the future, how do we know if we're imagining it correctly? Concerning the apocalyptic imagination, if part of what is happening is that you feel a new world has been revealed to you, then who or what enabled that revelation? What is the relationship between imagination and faithfulness to a tradition? How do we determine what "God really wants" as opposed to what "we really want and want to use God to justify?" How can we discern between imagination and delusion? These questions are considered in the next chapter.

Questions for Reflection

1. Why doesn't this chapter use the terms "the hermeneutic imagination" and "the apocalyptic imagination" as separate things, instead talking

about the hermeneutic and apocalyptic "aspects" or "functions" of imagination?

2. Has reading this chapter changed how you think about imagination or interpretation at all? If so, how?

3. Is there anything you find yourself curious, concerned, or worried about from this chapter? If so, what is it and why?

4. Are there any experiences you've had where how you interpreted or imagined something shifted how you saw things afterwards? Have you heard any stories of this happening to others?

5. How would you describe the difference between the scientific "paradigm-shift" model and the political "Overton window" model? Which one seems like a better fit for describing imaginative innovations to you? Are there any other models or metaphors that you can think of that might be useful?

Related Readings

Alves, Rubem A. *Tomorrow's Child: Imagination, Creativity, and the Rebirth of Culture.* New York: Harper & Row, 1972.

Brueggemann, Walter. *Texts Under Negotiation: The Bible and Postmodern Imagination.* Minneapolis: Fortress, 1993.

Kearney, Richard. *Poetics of Imagining: Modern to Post-Modern.* New York: Fordham University Press, 1998.

Levy, Sandra M. *Imagination and the Journey of Faith.* Grand Rapids: Eerdmans, 2008.

Vanhoozer, Kevin J. *Is There a Meaning in This Text? The Bible, the Reader, and the Morality of Literary Knowledge.* Grand Rapids: Zondervan, 2009.

3

Delusion and Suspicion

LAST CHAPTER I DISCUSSED how the hermeneutic function of imagination helps us interpret the people and events around us, shaping our views and providing interior sketches of the results of our actions. I distinguished it from the apocalyptic function of imagination as experienced as an event or catalyst that changes not just how you interpret things but how you understand yourself, the world, God, and your relationship to those concepts. Hermeneutically, imagination invites you to interpret *things* in new ways. Apocalyptically, imagination invites *you* to be reinterpreted.

Given the above, two important and related questions should be answered, especially for Christians reading all of this to consider how it might relate to their faith life. First, regarding the hermeneutic imagination, how can we tell if the meanings we interpretively imagine about the present are true? Relatedly, when we interpret the present and imagine the future, it cannot be the case that anything we imagine is also certainly accurate, so how do we assess this? What is the relationship between imagination, accuracy, and truth? Second, regarding the apocalyptic imagination, if part of what is happening is that you feel a new world has been revealed to you, then who or what enabled that revelation? What is the relationship between imagination and faithfulness to a tradition? Given that imagination is bivalent, enabling "one to flee one's socio-cultural reality and to constitute one's sociocultural world,"[1] how do we determine what "God really wants" as opposed to what "we really want and want to use God to justify?" How can we discern between imagination and delusion? In this chapter, I'll explore some of the concerns that imagination can produce, considering how to respond to those concerns in the next chapter.

---

1. Geniusas, "Between Phenomenology and Hermeneutics," 223–41.

Imagining the Truth

Part of what I suspect is going on in anxieties related to the imagination is a question of the muddy relationship between truth and imagining. We can see this, for example, in the phrase "imagining the truth," which suggests imagination is like guessing. However, "to guess" didn't come up as a definition, so what's happening? To explore this muddiness, let's look at a scenario.

Consider that it is Christmas morning, and your family has a Christmas tree. Sitting beneath the tree is a gift with your name that you did not expect. As you look at it, you say to yourself, "I wonder what it is . . ." This sets you off on a path of trying to imagine what might be in there. As part of your imagining, you are drawing on your conversations of the last few weeks, considering the size of the box, and possibly consulting your own desires and hopes, looking for clues as to what might be in there. You imagine several things it might be, one of which is a new leather journal.

Now, if, by some chance, the image you had in mind *does* correspond to material reality and the gift is a leather journal, there are still several *ways* it could be right. It could be that it *is* a journal, but it is a different color from the one you imagined. Or it could be much larger or have a strong smell that wasn't part of what you imagined. Maybe you imagined real cow leather and it is faux leather. In any event, there seems to be only one situation in which what you imagined to be in the box is precisely what is in the box. In all the other imaginings, the journal was too heavy, too green, or too fragrant . . . none of those were "right." It is possible to have imagined "a leather journal," and it was one, but the sensory specifics of the image pictured were off. Did you imagine correctly if you imagined the smell wrong? I see at least two dynamics in this situation worth exploring directly.

First, part of what is going on is the difference between language-based and sense-based operations. If I said to you "Guess what is in that box," and you simply replied, "I guess it is a leather journal," and it *was* a leather journal, it would be easy to say your guess was correct. You guessed the truth. The words you used for your guess exactly point at what is, in fact, in the box. However, when you *imagined* what was in the box, the activity seems not to be language-based in the same way and, therefore, harder to assess as clearly. You could have imagined a heavy, orange leather journal that smelled of raspberries but said aloud, "My guess is a journal." Then, if what you open is a small, unscented, blue journal with light canvas covers, your spoken guess of "a journal" is correct, but your imagination is not. Or, at least, it certainly wasn't perfectly accurate. Language can be more abstract than sense-based operations which work with specifics.

Putting things into words helps us communicate with others but isn't a perfect expression of our interior experience.

Part of what I think contributes to the muddiness is that underneath the conversation about imagination there is an often-unexamined series of beliefs and expectations about what truth is. These expectations have a significant bearing on the conversation about imagination. This is not the book to go into detail about the nature of truth and knowledge, but some brief discussion will be useful. Specifically, we ought to look at two ideas that philosophers call the "correspondence theory of truth" and the "principle of noncontradiction." These are technical academic phrases, but you probably already intuitively know what they mean even if you haven't heard them before.

The "correspondence theory of truth" goes way back, with some debate about whether it was first posited by Plato or Aristotle. In any event, we get a clear and well-cited articulation of it in Thomas Aquinas, who wrote that "a judgment is said to be true when it conforms to the external reality."[2] This seems self-evident: if I say "there is a leather journal in the box" it has to be the case that, in fact, there *is* a leather journal in the box for it to be true. Presumed within this "correspondence theory" is the "principle of noncontradiction" which says a judgment cannot be both true and not true at the same time. In this example, it cannot be the case that there *is* and *is not* a leather journal in the box. That isn't how truth works in "correspondence theory." This seems to be relevant in Scripture as well.

For example, there are numerous places where truth plays a central part of the conversation in the Bible. Consider 1 Cor 15:13–14: "If there is no resurrection of the dead, then Christ has not been raised; and if Christ has not been raised, then our proclamation has been in vain and your faith has been in vain." Underneath this verse, the "correspondence theory of truth" and the "principle of noncontradiction" are both operating. Either Christ rose on the third day or he didn't. If he didn't, then proclamation and faith have been in vain.

But what does resurrection mean in this context? Must this text be read as a strict realism where Jesus had to have observably died and come back to life? Dead by what standards, first-century or modernity? Are poetic or spiritual understandings of this event possible, or must they be strictly material and physical? Is what Paul meant by this the only way to understand it correctly?

Once again, we're back into hermeneutic and biblical interpretation issues for which other books are far better to consult. The point I want to emphasize here is that the above paragraph of questions primarily emerges

2. Aquinas, *De Veritate*, Q.1, A.1–3.

because of the discreteness and interpretability of language and text. It is easier to test the truth of a discrete claim when it is clear on the page. But is truth-testing a worthwhile activity for imagination? It depends on what your definition of imagination is.

Early forms of philosophy of imagination in Western thought—like Aristotle—tended to focus on the visual image form of imagination, not including the broader dimensions of other senses.[3] In this form, the question of truth was more challenging to assess than discrete claims in language, but it was still feasible. The idea was to take a mental snapshot of the image you had imagined and then if that thing was materially present somewhere, compare the actual object (or scene, or person, etc.) to the imagined object. If they matched, it was true. If not, the image was false. This is why, for Aristotle, "most cases of imagination were false."[4] However, as we've covered in the last two chapters, imagination can have a broader meaning than just "mental visualization."

Consider the example from the last chapter where Dr. King "had a dream" and imagined that "on the red hills of Georgia the sons of former slaves and the sons of former slave-owners will be able to sit down together at a table of brotherhood." It seems clear that King's full vision of justice has not been entirely achieved yet, so does that mean his imagination was false? Taking another tact, I *do* think that there must have been at least one moment in history in which sons of formerly enslaved people and the sons of former enslavers sat together at a table. However, it seems petty and legalistic to say that since it happened once King's imagined dream was proven "right," when we know his vision was more extensive than a single table. How are we to think about truth and imagination when our understanding of imagination extends beyond mental pictures and logical language-based claims, addressing other senses, other possibilities, and apocalyptic unveiling?

In situations where the product of the imagination is both external and predictive (I imagine my gift is a leather journal), I think it is viable to apply considerations of truth. What is being imagined is a possible state of the material world outside me. It is a kind of sensorial guess. I think this also applies to discrete and explicit predictive imagining such as "I imagine the world will end on December 21, 2028," "he imagined he'd be married and have two kids by the time he was thirty years old," "I imagine my wife will not be bothered by my heavy investment in cryptocurrency," or any other such imagined prognostications. For these kinds of situations,

3. Engmann, "Imagination and Truth in Aristotle," 259–65.
4. Engmann, "Imagination and Truth in Aristotle," 262.

I'm with Aristotle: most of these imaginings are false. However, the imagination isn't limited to predictive activity.

When I speak with a couple considering marriage and ask them—individually and jointly—to imagine what marriage will be like and what it will mean, the imagining itself can be transformative. In these non-predictive situations, I don't think application of the "correspondence theory" or "principle of noncontradiction" seems warranted. Checking to see if an imagined possibility "conforms to the external reality" isn't as applicable when the imaginative product being considered isn't an interpretation of a certain state of affairs but a broader, hypothetical future. It is functioning less as a prediction and more as an anticipation. As Paul Avis says, imagination allows us "to see the end from the beginning and to anticipate what it will be like to arrive at our destination. It is imagination that responds to the invitation in the Psalms: 'O taste, and see, how gracious the Lord is (Psalm 34.8).'"[5] Tasting, seeing, or feeling even a fragment of the anticipated destination can be powerful.

Mary Warnock suggests that an event like this—one of an excess of grace and the overflow of experience when moments seem overly full and saturated with meaning—might have its experiential roots in imagination.

> The sense that there is something more, that there is never an end, is the sense generated, I believe, by imagination, whether exercised on something apparently trivial, as when a child has an overwhelming passion for cars or for birds' eggs; or in the mysterious powers of memory, nature or art. It is a sense akin to the Christian quality (whether virtue or natural gift) of Hope. I can find no reason to suppose that the human imagination cannot function as much in the same way.[6]

Recognizing parallels between anticipation of "something more," the fruits of hope, and imagination of the future provide a fertile ground for theological reflection. This is imagination understood *not* as a type of sensorial guess or forecast, but a wondering and apocalyptic explanation of what might be possible.

However, problems can emerge when a transformative imagining or possibility begins to be treated as if it is inevitable or inherently predictive of actual circumstances. Interestingly, there are two kinds of critiques connected with religion and imagination that are quite different from one another but both rest on the problem of the imagination being experienced

5. Avis, *God and the Creative Imagination*, 75.
6. Warnock, "Religious Imagination," 151.

as true and predictive when, in fact, it might not be. I think about them as the "bad influence" and "religion is delusion" critiques.

Imagination as Bad Influence

Literary scholar and historian Jacqueline Pearson provides an excellent example of the "bad influence" type of critique, which, while still present today, was particularly strong in American Protestantism in the eighteenth and nineteenth centuries.[7] Between 1815 and 1816, an exchange in the evangelical magazine, *Christian Observer*, captures this concern concisely. The *Observer* published a debate between two pastors about whether or not a novel could be considered to have any redeeming qualities. On the attack against novels was the claim that based "on man's total depravity," it was advisable "to avoid reading matter which could in any way imperil the soul."[8] The act of reading and imagining something was itself dangerous.

Reading a novel, one was too likely to be caught up in the story, feeling it too keenly so that the "reader becomes caught up in a simulacrum," in which "virtue, religion itself, becomes a mere play of the imagination, influencing neither the heart nor the conduct."[9] As Pearson puts it, the novel was objectionable because "it produces a fictitious acquaintance with the reader's own subjectivity and her everyday life."[10] Within this frame, one of the consequences of humanity's fallen nature is an inherently "depraved imagination" that is "therefore innately fallen, capable of working evil but not good."[11] That is why even "good novels" are unacceptable: "the foundation of the building is radically wrong, and the superstructure and ornaments are of little consequence."[12] Imagination is critiqued here based on theological anthropology and a claim about sin.

Given the fall and human depravity, anything that emerges from the human mind must be viewed with suspicion as it inherently bears some mark of the taint of sin. Though the claim was that in fiction "religion itself, becomes a mere play of the imagination, influencing neither the heart nor the conduct," I am much more inclined to think that the impulse of the critique is actually more something like "religion itself, becomes a mere play of the imagination, influencing the heart and the conduct in a

7. Pearson, *Women's Reading in Britain*.

8. Pearson, *Women's Reading in Britain*, 513.

9. Pearson, *Women's Reading in Britain*, 513.

10. Pearson, *Women's Reading in Britain*, 514.

11. Pearson, *Women's Reading in Britain*, 516.

12. Pearson, *Women's Reading in Britain*, 516.

way that is depraved instead of focused on God." In any event, the worry is that fiction will *seem* to be profound or transcendently truthful but really will just be a delusion or a "simulacrum." I believe this emerges from a concern about idolatry.

The argument suggests that since novels come from human imaginations and require human imaginations to interpret, any content within that seems wholesome or connected to God can't actually be wholesome or a true connection. I hear in this critique an echo of biblical warnings such as Jer 23:16, "Do not listen to the words of the prophets who prophesy to you; they are deluding you. They speak visions of their own minds, not from the mouth of the Lord." Within this view, at best, the God of a novel is a frail shadow of the actual God, far less than what God is in truth. The narrative of God via such a human lens as a novel says more about the author than Christ. As Elizabeth Sewell puts it, "it is no use pretending that with the Fall behind us the imagination is not, like all man's other powers, liable to corruption and disease and death."[13] At worst, the God of a novel is not just a bad copy resulting from a cracked photocopier screen but is an outright work of sin, a consequence of the fall and best to be avoided entirely.

I was just talking about novels in the nineteenth century, but Christian critiques of various forms of media still exist today. However, one thing that I think is important to note is that in the novel example above, the problem was inherent to the medium itself, not the *content* of that medium. Even if a novel had a good story with good values that seemed Christian and faithful, it ought not to be read by virtue of its nature as a novel.

This level of resistance largely seems to have passed, and suspicion about books, films, and television seems largely to be about the *content* of those forms, not just their existence per se. Indeed, the entire industry of Christian cinema is premised on the idea that films *can* be acceptable, but only if their content is wholesome and Christian. The fear seems to be that exposure to unsavory images and ideas in fiction might disrupt appropriate Christian behavior. Rather than risk it, say some, just skip them altogether.

This is a substantively different resistance than the critique of the novel, but it is functionally premised on the same advice: given "total depravity" it is advisable to avoid anything "which could in any way imperil the soul."[14] The mind should be kept focused on God. Becoming overly interested in other things runs the risk of having those things captivate us so much that we look to them and think we see God in them when what is actually there is just a reflection of our fallen nature masquerading as God. Or, just as bad,

13. Sewell, "Death of the Imagination," 178.

14. Pearson, *Women's Reading in Britain*, 513.

something that will tantalize our fallen nature to such a degree we forget God for a time. We see a similar warning in the Orthodox text, *Philokalia*.

In "On Prayer," Evagrios reminds the reader that "when you are praying, do not shape within yourself any image of the Deity, and do not let your intellect be stamped with the impress of any form approach the immaterial in an immaterial manner." Likewise (and with more intensity), he adds: "never try to see a form or shape during prayer."[15] The idea here is that the experience of God, if encountered in the context of explicitly imaginative prayer, is inherently suspicious. Callistus and Ignatius of Xanthopoulos provide another excellent example of the intense suspicion many Orthodox theologians maintain.

> Imagination, according to the holy fathers, serves as a bridge for the demons, over which these murderous miscreants cross and recross, commune and mix with the soul and make of it a hive of drones, the abode of barren and passionate thoughts. This imagination must be firmly swept away, even if sometimes one does not so wish, for the sake of penitence and contrition, of mourning and humility, and especially for the sake of putting this chaotic imagination to shame; and one must attract and oppose to it well-ordered imagination, and by mixing the two together incite them to battle with one another, and so strike down the former as dishonorable and shameless, and triumph over it.[16]

Additional Orthodox perspectives on imagination and prayer will be considered in chapter 8, but here it is worth noting that even though imagination serves as a bridge to demons, it was nonetheless possible to develop a "well-ordered" imagination that would be of service to the faith. However, without training and discipline, a person's natural state is overly open to evil forces, and things they imagine are positive will actually be demonic trickery trying to make their mind and spirit too passionate. Suspicion of the imagination is a common theme, especially as it is connected to overly passionate emotions. This was also the concern of the eighteenth-century American preacher and theologian Jonathan Edwards.

Worried about the role of emotions in experiences of God, Edwards wrote disparagingly of "enthusiasts," who felt emotionally and spiritually filled with God.

> Enthusiasm is a vicious circle, whose wheel is driven by the overheated imagination: one believes one is inspired by God because one feels so strongly, and one feels so strongly because

15. *Philokalia*, 68.
16. *Philokalia*, 234.

> one believes one is inspired by God. Any experience will appear
> authentic if one mistakes the workings of his own passions for
> divine communications, and fancies himself immediately in-
> spired by the SPIRIT of God, when all the while, he is under no
> other influence than that of an overheated imagination.[17]

Kathryn Reklis, a theologian and Edwards scholar, suggests that as Edwards
understood it, imagination is simply "another name for the understanding
disordered by the passions." Whereas the "enthusiast mistakes her imagined inspiration for true understanding," it is actually "a disease of disorder
in which the faculties are thrown out of true alignment."[18] Worries about
"mis-alignment" seem to run through not only Edwards but also writers in
the *Philokalia* and those critical of Victorian novels.

How you decide to engage with "non-Christian" media is up to you.
For our purposes, the thing to focus on is that if imagination shapes how
we interpret and engage with the world, then things that shape our imagination influence how we engage with the world. One response to this can
be to avoid certain kinds of media so that they cannot as easily shape your
vision of the world. Another might be to acknowledge that imagined worlds
encountered in books and movies may well transformatively influence *how*
you imagine but do not necessarily have to become specific imaginative
predictions of *what* the future will bring. In any event, this book isn't the
place to make pronouncements on what constitutes good media consump-
tion habits. However, I felt it was relevant to bring up these examples because they have very significant similarities to another type of critique, even
though they come from a radically different point of view.

Religion as Delusion

In the next chapter, I'll discuss more of the work of Paul Ricœur, who wrote
about the "masters of suspicion" being Karl Marx, Sigmund Freud, and
Friedrich Nietzsche. Before getting there, it is worth recognizing that behind those "masters" is the work of Ludwig Feuerbach. Having a sense of his
arguments is important for setting the context of Ricœur and contemporary
religious doubt in the academy more broadly.

Relevant to the topic of imagination, Feuerbach's project was to argue that, historically speaking, people developed religion as a way to think
and communicate about the parts of themselves that are hardest to find

17. Chauncy, "Enthusiasms Described," 231.
18. Reklis, "Imagination and Hermeneutics," 313.

evidence of in our day-to-day lives. According to Feuerbach, the qualities assigned to God are projections of human values and hopes for ourselves as individuals and as a species. For Feuerbach, all religion is the result of human projection, and the concept of God is just the echo that humanity hears of its own voice.

In his *The Essence of Christianity*, for example, Feuerbach argued that God's omnipotence is a projection of the human experience of vulnerability and desire for agency. Similarly, God's omnipresence is a projection of the human experience of disconnection from others and a desire for accompaniment and constant relationship.

> It is pleasanter to be passive than to act, to be redeemed and made free by another than to free oneself; pleasanter to make one's salvation dependent on a person than on the force of one's own spontaneity; pleasanter to set before oneself an object of love than an object of effort; pleasanter to know oneself beloved by God than merely to have that simple, natural self-love which is innate in all beings; pleasanter to see oneself imaged in the love-beaming eyes of another personal being, than to look into the concave mirror of self or into the cold depths of the ocean of Nature; pleasanter, in short, to allow oneself to be acted on by one's own feeling, as by another, but yet fundamentally identical being, than to regulate oneself by reason.[19]

His claim here is that religion is a kind of fantasy-prone imagination, an appealing imaginative fiction that people treat as if it was actual. God is a pleasant—though false—shield protecting people from hard truths.

In some ways, I see Feuerbach's argument as an amplified version of the same concern that led to the suspicion of novels and the implicit fear that Christians would mistake their own vision of God for God. As I see it, Feuerbach says, "You're right to be suspicious of novels and think you'll only find the God you imagine there. But . . . that is because you'll only *ever* find the God you imagine no matter where you look." As he puts it, "to reason, the divine persons are phantoms, to imagination, they are realities."[20] The phantoms of divinity are the echoes of the depths of human hope and longing bouncing back to us from such a distance we perceive them as separate from ourselves. Or, so says Feuerbach.

For Feuerbach, religion was part of an early stage of human development that emerged so that humanity could develop an awareness of itself as a collective. This was fine to the extent that it was a helpful part of human

19. Feuerbach, *Essence of Christianity*, 167.
20. Feuerbach, *Essence of Christianity*, 232.

development. Today, though, we should realize that while religion still has things to teach us, the content of those lessons comes from us. Feuerbach's line of reasoning is that we think about God as an omnipotent creator because we want to believe in a God able to give us anything we lack, including better material conditions and/or a perfect future in heavenly eternal life.

In this perspective, each of God's essential metaphysical qualities results from humanity's deep-seated lacks and desires. It isn't so much that each individual person ascribes values to God they wish to be true—although given the vast array and conflicting claims that God's morality supports particular political platforms, this seems worth considering too. Rather, the idea is that humans in general, by virtue of our finitude, limited life spans, and experiences of loss, have not just specific wishes for particular things to be different in our lives but also "the unspecific overall wish that there be in general no natural necessity; no limitations, no opposition to the human being and to human wishes."[21] It is no coincidence, says Feuerbach, that our idea of God is precisely the same shape as human insecurities and hopes.

One of the consequences of Feuerbach's claims is that looking at religion and examining Christ makes it possible to better understand humanity's goals for itself. He argues that "Christ is the blending in one of feeling and imagination,"[22] and that "all religious cosmogonies are products of the imagination."[23] As he puts it, "the Son is the reflected splendor of the imagination, the image dearest to the heart; but for the very reason that he is only an object of the imagination, he is only the nature of the imagination made objective."[24] Feuerbach's project is an argument that theology is just the echo of idealized anthropology. Studying God is a form of studying humanity in concentrated form.

Though his work certainly disrupts classical theology, it seems to me that there is just as much of an argument for him being "pro-humanity" as there is for "anti-religion." He thought that humanity as a species was an incredible achievement. His argument, at least in *The Essence of Christianity*, wasn't that religion was worthless per se, just that theology was helping humanity hide from itself by faith. The truths of God and religion *are* human truths and are worth exploring; it is just a mistake to think they first came from anywhere other than humanity.

21. Feuerbach, *Essence of Faith According to Luther*, 372.

22. Feuerbach, *Essence of Christianity*, 197.

23. Feuerbach, *Essence of Christianity*, 99.

24. Feuerbach, *Essence of Christianity*, 75.

Before leaving Feuerbach, I want to note one thing that has always stuck with me about him. While the consequences of his argumentation are certainly unsettling for those of us looking for an account of theological realism, the thrust of his project doesn't seem to come out of an explicit disdain or outright dismissal of religion—as we see with Nietzsche and Marx, for example. Instead, he is concerned that humanity's failure to see God as an imaginative projection and reflection masks us from ourselves. For Feuerbach, the symbol "God" might be recuperated and still be helpful for moral and social reflection, but only if people recognize that we can find a larger sense of ourselves by looking at it. Failure to do so keeps us from seeing some of how material injustices are legitimated by theological justification. This last point especially seems like one worth considering.

Even if the larger arc of Feuerbach's work is disconcerting for a Christian, I think there is something in there for us. For example, Feuerbach notes that "just as the Christians are equal in heaven, but unequal on earth, so the individual members of the nation are equal in the heaven of their political world, but unequal in the earthly existence of society."[25] As a consequence of claiming that human moral values are derivative of a divinely ordained moral order which *precedes* humanity, theological concepts are pointed to as justification for material conditions. There is rarely recognition that the "evidence" of religion is functionally self-supporting.

Later philosophical and theological scholarship—via Marx—will pick up this sense of misattribution, misrecognition, and miscategorization and refer to it as the "alienation" of individuals from a true sense of themselves. The results of alienation on people are a limited ability to feel like they have options and can explore possibilities within the world. Put more simply, if everyone you know and love—and everyone *they* know and love—repeats the story that life is hard, low wages are just how things are, things can't change, and it will all be worth it when rewards are divvied out in heaven, it will be harder for you to imagine other options.

Beginning in the mid-1900s, the idea that imagination had social and individual dimensions became increasingly common in theological scholarship. This content is explored for the entirety of chapter 7, considering "Christian Imaginaries," so I won't discuss it here with any detail. However, given that suspicion may seem like a dubious candidate for a useful theological tool, I'll give a couple examples below to show how this thinking has fruitfully entered theological scholarship. An energetic willingness to interrogate content presumed to be untouchable or universal can yield life-giving realizations. Given that your imagination is related to the vision

---

25. Feuerbach, *Essence of Christianity*, 79.

of the world being produced and sustained by others, being curious about that production can be fruitful.

The Power of Suspicion

Uniting the concepts of "imagination as bad influence" and "religion as delusion" is a concern that imagination can unduly influence how we see the world. We can be "duped" by imagination to think the world is one way when something else entirely is the case. Beginning to wrestle with the possibility that this may be true can lead to investigating what assumptions we are making that might not actually be the case and are just something we continue to assume out of habit and an unrecognized imagination. I want to consider two instances where scholarly suspicion yielded fruitful theological growth.

For the first example, consider the work of trailblazing American feminist theologian Valerie Saiving. In her groundbreaking essay, "The Human Situation: A Feminine View," she showed how a default presumption of male experience as universal made for faulty theological arguments.[26] In the 1960 essay, she focused on the work of two well-known male theologians and how their articulations about the nature of sin and love are presented as universal but are, in fact, particular to maleness.

In the essay, Saiving noted how the famous theologian Reinhold Niebuhr argued that the nature of human sin was tied to pride and self-assertiveness. Adam was too bold in the garden: his willfulness and dismissal of God's invitation led to the fall. Given that sinfulness is about pride and excess self-aggrandizement, the appropriate response is sacrificial self-negation and recognition that "He must increase, but I must decrease" (John 3:30). This, says Saiving, may be true of men, but to claim the same truth and response applies to women is not a helpful way to proceed.

As Saiving saw it, in Western society, the default assumption about women had *already* been self-denial, self-sacrifice, and an enabling love for service to others.

> The moments, hours, and days of self-giving must be balanced by moments, hours, and days of withdrawal into, and enrichment of, her individual selfhood if she is to remain a whole person. She learns, too, that a woman can give too much of herself, so that nothing remains of her own uniqueness; she can become merely an emptiness, almost a zero, without value to herself, to her fellow men, or, perhaps, even to God. For

26. Saiving, "Human Situation," 100–112.

the temptations of woman as *woman* are not the same as the
temptations of man as *man*.[27]

By imagining that the experience of men was the experience of humanity
writ large, theology was making a crucial mistake.

To say that women need to be *more* self-negating, decrease further,
and be less self-assertive could result in the "underdevelopment or negation
of the self."[28] In a society where male dominance has been a social norm and
presumed truism, a male view saying that pride was the issue is sensible . . .
for *men*. For women, though, the problem of sin is far more likely to be a
lack of self-realization: hiding light under the bushel basket.

> Today, when at last women might seem to be in a position to
> begin to be both feminine and fully developed, creative human
> beings; today . . . theology, to the extent that it has defined the
> human condition on the basis of masculine experience, contin-
> ues to speak of such desires as sin or temptation to sin. If such
> a woman believes the theologians, she will try to strangle those
> impulses in herself.[29]

Later scholars like Judith Plaskow, Mary Daly, and Rosemary Radford Ruether
would push feminist thought within theology even further. Today, scholars
may well be critical of what—in Saiving—seems like a presumed assumption
of a fixed notion of what a woman experiences. However, what Saiving argued
here was the beginning of theological feminism in the academy: a recognition
that not all stories, symbols, and assumptions have the same resonance and
truth for people. We can see a similar recognition in Robert Allen Warrior's
1989 essay, "Canaanites, Cowboys, and Indians."

Though Warrior, who belongs to the Grayhorse District of the Osage
Nation, is now a literature scholar, he was initially trained as a theologian
and this piece was written from that perspective. The short essay recognizes
that the power and hope of the biblical narrative for a "chosen land" in the
Exodus story is highly problematic for Indigenous people.

> No doubt, the story is one that has inspired many people in
> many contexts to struggle against injustice. Israel, in the Exile,
> then Diaspora, would remember the story and be reminded of
> God's faithfulness. Enslaved African Americans, given Bibles to
> read by their masters and mistresses, would begin at the begin-
> ning of the book and find in the pages of the Pentateuch a god

27. Saiving, "Human Situation," 108.
28. Saiving, "Human Situation," 109.
29. Saiving, "Human Situation," 110.

who was obviously on their side, even if that god was the god
of their oppressors. People in Latin American based communities read the story and have been inspired to struggle against
injustice. The Exodus, with its picture of a god who takes the
side of the oppressed and powerless, has been a beacon of hope
for many in despair.[30]

The problem with this narrative is that the God who takes the side of the
oppressed Israelites does so against those in Canaan.

Other passages could be considered, but Deut 20:16–18 is sufficient to
see the point Warrior makes. Here we read instructions given to the Israelites as they prepare to enter the land God promised them.

But as for the towns of these peoples that the Lord your God
is giving you as an inheritance, you must not let anything that
breathes remain alive. You shall annihilate them—the Hittites
and the Amorites, the Canaanites and the Perizzites, the Hiv-
ites and the Jebusites—just as the Lord your God has com-
manded, so that they may not teach you to do all the abhorrent
things that they do for their gods, and you thus sin against the
Lord your God.

Warrior reads passages like this and contrasts how from the Israelite perspective, Canaan is a gift and inheritance of "flowing milk and honey," but
from those in Canaan, the view must have been entirely different.

The land, Yahweh decided, belonged to these former slaves
from Egypt and Yahweh planned on giving it to them—using
the same power used against the enslaving Egyptians to defeat
the indigenous inhabitants of Canaan. Yahweh the deliverer became Yahweh the conqueror. The obvious characters in the story
for Native Americans to identify with are the Canaanites, the
people who already lived in the promised land. As a member of
the Osage Nation of American Indians who stands in solidarity
with other tribal people around the world, I read the Exodus
stories with Canaanite eyes.[31]

The promises made to Abraham and Moses are about to come true but at the
cost of the expulsion and extermination of those already in Canaan. Given
this text, his identity, and his solidarity, Warrior has three suggestions.

---

30. Warrior, "Canaanites, Cowboys, and Indians," 261–65.
31. Warrior, "Canaanites, Cowboys, and Indians," 262.

First, "the Canaanites should be at the center of Christian theological reflection and political action."[32] Second, we "need to be more aware of the way ideas such as those in the conquest narratives have made their way into Americans' consciousness and ideology." For example, there is ample historical record that many early colonial preachers referred to Native peoples as Amalekites and Canaanites. Such perspectives allowed for the colonization of the North American continent. What do we do with this knowledge today? Third, "we need to decide if we want to accept the model of leadership and social change presented by the entire Exodus story."[33] As Warrior sees it, the Exodus story is not nearly so much one of liberation for all but one in which "a society of people delivered from oppression . . . become oppressors themselves."[34] Is this the model that should be advocated? Warrior is not convinced.

The essay closes with the haunting suggestion that for Native peoples, figuring out how to manage the above three things might not be worth it.

> With what voice will we, the Canaanites of the world, say, "Let my people go, and leave my people alone?" And, with what ears will followers of alien gods who have wooed us (Christians, Jews, Marxists, capitalists), listen to us? The indigenous people of this hemisphere have endured a subjugation now 100 years longer than the sojourn of Israel in Egypt. Is there a god, a spirit, who will hear us and stand with us in the Amazon, Osage County, and Wounded Knee? Is there a god, a spirit, able to move among the pain and anger of Nablus, Gaza, and Soweto? Perhaps. But we, the wretched of the earth, may be well-advised this time not to listen to outsiders with their promises of liberation and deliverance. We will perhaps do better to look elsewhere for our vision of justice, peace, and political sanity—a vision through which we escape not only our oppressors, but our oppression as well. Maybe, for once, we will just have to listen to ourselves, leaving the gods of this continent's real strangers to do battle among themselves.[35]

As you might guess, Warrior's essay is frequently cited and sometimes challenged, especially by Native Christian thinkers with a more optimistic perspective. Key for us is the recognition that what Warrior has done is to interrogate a central story of Christian teaching and question to what degree

32. Warrior, "Canaanites, Cowboys, and Indians," 263.
33. Warrior, "Canaanites, Cowboys, and Indians," 264.
34. Warrior, "Canaanites, Cowboys, and Indians," 264.
35. Warrior, "Canaanites, Cowboys, and Indians," 265.

it should be lifted up as normative and precedent-setting for all Christian people. What kind of world is imagined in the Exodus story? Who sees it that way and who can't? These are questions of critique and a suspicion that not everything should be accepted at face value.

If this kind of critical material is new to you, this section may have felt challenging. Actually, even if you've thought about male-dominated society and colonization a lot, it can still be challenging. Both intellectually and spiritually, it can be exhausting to consider how we believe and act has been shaped by contexts we may not have considered previously. However, it is worth noting that this content may feel liberating for some of you. Others still will feel it is difficult *and* liberating. It is precisely because both of these dynamics may be in play that these ideas are worth exploring. Let's consider how the examples of both Saiving and Warrior show the interaction between suspicion and imagination.

In chapter 1 we discussed how one of Kant's aspects of the imagination could be described as "schematic." This function of the imagination works like a dynamic switchboard or database where perceptions, symbols, and memory get associated with one another. Imagination operating this way helps us to "see the whole picture" even when we don't *actually* see the whole picture. In the example I gave, I noted that if I was in a city and saw a taxicab from the side, I would be able to imagine that the car has another side and isn't just the cardboard cutout of a car.

The connective and schematic aspects of imagination help us to fill out the fuller picture when we only have limited direct data (I can only actually see one side of the cab) but enough experience to be able to assume the context (I've never seen a flat cardboard cutout of a cab on the street, but I have seen thousands of actual automobiles). What we're seeing in the Saiving and Warrior examples is that sometimes assumptions and imagination misfire or produce interpretations that seem like they ought to be broadly applicable for all people but are either only valid for a subset or might be entirely problematic. In either case, these scholars have pointed out some of the problematic interpretations that arose from presuming a particular view could be universalized. The power of a "hermeneutic of suspicion" is the recognition that not everything may be as straightforward as it seems, and that further investigation might be worthwhile. Imagination isn't just something that comes into play in idle times: it is often what we turn to when we feel that what we've been told is real cannot be all there is. Trevor Hart makes this point poignantly in a recent essay:

> To imagine what is not actually or apparently the case takes
> effort, and such effort is unlikely to be deemed either necessary

or worthwhile by those wholly contented with their lot. Our imaginings are, we might say, born of an insatiable itch for something more, something other, and mostly something better than we currently enjoy or must endure. They are, in other words, born of desire.[36]

While learning to see and be in new ways can be freeing, it is nonetheless a lot of work. And to be constantly on guard to the ways in which there's more to uncover . . . well . . . that's even more tiring.

All of the above raises some pretty important questions for Christian theology. Even if we accept that sometimes suspicion and critical questioning can be helpful, what happens if that never stops? The philosopher Paul Ricœur referred to the paralyzing effect of constant suspicion as the "desert of criticism." If we're constantly looking for ways we've been fooling ourselves with our imagination, how can we ever actually feel like faithfulness is possible? How do we know if what we imagine as possible is good? What—if any—difference is there between imagining in general compared to *faithfully* imagining something? Is it possible to be a person of faith if you're constantly suspicious of the stories and assumptions you think are important? These questions are all considered in the next chapter.

Questions for Reflection

1. What is the distinction between the imagination used predictively and it used transformatively? Do you think that people actually do use their imagination transformatively or is this just hollow theorizing? Somewhere in between?

2. Early in the chapter there was a discussion about the difference between language compared to sense-based imagination and how words provide a clearer basis for testing truth than do imagined scenarios. What does it mean for you that "testing for truth" isn't as feasible with transformative imagination? Does it make you feel like imagination should be avoided? Something else?

3. Have you ever—or known someone who has—avoided certain types of media because you felt like they would somehow be detrimental to your faith? If so, how do you feel about that avoidance now in light of what we have been discussing so far?

36. Hart, "Why Imagination Matters," 142.

4. Whether you agree with him or not, do you feel like you have a clear sense of Feuerbach's argument? What is it? Is this kind of thing something you've heard of or thought about before?

5. In the examples from Saiving and Warrior we saw scholars pointing out that stories, symbols, and ideas that are supposed to "be for everyone" might actually only work for folks who see the world a certain way because of their own experience. Have you ever encountered someone who didn't realize that their own experience wasn't the same as everyone else's? Or who made an assumption about something based on their own limited experience? What happened in that circumstance?

Related Readings

Blackburn, Simon. *Truth: A Guide.* Oxford: Oxford University Press, 2005.
Dyrness, William. *Reformed Theology and Visual Culture: The Protestant Imagination from Calvin to Edwards.* Cambridge: Cambridge University Press, 2004.
Harvey, Van. *Feuerbach and the Interpretation of Religion.* New York: Cambridge University Press, 1995.
Rollins, Peter. *How (Not) to Speak of God.* Brewster, MA: Paraclete, 2006.

Part II: Interpretation and the Theological Task

4

Hope and Grounding

THE IMPACT OF CRITICISM and critical suspicion has been profound within the academic study of theology. Some scholars, having wrestled with the implications of Feuerbach and the "masters of suspicion," ultimately found themselves unable to remain Christian. Famously, this happened with the British theologian Daphne Hampson, who substantively and fruitfully engaged with theology and the work of continental philosophy, including Luce Irigaray's study of Feuerbach.

Eventually, Hampson concluded that "Christianity is neither true nor moral" and "'that which is God' is based in human religious experience."[1] She consequently took a position in "Post-Christian Thought" at the University of St. Andrews in Scotland. It is, however, a mistake to presume that recognizing the power of a hermeneutics of suspicion somehow leads down a slippery slope that always ends outside the church.

Some of the most significant theological figures of the late-twentieth century were scholars whose use of criticism deepened their faith. Trailblazing Peruvian Catholic theologian Gustavo Gutiérrez famously explored the implications of some aspects of Marxism for theologies of liberation, considering the relationship between theological work, material economic conditions, and political change. Similarly, black liberation theology innovator James Cone, a member of the African Methodist Episcopal Church, interrogated how Eurocentric views of Christianity were often accepted as if they were the only way to view Christianity.

American theologian Kwok Pui-lan, an Anglican, has written in resonant ways, developing her work on postcoloniality and feminist theology. She writes that "the most important contribution of postcolonial feminist theology will be to recapitulate the relation of theology and empire

---

1. Warwick faculty website. https://warwick.ac.uk/fac/arts/english/research/current projects/coral/events/hampson/.

through the multiple lenses of gender, race, class, sexuality, religion, and so forth."[2] This "recapitulation" is a consequence of the recognition that straightforward appearances of texts and traditions may be incomplete and more contextualized readings can reveal meanings or implications not initially apparent.

Each of these theologians—and dozens more—recognized that a hermeneutics of suspicion can help reveal how our imaginations have been shaped by patterns and forces that are not always immediately evident. Rather than running from suspicion and criticism while denying its relevance to the task of theological inquiry, it can be used as part of faithful work. Suspicion can help to bring to light previously tacit and unexamined presumptions and norms.

It is also the case that past these hermeneutics of suspicion there can be a hermeneutics of faith, retrieval, and affirmation. This chapter will explore how Ricœur grappled with suspicion, how he felt faith was possible after it, and what role the imagination played in his thinking. Recognizing that Ricœur was not a theologian, but a philosopher, the second half of the chapter will turn to the work of Garrett Green and Ada Maria Isasi-Diaz, theologians whose work powerfully wrestles with questions of interpretation and imagination.

A Second Naïveté

Paul Ricœur was born in France in 1913 to Protestant Huguenot parents in a region where Catholicism was the dominant religious context. He published consistently for the entire second half of the twentieth century and has significantly influenced theology. His work is complex and vast, so what I'll discuss here should only be taken as a faint sketch of his work. However, even that sketch may prove enlightening. Given the emphasis on suspicion in the last chapter, I think it is helpful to start our exploration of Ricœur with an introduction to his idea of "The Second Naïveté," before moving on to his direct consideration of interpretation and imagination.

Ricœur tasked himself with seriously considering the work of those he saw as coming in the wake of Feuerbach and asking what faith could viably look like given their scholarship. He grouped, by name, Sigmund Freud, Friedrich Nietzsche, and Karl Marx as the "masters of suspicion." He didn't buy every argument they made, but he did acknowledge that they certainly raised some ideas he felt were worth seriously engaging. Though he was a philosopher and not a theologian, his Christian faith was

2. Kwok, *Postcolonial Imagination and Feminist Theology*, 144.

important to him, and he deeply felt the need to consider whether he could affirm the possibility of faith's relevance in light of some of the events of the twentieth century. The horror of two world wars and the devastation of both the Holocaust and nuclear war left many, including Ricœur, wondering how to make sense of it all.

In 1960 Ricœur wrote *The Symbolism of Evil*. In it, he acknowledged that how people think about religion and Scripture is changing, and people will never be able to believe the same way it was possible to believe hundreds of years ago. For some, this will be because they continue to desire to believe in a way that dismisses historical-critical perspectives on the Bible, continually amassing scientific data that contradicts older beliefs, and the increasingly pluralistic world in which Christians live alongside those of other or no faiths. For these folks, the irrevocable change is that their commitments to a particular type of biblical interpretation are likely to feel consistently under scrutiny and disjointed from broader society. It is no longer possible to think about religion the ways our forebears thought about it and accurately presume that is how most other people still think about it today.

In light of the developments of the last century, attempting to maintain a "pre-critical" view of religion is challenging. Believing now is not the same as believing in, say, the 1600s because you will either (a) not see your faith reflected around you as normative or you will (b) increasingly need to isolate yourself from the broader community so that you hear from only those who think like you. Either of these options is a change from what was the case centuries ago.

Conversely, for those who are people of faith trying to engage and positively integrate historical criticism, scientific discovery, and a diverse democratic pluralism, it can feel daunting. What viable religion is left after all the doubt and criticism? It is to those asking questions like these that I think Ricœur has the most to say.

> It is in the age when our language has become more precise, more univocal, [and] more technical . . . that we want to recharge our language, that we want to start again from the fullness of language. . . . Beyond the desert of criticism we wish to be called again . . . to a world in front of the text, a world that opens up new possibilities of being. . . .
>
> In every way, something has been lost, irremediably lost: immediacy of belief. But if we can no longer live the great symbolisms of the sacred in accordance with the original belief in

them, we can, we modern people, aim at a second naïveté in and through criticism.[3]

For Ricœur, the insights of interpretation and criticism eventually point to a place that is both beyond criticism and yet doesn't retreat to "pre-critical" silos. Ricœur identified this possibility as the "second naïveté."

In the next section, we'll consider how Ricœur thought it was possible to arrive at this space of second naïveté, how this arrival is fueled by the imagination, and some of the ways Christians might discern how appropriate their imaginings are. Specifically, we'll look at his "hermeneutic arc" or "hermeneutical spiral" and consider how this relates to imagination and what it has to say about the desert of criticism.

Spirals in the Desert

Sometimes religious belonging and faith are treated as all-or-nothing scenarios. Either you are 100 percent on board with 100 percent of a tradition's commitments and practices, or you ought to get out! Interestingly, I've seen this happen in conservative Christian communities and anti-church atheistic groups. On the religious side, the basic argument is something like "Our religion and tradition means feeling X, believing Y, and doing Z. If you are not doing those things, then you are not participating in our community correctly." Those critical of the church say almost exactly the same thing, usually basing their critiques on conservative theological positions and biblical interpretations. This argument is functionally, "Look . . . your religion wants X, Y, and Z from you. You know you're not really 100 percent on board with any of those things! Why bother with the mental and emotional gymnastics? Just admit your religion is ridiculous and get out of there!" In general terms, these are "precritical" and "critical" positions. The precritical perspective rejects new interpretations and emerging perspectives, maintaining that the traditions of X, Y, and Z are correct because they have always been correct, and this has been revealed in some way that cannot be challenged by human reason. The critical perspective points out inconsistencies in precritical traditions, attempting to discredit them by showing logical flaws and empirical evidence that contradicts assertions of the unassailable necessity of X, Y, and Z. What Ricœur proposed was a third way forward, something that often gets called "postcritical."

As a consequence of philosophical debates in the mid-twentieth century, Ricœur began to develop a new method of thinking about the

3. Kwok, *Postcolonial Imagination and Feminist Theology*, 349.

interpretation of texts. In his model, individuals hold their experience and understanding in tension with broader social interpretations and objective meanings. Rather than focusing on either (a) subjective and wholly individualized approaches or (b) attempts to develop depersonalized and wholly objective ones, he suggested that both kinds of focus could be brought together. He felt this was important to do as an overly personalized, "texts mean whatever I feel like they mean" approach was equally as problematic as the assumption that "there is only one true and perfect interpretation of this text." Finding a path down the middle of these approaches was his goal. As he developed it over decades beginning in the 1970s, the "critical hermeneutic arc" eventually came to be described as a process of interpretation having three distinct "moments." In a simplified form, they are "understanding," "comprehension," and "appropriation." We'll get to the details shortly, but first, we need to understand what Ricœur thought about texts in general.

Ricœur considered text a kind of temporary freezing of conversation. It is the concretizing of thinking and dialogue that had previously been interactive. This is perhaps most obvious at a superficial level if you compare two people having a conversation in real time with their voices and bodies present versus a transcript of that conversation considered after the fact. Writing puts some distance between the event and the record of it. Ricœur thought this was true not just of transcriptions of conversation, but of *all* writing.

When I write this sentence, the back-and-forth of thinking and the weighing of various other things I have read are a kind of rushing flux. Eventually, to communicate to you, I must decide to write specific words on a page and try to have them capture some sense of what I intend. Reading these words as I type them is an experience of having them extracted from the broader dialogues and discourses I carry within me. As I write, I am crystallizing the internal dialogue of thoughts into a form that alludes to other ideas and conversations but is fixed in a way that thinking and conversation are not. Whether or not you ever read this, the act of writing itself puts distance between me and the text. Putting thoughts into writing is, for Ricœur, one of the forms of "distanciation."

Ricœur argued that when I get ready to read a text for understanding, I'm in the first "moment" of interpretation. That initial reading attempts to explain the text on its own terms, a "naïve grasping of the meaning of the text as a whole."[4] The first moment of interpretation begins with a guess at what a text means. Because the text is distanced from its origins in the mind and life

4. Ricœur, *Interpretation Theory*, 74.

of its creator, "the author can no longer 'rescue' his [sic] work."[5] The reader must strike out on their own without the author as guide. Though this might feel daunting, one of Ricœur's insights is that without the ability of a "rescue," in which a text is only understood to have the single meaning the author intended to give it, we discover that there is a "surplus of meaning" that the text can contribute. One of the marks of a text that is experienced as powerful or transformative is that it can be interpreted in multiple ways, continually providing the reader with material for meaning making.

Ricœur's first moment is actually its own little interpretive circle. The first guess at a "naive reading" of the text is considered—to the extent possible—on only its own terms. Then it is considered more analytically. As he puts it, "in the beginning, understanding is a guess," and there are "methods for validating those guesses we do make."[6] This process of validation is its own kind of distanciation because, as a reader, I want to ask myself why my first guess *was* my first guess and what habits and patterns of my own thinking might have shaded my initial pass at things. As a reader, "in order to make sense of my own motives,"[7] I must not just understand the text but explain why that understanding makes sense.

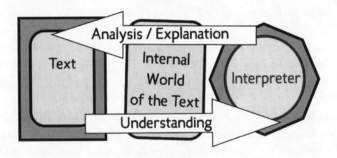

Figure 4.1: A diagram of understanding: The first movement
in Ricœur's hermeneutic spiral.

This analysis emerges from a suspicion that my initial understanding of the meaning of the text somehow missed other relevant dimensions of possible meaning. Instead of just accepting that the first reading of a text is the only way to understand it—as if the text just offers pure information to you—you can take that initial understanding and begin to question it, turning back to the text again for more analysis and reflection. In simple

5. Ricœur, *Interpretation Theory*, 75.

6. Ricœur, *Interpretation Theory*, 75–76.

7. Ricœur, "Model of the Text," 214.

terms, Ricœur argued that "understanding" a text was the process of (1) guessing at the meaning of a text, (2) asking ourselves *why* we guessed that way, (3) reflecting on both the text and our own habits, (4) considering other possible guesses, (5) repeating as needed, and eventually (6) settling on a tentative interpretation.

Even before getting into the second and third "movements" of interpretation, we can hear echoes of Feuerbach, modified by Ricœur into the development of what he called a "hermeneutics of suspicion." Instead of just presuming that what the text first seems to say is all it can say, Ricœur encouraged interpreters to explore the possibility of "the latent meaning" in language.[8] He was aware of how alienation can produce a "false consciousness," in which people fail to recognize they are sometimes complicit in maintaining their own unideal circumstances because of the momentum of social systems and personal habits.

For example, let's consider a recent political situation in the United States and its interpretation. In 2017, a flurry of popular support for a tax bill emerged within the first year of Donald Trump's presidency. Nonpartisan analysts concluded that the bill would "lower taxes on the wealthy and raise them for the working class." Despite this, it was widely supported by poor and working-class whites.[9] Why would such a bill find support among those it would harm?

Some critics suggested that support emerged as a result of a false consciousness in which Trump's promises to build a wall on the Mexico border, declaration of being a "law and order" president, and support for maintaining confederate statues intimates the vision of a world which some supporters would like, even if at the cost of their own economic well-being.[10] What Ricœur would point out is that even if that *is* the reason why this support exists, the logic of it isn't direct. It is not as if the tax bill is explicitly framed as "an offer to working class whites that though the policy will hurt them financially, it will be worth it because they'll get some socio-cultural benefits." No one ever said this. That level of things can rarely be seen on the surface, only emerging from some further analysis caused by the suspicion that things often mean more than what they seem to mean at first.

Suspicion-caused analysis is part of the interpretative move "between a naïve interpretation and a critical one, between a surface interpretation and a depth interpretation."[11] It is only after a few loops through understand-

---

8. Ricœur, *Freud and Philosophy*, 17.

9. Zeitz, "White Working Class."

10. Zeitz, "White Working Class."

11. Ricœur, *Interpretation Theory*, 87.

ing, explaining, then understanding again that a reader moves on. The text, having already been distanced from the author, is now distanced from the reader too. The reader has suspiciously interrogated their own initial understanding to see what more might be found. After some initial cycling of suspicion and interpretation, the process moves toward what Ricœur called "comprehension." As Ricœur sees it, this kind of deep interpretive reading allows the text's internal world to affect the reader's inner world.

In comprehension, new ways of being or seeing that the reader found in the text have become available and the world of the text shines a light into previously unexplored areas in the reader's inward landscape. Reader and text do not merge or fuse together, but there has been some contact between the world envisioned in the text and the world envisioned by the reader. In comprehension, a reader "seeks to grasp the world-propositions opened up by the reference of the text . . . to follow its movement from sense to reference: from what it says, to what it talks about."[12] Past naïve understandings and purely factual interpretations, a reader can experience the text as "a new way of looking at things" as the "text speaks of a possible world and of a possible way of orienting oneself within it."[13] Understanding that a text offers a new way of "orienting oneself" is comprehension. Only after the awareness of a possible new orientation can the third movement of "appropriation" occur.

Appropriation is when an interpretation of text results in a reader's self-interpretation that makes the reader realize the text helps them to understand themselves better, differently, or, as Ricœur wrote, "simply begin to understand himself."[14] The consequence of appropriation is that the reader feels some greater sense of herself in the world. Reading a very compelling or eye-opening text can make the reader feel like their own sense of self is enlarged. This doesn't always happen when someone reads a text, but when it does, the reader finds herself—even if only in small ways—transformed.

Importantly, this transformation isn't a mechanical or inevitable process. Self-help claims that "reading this book *will* change your life" are not what we are talking about. Instead, Ricœur thought that powerful texts could be returned to again and again, and their well of meaning would never run dry. For Ricœur, the goal of interpretation was *not* to project oneself into the text but "to expose oneself to it: to receive a self enlarged by the appropriation of the proposed worlds which interpretation unfolds."[15]

---

12. Ricœur, *Interpretation Theory*, 87–88.

13. Ricœur, *Interpretation Theory*, 87–88.

14. Ricœur, *Hermeneutics and the Human Sciences*, 158.

15. Ricœur, *Interpretation Theory*, 91.

And how are the worlds within a text possible? What is the human capacity that allows for this new way of being to emerge from interpretation? The imagination.

Ricœur was clear that "there is no such thing as a brute impression, an impression that is direct and unadorned by human structuring. Instead, perception is always structured by physiological and imaginative processes."[16] His position is not just that interpretation requires imagination, but that *all* perception does. If "there is no such thing as a brute impression," then the act of perception is interpretive and meaning making. For Ricœur, "imagination comes into play in that moment when a new meaning emerges from out of the ruins of . . . interpretation."[17] Ricœurian imagination allows us to hope for water even as we stand by ruins on the sands of the desert of criticism.

I think about Ricœur often in my work as part of a small church-planting team. Following a vision first articulated by my wife, we're trying to bring a new congregation into being. Church planting is challenging work anywhere, but in our context, the situation is unusual in particular ways. We are Quakers living near Boston, and in our tradition, there hasn't been a new Quaker meeting started in our area for *decades*. The details of our story are less important than the fact we are clear to say that part of the inspiration is a passion to "reclaim and reinterpret Quaker practices for our current times."[18] We have a deep-seated conviction that giving greater attention to our tradition and traditional practices can result in insight and *new* ways of doing and being church. We strive to be deeply rooted in our tradition and open to new interpretations of that tradition.

Ricœur's tactic is not to ignore or reject critical suspicion but to use its analytic and critical power to "clear the horizon for a more authentic word, for a new reign of Truth, not only by means of a 'destructive' critique, but by the invention of an art of interpreting."[19] I am of the mind that attempting to entirely dismiss the points made by critics of religion misses the opportunity to find a space for a faith that is larger than before. I think it is possible to acknowledge the changing times and find a grounded and nourishing faith that can encompass new visions. Ricœur is undoubtedly not the only scholar to try to think through faith in the light of criticism, but he is someone who has had an outsized impact on theology, especially theology that discusses imagination.

16. Taylor, "Ricœur's Philosophy of Imagination," 94.
17. Kearney, *Wake of Imagination*, 148.
18. See https://www.threeriversmeeting.org/.
19. Ricœur, *Freud and Philosophy*, 33.

It isn't so much the idea that imagination swoops in like a superhero to fix everything, but that imagination can hold together religious commitments and poetic, reflective thinking about faith. In fact, Ricœur is clear that without some aspect of self-transcendence, imagination can just become an aesthetics: lots of appealing talk without substantive change.

> There is an element of promise and commitment in the religious attitude which is different from the pure play in imagination and through imagination that takes place in poetry. That is why I should preserve both a strong kinship and a precise difference between the two, because I neither want to make everything poetical in religion nor to make everything religious in poetry - and to preserve this dialectic.[20]

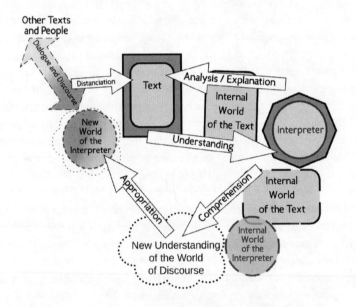

Figure 4.2: A diagram of understanding: Ricœur's hermeneutic spiral.

Ricœur wants an unending dance between poetic interpretations and faithful convictions. It is important to him that these not get seen as collapsing into a single category: they are supposed to remain in motion.

As I read Ricœur, his approach is not severed from tradition, just pragmatic about what is possible given the current moment. I agree with him

20. Ricœur, "Poetry and Possibility," 455.

that tradition is "not the inert transmission of some already dead deposit of material but the living transmission of an innovation always capable of being reactivated by a return to the most creative moments of poetic activity."[21] Part of what makes my faith a living faith is precisely its ability to adapt and grow as we discover new things about the world.

There is no reason why the witness and testimony I give has to sound exactly like what my forebears would have said. Its roots should be traceable to what has come before and it should be nourished by that connection, but to think that what has come before must be all that continues to be available is not honoring tradition but worshiping at the idol of traditionalism. New faith commitments and expressions emerge in the dynamic tension between knowledge of what has come and the imagination of what might yet be.

> The contrary of suspicion, I will say bluntly, is faith. What faith?
> No longer, to be sure, the first faith of the simple soul, but rather
> the second faith of one who has engaged in hermeneutics, faith
> that has undergone criticism, postcritical faith.[22]

This raises a question.

For the sake of argument, let's say the imagination *is* as powerful as Ricœur thinks it is, and reading can "open new worlds." How do we know the worlds being opened are good? Ricœur provided the vision of a second naïveté, but by what means are we to assess the images of the future that emerge from that space? How do we determine what "God really wants" instead of what "we think God wants?" What does it mean to faithfully read Scripture and religious texts in the wake of criticism and suspicion? Though Ricœur was a man of faith and often wrote about philosophy and religion, these questions are far more related to the work of theology. And so, we turn to the contemporary American, Reformed theologian Garrett Green.

Green's Trust

Among the few theologians who have written on the imagination at length, Green is among the most cited. As I mentioned in chapter 2, I'm not convinced that his use of the paradigm model is the best approach; however, dismissing Green because of his use of the paradigm metaphor would be a mark of hubris. His work is useful and lucid. With multiple lengthy volumes dedicated to thinking about imagination and theology, his work is required reading if you are interested in scholarship about those topics.

21. Ricœur, *Time and Narrative*, 68.
22. Ricœur, *Freud and Philosophy*, 28.

Though I am not convinced of the fit of the Kuhnian paradigm if it is used more expansively and metaphorically with the recognition that there are multiple contesting paradigms within theological and biblical studies, there is a viable way forward. In his trailblazing 1989 book, *Imagining God*, Green pointed directly to the problem that arose at the end of the last chapter: how do we know we can trust our imagination?

Green's work very much follows in the lineage of the Neo-Orthodox German theologian Karl Barth, specifically in the sense of their shared ideas about revelation. One of the major twentieth-century theological debates was an ongoing argument between Barth and Swiss theologian Emil Brunner about the degree to which the natural world and human reflection upon it can yield any dependable knowledge of God. This debate is highly relevant regarding how to think about the role that imagination is seen to play in a life of faith. Before digging into Green, we should look at the pivotal point of conflict between Barth and Brunner. Not only will this help contextualize Green's work, but it is also the case that the Barth-Bruner debate was a massive event in twentieth-century Protestant theology, and Green thinks imagination helps to provide a way forward between both positions.

In a simplified form, Brunner's argument was that humanity possesses the capacity to reliably gain knowledge of God independent of the revelation that is Christ and the Scriptures that bear witness to him. Some sense of God can come from the world. This concept of "natural theology" has deep roots within the history of Christian theology, with Augustine originating the phrase via *theologia naturalis*, later developed further by Anselm and Aquinas. The debate started in 1934 when Brunner authored an essay called "Nature and Grace." In that essay, he suggested that Barth had gone too far in denying the validity of natural theology. Even given the fall and its tainting of human being, surely *some* part of human reason and observation of the world had to be worth something. Right? Barth replies with a "No" just about as firmly as is possible.

Barth's position is that Jesus the Christ himself is the only way to come to authentic knowledge of God. Only through an authentic knowledge of God's humanity in Christ can we come to know what a human truly is. As Barth himself argues,

> Humanity is grounded in the fact that one man among all others is the man Jesus. So long as we select any other starting point for our study, we shall reach only the phenomena of the human. We are condemned to abstractions so long as our attention is riveted as it were on other men, or rather on man in general, as if we could learn about real man from a study of man in general,

and in abstraction from the fact that one man among all others is the man Jesus. In this case we miss the one Archimedian point given us beyond humanity, and therefore the one possibility of discovering the ontological determination of man.[23]

We can know how we are supposed to be as humans only in and through the person of Jesus Christ.

If we turn our attention to "man in general" instead of to the "Archimedian point" that is Christ, we will arrive at some sense of humanity that is nearly infinitely less than humanity in its fullness. Barth writes that the sin in the garden was so rupturing that humans have become "radically and totally evil, without qualification."[24] Thus, looking at other present-day humans and expecting to discover humanity's nature is more than a fool's errand. It is reprehensible. If other people are the basis for the development of a theological anthropology, the developed construct will be based on radically broken people, reflecting that sin and not God's intention for humanity.

The entirety of humanity "constantly reenacts the little scene in the garden of Eden. There never was a golden age. There is no point in looking back to one. The first man was immediately the first sinner."[25] We ought not to base our understanding of humanity as it *should be* on humanity as it *is*. The problem isn't that Creation doesn't bear some traces of the Creator, but that as fallen creatures, humans both (a) cannot be trusted to find God accurately in it and (b) commit an enormous act of hubris if we think our reason, reflection, and will can get us to an accurate encounter with God. According to Barth, "natural theology is the doctrine of a union of man with God existing outside God's revelation in Jesus Christ,"[26] and it should be "treated only as non-existent. In this sense, therefore, it must be excised without mercy."[27] The baseline Barthian position is that God revealed God-self in Christ, and this revelation was made known to us *only* via the person of Jesus, knowledge of which is today accessible solely via Scripture. God's grace is the only singular means of coming to know God. No human efforts can help us gain knowledge of God. Intense, right?

It has to be noted that Barth's context here is supremely important. Barth was a German theologian writing during Hitler's attempt to ideologically weaponize Christianity via the *Reichskirche*, the Church of the Third

23. Barth, *Church Dogmatics III.2*, 132.

24. Barth, *Church Dogmatics IV.1*, 500.

25. Barth, *Church Dogmatics IV.1*, 508.

26. Barth, *Church Dogmatics II.I*, 168.

27. Barth, *Church Dogmatics II.I*, 170.

Reich. His essay "No! A Reply to Emil Brunner [*Nein! Antwort an Emil Brunner*]" was published just one year after Ludwig Müller, a pro-Nazi pastor, was installed in the created position of "Reich Bishop" and proceeded to merge all German Protestant youth organizations into the Hitler Youth programs.[28] Barth's "No" to natural theology must be understood in the context of his motivation to reject any attempts to say that the events of the world could be seen as signs of God's nature, presence, or plan. As decades went on, Barth's position shifted some, and by the end of Brunner's life, the two men reconciled personally and—to some degree at least—theologically as well.[29] It is in the wake of all this that Green writes.

Green's thesis is a kind of meeting point between Barth and Brunner: imagination is "the link between divine revelation and human experience,"[30] the "point of contact" (*Anknüpfungspunkt*, which is a concept directly from Brunner) where human experience encounters revelation.[31] Green provides a spatial kind of metaphor as a definition of imagination, identifying it as "that specific point where, according to Christian belief and experience, the Word of God becomes effective in human lives."[32] Framing it this way allows Green to maintain a strong sense of dependence and priority on grace while providing a means for human analysis and reflection to have some worth. Bringing imagination into the conversation allows Green to come alongside Barth *and* Bruner.

He maintains the idea that humans have no direct access to ultimate truth outside of revelation in Scripture, suggesting that theology's function is not to proclaim—or refute—the ultimate nature of things and the nature of their being (their "ontological" status), but to help faithful people develop opportunities for an experience of meaningfulness shared by Scripture. As Green puts it, there's a divine two-step taking place. First, God "impressed his image, embodied in Jesus Christ, on the original witnesses, who have in turn expressed that image in certain texts." Second, Scriptures can "impress their form on us, the modern hearers, reshaping us in the image of God."[33] The contours of Scripture reflect the shape of God, so allowing the Bible to mold us leaves us indirectly shaped by God as well.

One of the consequences of this way of seeing things is that the concept of a "faithful imagination" isn't about philosophical truth in any

28. Romocea, *Church and State*, 54–64.

29. Barth, *Letters, 1961–1968*, Letter #207.

30. Green, *Imagining God*, 42.

31. Green, *Imagining God*, 5.

32. Green, *Imagining God*, 40.

33. Green, *Imagining God*, 106.

metaphysical sense so much as it is about conforming to a vision of life Green sees captured in Scripture. This vision provides the "paradigm" for how Christians ought to see the world.[34] The role of paradigmatic thinking is essential for Green primarily because it is a *shared* paradigm tacitly agreed upon between Christians. We need this sense of mutual concern because, at least in terms of religion, imagination does not self-justify.

As Green puts it, "imagination as a subjective experience contains no clue to the truth of what is imagined, since imagination can serve also as the organ of fiction and deceit."[35] Something other than the imagination must be relied upon to assess the appropriateness of the products of imagination and ward off idolatry. Green also recognizes the impact of Feuerbach, suggesting that "not *whether* to imagine but *how* to imagine rightly is the central theological question to emerge from the conversation with Feuerbach."[36] Given that humans are imagining creatures, the task isn't to try to stop people from imagining and start only using non-imaginative thought but to develop normative marks against which to measure faithful imagining. Green's most recent work helps significantly in this regard. In 2020's *Imagining Theology*, Green developed six facets for "normative use of theological imagination in Christianity."[37]

First and foremost is a norm that provides the foundation for the following five: "the Bible embodies the concrete paradigm on which all genuine Christian theology is based, enabling the faithful to rightly imagine God."[38] Importantly, Green distinguishes between thinking of the Bible as foundation in a literalist way—which he rejects—and thinking of it as Calvin did, like spectacles, a "pair of corrective lenses that refocus our flawed spiritual vision."[39] Scripture is meant to be seen as the *account* of the word of God, Jesus Christ, not taken as if the Bible itself was equal to Christ. Elsewhere Green has a line that captures this well, writing that Jesus Christ is "the first, original, and governing sign of all signs."[40] Since the Bible is a record of the revelation of Christ and given that Christ is the point through which other things should be interpreted, Scripture serves as a necessary grounding to any attempt at faithful Christian imagination.

34. Green, *Imagining God*, 135.

35. Green, *Imagining God*, 84.

36. Green, *Theology, Hermeneutics, and Imagination*, 104.

37. Green, *Imagining Theology*, chapter 1 contains this list.

38. Green, *Imagining Theology*, 28.

39. Green, *Imagining Theology*, 31.

40. Green, *Theology, Hermeneutics, and Imagination*, 162.

Second, "right imagination of God is a movement not only of the head—our mind or intellect—but also of the heart, our feelings and affective responses." Central to this norm is Green's assertion, which occurs in numerous places, that attempts to develop a "religion of reason" or to read Scripture "without interpretation" are a result of the folly of attempting to overemphasize the rational and the unintentional absorption of the "unacknowledged metaphysics of modern science" into Christian theology.[41] Scripture gives an account of reality not by cataloging truths as if an encyclopedia but by providing the story through which we are invited to experience and interpret all other stories.

Third, "the theological use of imagination must always remain open to the Mystery of God, resisting every temptation to rationalize, demystify, or control the divine."[42] It is an error to think about the task of a theologian as someone out to solve the riddle of God, as if there is an answer, explanation, or argument that will conclusively fulfill all questioning and seeking. As Green puts it, "the wise person is open to the possibility of genuine mystery, which implies that there is more to reality than we are able to comprehend; the foolish person assumes that anything beyond our rational grasp is unreal or untrue."[43] Mysteries are not riddles.

Fourth, "in accordance with its biblical paradigm, theological imagination always remains open to novelty, eschewing every attempt at metanarrative or systematic closure."[44] One of the interesting positive benefits of thinking about the imagination as the paradigmatic imagination is that, as with modern science, it has to be seen as open-ended. In 1874, a promising physics student sought guidance from his mentor, Phillip von Jolly, asking about where and how he should pursue the life of a research scientist. Von Jolly's reply was disheartening and included the line "there might still be a little dust or bubble at one or the other angle to check and classify, but the system as a whole is quite secure."[45] The study of physics is almost complete, don't get into that field if you want significant discoveries.

The student was Max Planck, who proceeded regardless and forty-four years later won the Nobel Prize for his discovery of energy quanta and the initial development of what is now known as quantum physics.[46] As Christians, we must hold open the possibility of a new vision. As Green

41. Green, *Theology, Hermeneutics, and Imagination*, 28.

42. Green, *Theology, Hermeneutics, and Imagination*, 33.

43. Green, *Theology, Hermeneutics, and Imagination*, 34.

44. Green, *Theology, Hermeneutics, and Imagination*, 34.

45. Planck, *Year Million*, 104.

46. To be precise, Planck won the Nobel Prize in Physics (1918).

puts it, given human finitude and the ongoing movement of God's Spirit, all attempts at certain closure must be seen as a "betrayal" of the mission of theology.[47] God continues to do a new thing.

Fifth, "because theological imagination is dependent on the Holy Spirit, it is an enterprise of faith, appearing uncertain and circular from a worldly perspective, depending on the certainty of God's revelation for its claim to truth."[48] Green is—rightly in my opinion—dismissive of Christian attempts to prove theological claims in the lexicon of science. From his perspective, the goal of a Christian, theologian or otherwise, is never to attempt to arrive at some unassailable fact or argument from which Christian truth is undeniably seen as ultimate truth. That misses the point that as "an enterprise of faith," we proceed *without* the world's certainty.

We see this scripturally, for example, in Paul's declaration that "in hope we were saved. Now hope that is seen is not hope. For who hopes for what is seen? But if we hope for what we do not see, we wait for it with patience" (Rom 8:24–25). Green is aware that this fifth normative position could skirt against the edge of "fideism," or the idea that reason and faith can have no interaction, thereby shielding the believer from any need to engage in critical or analytic thinking about their commitments. He has an interesting discussion of just this issue elsewhere, arguing that the charge of "fideism" is appropriately applied not when someone appeals to faith rather than reason but only when that appeal is cited as therefore requiring a refusal to engage in critical dialogue with those who do not share faith commitments.[49] Though the Christian imagination is open-ended and built on God rather than on fact verifiable through material science, the claims made in Christ's name should not be arbitrary. Indeed, the intended function of these six facets for the normative use of theological imagination is one way of staving off arbitrariness.

Sixth and finally, Green offers that we must acknowledge that "theological imagination belongs to the present age, the *regnum gratiae*, the era of our earthly pilgrimage, when we 'see through a glass, darkly.'" Once the reign of God is fully present "we will no longer need to imagine God in the world to come" because "we shall see him 'face to face.'"[50] Imagination is only important in the *present* moment. Later we will experience everything fully. The issue is just that right now, prior to new Jerusalem, we don't have access to the whole picture. Consequently, we need imagination to help us

47. Green, *Imagining Theology*, 38.

48. Green, *Imagining Theology*, 37.

49. Green, *Theology, Hermeneutics, and Imagination*, 70–84.

50. Green, *Imagining Theology*, 40.

interpret and get properly formed by Scripture and the communities that form around it.

In Green's frame, theology is based on faith and has access to knowledge of God only indirectly via the testimony of the scriptural witnesses to the word of God. As a result, imagination is identified as the means by which we can gain that indirect knowledge while still physically present in this world. We need imagination now because we have no means of direct and full vision of God. Faith is, after all, "the assurance of things hoped for, the conviction of things not seen" (Heb 11:1). In our hope, exploring the edges of a mystery we know will never be exhausted, theologians will continue to find new ways to articulate what we have found.

> Just as the discipline of grammar does not prevent the poet or philosopher from employing the language in new and creative ways, so the church's doctrine does not confine the theologian to a boring traditionalism but rather provides guideposts and warning signs along the way to new insights into the meaning and application of the biblical witness to real life in the world today.[51]

Green's work in imagination takes seriously the critiques of suspicion *and* those who critique those critiques. He values the role of the imagination as the only means by which humans can gain access to knowledge of God *and* argues we need some guidance to make sure we stay on the course of faithfulness. Recognizing the simultaneous need for imaginative new ways of thinking about theology and some guidelines for how to do that faithfully is a theme that will return numerous times in the following chapters. It is important to note that while Green offers some compelling means of making the discerning assessment, his facets are not the only viable rubric. Below we'll consider some of the scholarship from Ada María Isasi-Díaz, an American Catholic theologian and Christian ethicist that had an explicit concern with imagination, change, and thinking about how to test the faithfulness of those changes.

Rooted in the Possible

Influenced by other Latin American liberation theologies but centered on the struggles of Latina women, Isasi-Díaz became a founder of the movement known as *mujerista* theology. This movement advocated for the importance of affirming how the daily experience of Latinas shapes their lives

51. Green, *Imagining Theology*, 22.

in faith. Vital to the work of theologizing in a *mujerista* way is the validation of *lo cotidiano* as a source of wisdom and knowledge.[52]

Lo cotidiano is Spanish (like the English word "quotidian") and refers to the multiple layers of daily life experience for Latinas. It is an intersectional category that considers race, class, gender, faith, and society's various privileges and marginalizations. As she puts it, it is the "stuff" of Latina women's reality.[53] In this theological tradition, reflection begins with an experience of the every day and imagination's role is held as important because it is often the means by which the hope of a better day tomorrow is sustained. The hope for a better world for our children and their children.

The insistence on particularity and dailiness of *lo cotidiano* is part of its power. The way that Isasi-Díaz frames it, an emphasis on the particular helps to push back against overly abstract and disembodied universalization (I know our lives are hard but if we are faithful, when we die, we'll get our just rewards in heaven). Focusing on the regular experience of living as a Latina woman brings a spirit of change and liberation. Inviting Latina women to think about God and the future using terms from the "stuff" of life instead of technical academic jargon can help clear away some clutter.

> Taking seriously the descriptive function of *lo cotidiano* makes it possible for new narratives to emerge, narratives created by the poor and oppressed who take charge of reality. In these narratives they find themselves and see themselves as moral subjects who exercise their right and power of self-definition. . . . New narratives help us to see and to value parts of ourselves that we have ignored or that we do not know well, and they help us to know ourselves differently from the way oppressors define us.[54]

Though the word imagination doesn't appear anywhere in the above paragraph, I think it is embedded throughout. "Conceiving of future realities" is all about the "capacity to bring into consciousness things that are not observably present." New ways of seeing things, new stories to be told, and new visions of the future and the self are all things associated with imagination operating hermeneutically and apocalyptically. Imagination allows us to call forth into the present hopes for what might yet be.

This spirit animates much of the conversation of Latin American liberation theology, running from Paulo Freire through to Gustavo Gutiérrez and then on to countless others. In that work, themes of utopia often surface

---

52. Isasi-Díaz, "Lo Cotidiano," 5–17.

53. Isasi-Díaz, *Mujerista Theology*, 66–67.

54. Isasi-Díaz, "Lo Cotidiano," 11.

and how important it is to dream for change so that change may come. Below, consider a passage from Gutiérrez that Isasi-Díaz cites herself.

> Utopia is also a proclamation, an annunciation of what is not yet, but will be; it is the forecast of a different order of things, a new society. It is the field of creative imagination which proposes the alternative values to those rejected.[55]

Isasi-Díaz is entirely supportive of this. . . . She just wants to remind us that the "forecast of a different order" must also be grounded.

> I think imagination has an enormous role to play in creating/building utopias. However, the imaginable has to be harnessed into the possible in order for it to be effective in the struggle for life-fullness of life.[56]

This "harnessing into the possible" is a kind of test for the rightness of imagination. Where Green has his six facets to help him discern, Isasi-Díaz starts with the stuff of everyday life and asks how new ideas and images might matter there.

I distinctly remember the first time I met Isasi-Díaz in person. I was at a conference at Drew Theological School, where she taught for years. Midway through the second day of papers and panel discussions, there was a break for some extended questions and comments from the audience. Isasi-Díaz, who appeared to have been listening intently to all the sessions, approached the microphone.

"I've found this all very fascinating," she said, "and I'm hoping it might be something I'll think about more. To help me with that, could one of you on the panel try to explain to me what we've all been doing here and why it matters? Oh . . . and imagine I never finished high school and need to work more than a full-time job to feed my kids." And she meant it. She wasn't being glib or mocking in any serious way. She wanted one of us to try and take the talk out of abstraction and see if we could ground it in something material. She stood at the mic for some time before someone tried.

In a chapter about the connection between hope in the face of suspicion, what Isasi-Díaz can show us is that imagination is a central process whenever the task at hand is trying to envision new ways of living and being in the world. Interrogating the present to see if more might be possible is itself an act of resistance and hope. Criticism need not lead to cynicism. Suspicion need not lead to faithless critique and could turn toward life-giving

---

55. Gutiérrez, *Theology of Liberation*, 135–36. As cited in Isasi-Díaz, "Burlando Al Opresor," 350.

56. Isasi-Díaz, "Burlando Al Opresor," 354n46.

theological renewal. What the concept of *lo cotidiano* offers is a reminder that when what we imagine is grounded in experience, it is easier to find ways forward from critique to construction.

The theologian Mayra Rivera addresses this dynamic well, noting that theology done from a Latina perspective already has as a starting point an "incarnational imagination" that affirms that "the incarnation, the presence of the greatest of mysteries in our flesh, is more than Jesus of Nazareth."[57] God's gift in the incarnation isn't only Christ, but also an invitation to see holiness in all the places and bodies that society marginalizes. Imagining leans on sensation and sensing is an embodied process.

> Attending to the spirit in the flesh of rejected, disorderly bodies is hardly to dismiss Jesus' body. Instead we read his body—a material, finite, stigmatized, vulnerable body—as revealing the scandal of divinity in the flesh, or more accurately, of the divine *becoming* flesh. . . . An interpretation of the incarnation as "the greatest of mysteries in our flesh," implies, methodologically, openness to learn from real, finite bodies, to seek the wisdom of body-words and their transformative power.[58]

Recognizing that "learning from real finite bodies" can be the means to catalyze radical transformation also entails recognizing that the answer we're looking for will not fall in our laps from on high. It will arise in the nit and grit of a manger where two refugees sought shelter for a night.

As I see it, substantive academic consideration of the power of imagination results in a call for a kind of critical hope. This hope rests on serious wrestling with the questions of interpretation, the issues raised by historical-critical biblical analysis, the discoveries of science, and a willingness to look at the material realities of those who suffer. Recognizing there are hosts of reasons why our relationship to faith cannot be—or sound—precisely the way it did for our forebears, there is still a deep movement into mystery to explore. Ricœur, Green, and Isasi-Díaz all point to a faith that imagines the future and refuses to support shallow certainty. In its place is a hope for *faith*: who hopes for what is already certain? For those who feel like their position accepts some of the work of critical suspicion and yet stays grounded in faith, how do they explain the task of theology? What does theology sound like when questions of uncertainty, faith, and imagination guide theological reflection? These are the questions of the next chapter.

57. Rivera, "Thinking Bodies," 222.
58. Rivera, "Thinking Bodies," 220.

Questions for Reflection

1. Paul Ricœur's theory of interpretation is complicated. Looking back to that diagram on page 82, are you able to explain all the different moments? Which ones—if any—are confusing?

2. How do you feel about the idea of a second naïveté? Do you feel like you've ever had an experience where you don't deny or ignore criticism but also somehow feel moved beyond it?

3. Garrett Green is definitely a thinker in the lineage of Karl Barth. How is his work on imagination connected to Barth's arguments?

4. What do you think about Green's argument that there need to be some explicit norms to help guide the faithful use of the imagination? Do you think that adhering to the norms that Green suggests is a kind of discernment? Why or why not?

5. Isasi-Díaz argues that an emphasis on the daily "stuff" of life is an aid to helping make sure our theologies don't become too abstract and disconnected from communities. What do you make of this argument? What are its strengths? Where might it struggle?

Related Readings

Green, Garrett. *Imagining God: Theology and the Religious Imagination.* Grand Rapids: Eerdmans, 1998.

———. *Theology, Hermeneutics, and Imagination: The Crisis of Interpretation at the End of Modernity.* Cambridge: Cambridge University Press, 2000.

———. *Imagining Theology: Encounters with God in Scripture, Interpretation, and Aesthetics.* Grand Rapids: Baker Academic, 2020.

Ricœur, Paul. *The Symbolism of Evil.* New York: Harper & Row, 1967.

———. *Lectures on Imagination.* Edited by George Taylor et al. Chicago: University of Chicago Press, 2022.

Scott-Baumann, Alison. *Ricœur and the Hermeneutics of Suspicion.* London: Bloomsbury, 2012.

5

Imagination in Method

WHEN GARRETT GREEN PUBLISHED *Imagining God* in 1989, academic work with theology and imagination was at a high point. If you flip to the back of this book and look at the bibliography timeline, you can see the intense cluster of scholarship from this period. The 1970s had seen significant book-length work on imagination by Brazilian Presbyterian liberationist Rubem Alves, Congregationalist minister and Bible scholar Amos Wilder, and United Church of Christ minister and Bible scholar Walter Brueggemann. In the fall of 1975, Ricœur gave his thirteen "Lectures on Imagination" at the University of Chicago. That same year, the Mennonite theologian Gordon Kaufman published *An Essay on Theological Method.*

Essay marks a turning point for Kaufman, beginning work on imagination in theological studies that he would continue to develop for the rest of his life, notably in *The Theological Imagination*, published in 1981. This is the same year David Tracy released *The Analogical Imagination.* Shortly after, John McIntyre wrote *Faith, Theology, and Imagination.* It was a busy time. Partly as a result of this rising attention to imagination, Green developed the work discussed in the previous chapter.

Though "imagination" was becoming a popular term for use in theological studies, very rarely was it clear how the authors were using it and what exactly they thought were the limits of what it could do. Green's *Imagining God* can be seen to serve two major purposes in response to this. First, it was an attempt to clarify the term "imagination," suggesting that if theologians start regularly employing this concept, it would be good to be more precise about what exactly it means and how it is connected to God. Second, and I think relatedly, it was a reply in the wake of the work of Tracy and Kaufman. One issue was that Green thought Tracy's use of the frustratingly jargony Ricœur resulted in a "conceptual Babel."[1] Kaufman's work he appreciated as

---

1. Green, Review of *The Analogical Imagination.*

clear and accessible but ultimately wrong.[2] *Imagining God* was written to address some of the weaknesses he saw in their work.

Though Tracy's *The Analogical Imagination* has had an outsized impact on academic theology, the fact is that the book isn't really centered on imagination. It is a book about Tracy grappling with the realities of religious pluralism and the appropriate role for systematic theology in the face of that diversity. His development of "the analogical imagination" is how he names his way of understanding how to think about theology as a whole. Tracy writes in the wake of Ricœur, affirming that one of the dimensions of religion is that it provides an interlocking system of symbols that can be drawn on to explain how we imagine the nature of the world and what our role ought to be in it. Religion is an imaginative symbol system that provides resources for articulating meaning and truth.

In this frame, "the analogical imagination" is Tracy's understanding of the dominant way that Catholic theological thinking has used the Christian symbol system it shares with other traditions. Analogical language seeks "ordered relationships articulating similarity-in-difference,"[3] that is, looking to see where there are connections with, and implications of, Christ's birth, death, and resurrection in the present. Our knowledge of God will not be direct but through analogy. How we marshal the resources of the symbol system to conceive of God—that is, how we imagine—is always about seeing God as something else.

As important as this book was in theology, it isn't a particularly useful place to linger long for our purposes. As Green wrote in his review of Tracy, "relating the human imagination with its analogical powers to God's revelation is an especially promising area of theological inquiry. It is therefore all the more disappointing that *The Analogical Imagination* sheds so little light on either analogy or imagination."[4] It was after Kaufman and Tracy published their books that Green released his text in an attempt to shed light on both. In this chapter, we'll take a look at Kaufman's project, following that up with an examination of some of the critiques it garnered, including Green's. The chapter closes by exploring some work that makes arguments that challenge the substance of Kaufman's claims.

---

2. Green's 1983 review of *The Theological Imagination* is clear on the importance of focusing on the imagination but contains a call for some theologian to proceed "with greater care" regarding the implications of imagination. Six years later Green himself published his first book on the topic.

3. Tracy, *Analogical Imagination*, 409.

4. Green, Review of *The Theological Imagination*, 421.

Theology as Imaginative Construction

Kaufman's writing on imagination and theology starts with a focus on method. However, by the end of his career, more than thirty years later, Kaufman's interest also extended to the importance of imagination (and creativity) as a specific area of doctrinal reflection. For Kaufman, imagination is relevant in terms of *how* theology is done (theological method) and *what* theology is talking about (doctrine). This chapter is about the method and the next one addresses doctrine.

At the root of Kaufman's early work is the removal of scriptural authority as the basis for assessing theological validity. In its place, Kaufman wanted theology to be assessed on how much it helped Christians interpret their experience towards the end of reconciliation and love. Rather than "good theology" being measured by the degree to which it coheres with tradition, previous theology, and prior scriptural interpretations, Kaufman wanted the test to be about the degree to which theology helped people.[5] The way he got to that point was, while potentially controversial, quite clear: theology is, has always been, and always will be, a construction of the human imagination.[6]

Kaufman's work can largely be considered a prolonged reflection on the theological consequences of the philosophy of Kant. One of Kant's arguments was that "God" is not a thing like any other thing. As a result, this means that references to "God" do not work the way that references to other things work. We have to realize, says Kaufman, that we will never be using the word God quite right because the thing it refers to is not referable like other things. God is so much more than we can understand that referring to God works differently than other words. For example, while we can use the word "God" without quotation marks, the word God still does not function the same way as the words coffee, person, or Wisconsin. The reality that the word "God" points to is so expansive that our reference to it in language operates differently than most other words.

Regardless of whether or not there *is* an actual, metaphysically real, ontologically distinct, agentive being—or force—to which "God" refers, humans can never have direct access to it in fullness. The truth of God's metaphysical existence is largely irrelevant to Kaufman's Kantian approach: everything that identifies itself as theology is only, and can only ever be, composed of human imaginative constructs built from human experience,

---

5. Kaufman, *Theological Imagination*, 272–79.

6. Kaufman, *Theological Imagination*, 11.

inherited language, and tradition. Theology is the structure of the *human* experience and rationalization of God, not a description of God.

Whether or not theology proves anything is utterly beyond Kaufman's point. The purpose of a theologically constructed concept of God is a way of "dealing with the inescapable human problem of orientation in life and in the world."[7] Theology is an articulation of "the human imagination's attempt to grasp and understand and interpret the whole within which human life falls."[8] God is the centerpiece of human orientation and how we consider all other things. Kaufman was aware that this sounded like an echo of Feuerbach, and he set out to show why their projects were different.[9]

Kaufman said that Feuerbach's assessment that Christian theology was all imagined is correct, but where Feuerbach was *wrong* is to assume that "imagined" must mean "false" or "fantasy." For Kaufman, "imagined" is simply a description of the necessary character of human language that intends to refer to the divine.

> The image/concept "God" is a humanly constructed symbol by means of which we (in western traditions) attempt to focus our consciousness on that ultimate resource of human being and fulfillment to which (we believe) we must relate ourselves if we are to become fully human, if we are fully to realize our potentialities.[10]

Kaufman argued that his work was not a projectionist theory like Feuerbach's because the constructed vision of God that humanity has produced is not all ideals and best human hopes.

Kaufman agreed that there was a dominant theological motif in which God is like us and through Jesus possesses traits of humanness that our values and ideals to strive toward, but . . . there is also the equally important motif of the infinite other-ness of God as judge and mystery beyond us who nevertheless sacrifices Godself on humanity's behalf. Kaufman said that if God were merely a human projection, then it would likely not have both those motifs present, just the "good" ones. Instead, theology *does* have "a center outside of and beyond ourselves,"[11] which means that it is still a helpful activity and not just a source of self-denial only worth being suspicious about.

7. Kaufman, *Theological Imagination*, 14.

8. Kaufman, *Theological Imagination*, 28.

9. This is all over his work, but a clear one from *Essay* is on p. 15 and in *Theological Imagination* on pp. 43 and 90.

10. Kaufman, *Theological Imagination*, 56.

11. Kaufman, *Theological Imagination*, 283.

Since those dual motifs (the humanity of Christ and the mystery of God) appear to refute a Feuerbach-flavored projectionist theory, does that mean we know the construct/concept "God" really *does* point to something we can know with certainty? No, it does not. This was a fundamental movement of Christian theology for Kaufman: the affirmation of a vast trajectory towards love and reconciliation as modeled in God has no proof that it is not an imaginative human construct. We must accept it on faith.

> Faith . . . lives from a belief in, a confidence that, there is indeed a cosmic and vital movement . . . toward humaneness, that our being conscious and purposive and thirsting for love and freedom is no mere accident, but is undergirded somehow in the very nature of things. God is the personifying symbol of that cosmic activity which has created our humanity and continues to press for its full realization.[12]

If, at any point, we find ourselves certain and resting on that certainty instead of using it to propel ourselves toward "full realization," we are engaged in idolatry. As Kaufman had it, the constructed concept of God "is the great relativizer of all false absolutes, the One who unmasks all the idols."[13] Proceeding in faith is required.

In an earlier book, *God the Problem,* Kaufman had already been richly exploring the possibility that theology is an imaginative construct. However, at that point his argument was a balancing act of sorts: he understood the concept of God to be "highly dialectical" and both "a construct of the human imagination" *and* "an objective reality."[14] However, by the time *An Essay on Theological Method* came out three years later, that balance had largely been abandoned. While Kaufman *might* be able to talk about God being a reality of some particular sort, it almost certainly would not be an *objective* one. So, what is the purpose of the theology that Kaufman proposes?

A theologian's role is to help others (and themselves!) consider existing "imaginative constructs" and ask what role they play in directing our intentional and moral activities. Contemporarily, we ought to accept that the only viable purpose of theology is as a corrective or justification for *practice*, not the means of securing the legitimacy of a *concept*. The unknowability of the God beyond "God" reminds us of the limitation of our own humanity.

---

12. Kaufman, *Theological Imagination*, 49.

13. Kaufman, *Theological Imagination*, 276.

14. Kaufman, *God the Problem*, 169–70. This more balanced idea of "imaginative construction" in theology is similar to the use of that phrase by John Thiel in *Imagination and Authority*.

The fact that we can't know with certainty the nature of God or human-ity means there is still good reason to explore and imaginatively work towards some better future. For Kaufman, regardless of the verifiability of "God exists" or whether or not "God" corresponds to a particular reality, the *cultural* power of religious thought is not diminished.[15] In fact, it is of profound importance to study and construct theology precisely *because* of how inherited cultural norms shape how we can name our present experience.

> There is no such thing as a raw prelinguistic experience of "tran-scendence," say, as distinguished from the experience of "ulti-macy" or of the "infinite." Each of these "experiences "is shaped, delimited and informed by the linguistic symbols which also name it. Without those symbols to guide our consciousness, these "experiences" would not be available to us at all.[16]

According to Kaufman, the peak of this shaping and symbol-making culmi-nated in the concept of God, which came into being "as our forebears sought ways (over many generations) to come to terms with the various issues with which life faced them."[17] God is the only thing that can "gather up, com-prehend, and hold together all reality and experience, all possibilities and imaginings in a meaningful connection that can orient human life."[18] To speak of God is to gesture at the mystery and possibility that pervades all life. This mystery ultimately resists all attempts to be enclosed and yet simul-taneously serves as the means of newness and transformation.

By 2001, Kaufman had settled on a phrase he felt captured the con-cept of God as he understood it: serendipitous creativity.[19] The significance of this decision is that it allows for a kind of realism in which Kaufman can say that God is demonstrably real because newness, change, and creativity are present throughout history. The name that various traditions give to the *experience* of that novelty will vary, but there is something to which the concept of God refers that is more than just wish fulfillment. With God as the endless possibility of all that might be, Kaufman's understand-ing of Christ is narrowing down of that possibility, showing only parts of it. If the concept of God is the symbol of endless mystery and possibility, then Christ serves as a particular possible vision for how people can be with one another in ways that contribute to greater human flourishing. The revelation in Christ points to

15. Kaufman, *God—Mystery—Diversity*, 109.

16. Kaufman, *Essay*, 7.

17. Kaufman, *In the Beginning*, 39.

18. Kaufman, *In the Beginning*, 27.

19. Kaufman, "On Thinking of God," 409–26.

> An inclusive egalitarian community welcoming all sorts and
> conditions of women and men, as the normative standard in
> terms of which humanity is to be understood. Though centering
> on the man Jesus, the Christ-symbol is regarded as referring not
> only to this solitary figure but also to the larger community of
> reconciliation that grew up in response.[20]

Jesus' ministry and self-sacrifice inaugurated a new way of being in the
world, offering a life pattern for those who came in his wake. This is em-
blematic of one of Kaufman's recurring themes.

One of the repeated points in Kaufman's work is the recognition that
human creativity in one area of life can profoundly shift ways of thinking and being in other areas. While the consequences of Christ may have
ushered in new ways of being, so did the creation of nuclear weapons that
can functionally end the world.[21] He had similar concerns with the realities of ecological disaster and felt it was necessary to continue to develop
a theology to manage the emerging understandings of the scientific world.
Major instances of human creativity have long-lasting repercussions for
humanity. This includes Christ and nuclear fission. For him, it was more
important that theology be able to meaningfully influence how people
think about the present and future than it was to maintain firm doctrinal
ties to traditions that struggled to address global realities like the possibility of nuclear holocaust and climate disaster.

Under Kaufman's frame, the evaluation of theological claims ought to
be based on the degree to which they are helpful resources and encourage-
ment for people to act in responsive and just ways in the world, forming
"communities of reconciliation."[22] Kaufman argues that the central issue
for Christians to wrestle with is not about salvation or faithfulness in some
metaphysical way concerned with heaven or hell, but how each of us can
live a life that continues to explore what is possible in a way that would be
resonant with the kind of solidarity we attribute to Christ.

> Claims are often made, by both Catholic and Protestant theo-
> logians, that theological work must begin with Christian faith,
> that it is essential to accept the Bible as God's revelation in
> order to do Christian theology, that the church's fundamen-
> tal affirmations must be regarded as authoritative for faith
> and life. I want to argue, however, that all such authoritarian

20. Kaufman, *God—Mystery—Diversity*, 117.

21. Ferguson Lectures at Manchester University in 1984, published in 1985 as *Theology in a Nuclear Age*.

22. Kaufman, *Jesus and Creativity*, 114.

> moves actually express not the vitality of faith but its threaten-
> ing breakdown. . . . Appeals to divine revelation as the ultimate
> authority in theology, therefore, should be regarded as a warn-
> ing flag: they are made when the theological conceptual frame
> is not working as well as it should, and needs careful scrutiny
> and possibly drastic reconstruction.[23]

Kaufman's project, taken as a whole, is fascinating. Though he knew many would identify his non-foundationalism as grounds for a slippery kind of relativism, his purpose was actually the opposite of this. He argued that understanding the constructed-ness of theology is crucial to recognizing it can (and *ought*) to be changed when warranted. Having theology be under-stood as imaginative rather than descriptive means that Christians—espe-cially theologians—have a distinct responsibility to be attentive to current needs and how tradition can be interpreted to bear on those needs. Far from having theology as "imaginative construction" be about diminishing the im-portance of theology, it is meant to accentuate it! Because imagined things have such power, we need to recognize theology's nature as an imaginative construct. An example may help clarify this point. Consider constitutional legal scholar Ian Haney López and his comments on race:

> Races are thus not biological groupings, but social construc-
> tions. Even though far from objective, race remains obvi-
> ous. . . . The absence of any physical basis to race does not
> entail the conclusion that race is wholly an hallucination. Race
> has its genesis and maintains its vigorous strength in the realm
> of social beliefs.[24]

From a strictly biological and materialist standpoint, the category of race is a human construct. However, attempts to ignore the social consequences of race because "race is just a construct" is an error.

Similarly, we know that though legal systems are socially constructed, they profoundly impact the material lives of us all. We are not called to ig-nore laws because they are "made up" or passively accept them because they have been important, and the rule of law is a founding pillar of all democrat-ic modern societies. Instead, it is precisely *because* of this importance that we are called to continually interpret, reinterpret, and allow for disputing the meaning of law. We know that law is imperfect and that some innocent people have been found guilty and vice versa. This doesn't mean that the concepts of guilt and innocence are irrelevant. The fact that these categories

---

23. Kaufman, *In Face of Mystery*, 47.
24. Haney Lopez, "Social Construction of Race," 61.

have such an impact on people undergirds the importance of imaginatively constructing them well, constantly revising them as time goes on.

As Kaufman put it, "all claims to truth made simply on the grounds of religious authority are in question: theological truth-claims are to be assessed strictly in terms of our present needs and our present moral insight (educated as much as possible, of course, by past experience and by tradition)."[25] Historical precedent is not to be ignored, but neither should it win out against the importance of material and spiritual flourishing for individuals and communities.

In some ways, this perspective ends up in a similar place to Isasi-Díaz as considered last chapter. For example, consider Kaufman's argument that theological truth-claims ought to be measured "in terms of our present needs." This seems quite resonant with Isasi-Díaz who writes that "liberation" is the criterion by which Latinas judge and is "the essential element of Hispanic women's morality and of all morality."[26] The test is not against some abstract sense of truth, but in material flourishing: "*lo cotidiano* makes it possible for us to see our theological knowledge as well as all our knowledge as fragmentary, partisan, conjectural, and provisional."[27] In both instances, each theologian asks us to consider what it would mean to have a test for the legitimacy of a theological claim be about the degree to which it tends to the hurt and harm we see around us today. What more might be possible to address the pain of the present?

As I see it, Kaufman's three-decade-long argument about imagination (in a significantly reduced form) is this:

- Many of us are born into a cultural context where the concept of God already has long-standing social power.

- We can recognize that such a concept is an imagined construction and that no human articulation of "God" will ever capture the fullness of God.

- Consequently, we can recognize that how we have imaginatively constructed that concept has objective and material consequences for many people.

- Since we know we cannot fully articulate the nature of God, recognize that theology is a human construct, and see that the consequences of that construct can positively or negatively impact people, we ought to continue the work of imaginatively constructing the concept of

25. Kaufman, *Theological Imagination*, 192.

26. Isasi-Díaz, *Mujerista Theology*, 69.

27. Isasi-Díaz, *Mujerista Theology*, 71–72.

God, intending to do so with a goal of making life materially better for people. We would do this knowing that the newly constructed theology doesn't "get it right" in a metaphysical sense any more than older models, but at least it would be honest about what it was doing and specifically prioritize the material well-being and health of communities and the planet.

Scholars vary widely in their support for Kaufman's project. However, even among his critics, it is generally accepted that what he accomplished was significant. Because of this, Kaufman had numerous detractors, not the least of which was Garrett Green.

Kaufman Contested

I noted in the preface that my goals for this book are tightly bound up in introducing you to some of the most influential thinking related to imagination and Christian theology. This goal means that there is not a single trajectory or argument in this book, instead, there is a kind of patchwork display of ideas connected not by the same endpoint but by wrestling with similar questions. Often those ideas are in tension or outright conflict. Instead of suggesting which is better, I hope to faithfully convey each perspective. This is relevant to reiterate as Kaufman's scholarship provoked a significant amount of critical response.

Kaufman's claim was that there is *no* direct contact point to the Truth of revelation and, if we're being honest, we can't even know for sure if there is such a thing as the God this revelation proclaims. But . . . we can have *faith* that this is the case and proceed, trusting that the modeling and consequences of Jesus can provide a framework of interpretation. We can operate within this framework even if we'll do so knowing it may well not ever be able to be objectively proven correct.

If you recall, Green argued imagination was "that specific point where, according to Christian belief and experience, the Word of God becomes effective in human lives."[28] Though imperfect and unable to receive the fullness of God, the imagination is the only site of connection to knowledge of the Divine. However, because the imagination can roam freely, Green asserted that Christians need to establish norms to ensure what we imagine is appropriate for Christianity. There seems to be no middle path between Green and Kaufman. Their positions cannot both be the case, and Green suggests he sees why Kaufman is incorrect. Remember,

28. Green, *Imagining God*, 40.

Green wrote the first of his books on imagination in the wake of the work of David Tracy and Kaufman.

In a review of *The Theological Imagination*, Green identified Kaufman's scholarship as "undeniable contributions to the seriousness and clarity of theological inquiry,"[29] but fiercely contested his conclusions. As Green saw it, Kaufman had made a foundational error in his thinking about how imagination functions. As Green wrote, "by conceiving imagination only under the metaphor of construction, [Kaufman] misses the fact that imagination has a passive as well as an active moment, that it not only shapes reality but is also shaped by it."[30] As Green sees it, Kaufman's theory of theology as imaginative construction might be correct, but . . . it would need to include a receptive or descriptive element to be considered viable. Without theology attempting to be *descriptive* of the actual God that is, the effort must be considered insufficient. As Green put it, "Theology which is merely constructive, which loses its resolve to reflect the glory of God and confines its work to building and rebuilding the image of 'God,' really has fallen prey to idolatry."[31] On this point Kaufman and Green are at an impasse.

Kaufman says that anyone who thinks it is the responsibility of theology to attempt to describe the nature of God and the church is committing an act of idolatry. The Great Mystery that is God as serendipitous creativity will always be beyond our attempts to capture it. As such, we should not try to do so. Instead, we are to look to the radical effect of Christ's life and sacrifice, building up a theology that supports communities of reconciliation modeled on that, using whatever means necessary. "You, sir," Kaufman might have said to Green, "are the one being idolatrous! I'm working very humbly, knowing that what I build cannot match God. You are the one who demands our work somehow describe a situation humans cannot ever fully comprehend."

Here I imagine Green shaking his head in frustration . . . "Of *course* our work will never comprehend God, but that doesn't mean we are to give up! You are too willing to give up the power and truth of tradition. We are to *describe*—however failingly—God's role in the world, not just make things up." And of course, Kaufman's reply would be clear: "You are also making things up, Garrett; I'm just willing to admit it. It's like Falcetano says: the intellect is never truly free of the imagination, so the only way it can truly fool us is when we fancy ourselves to be free of it."[32]

---

29. Green, Review of *The Theological Imagination*, 221.

30. Green, Review of *The Theological Imagination*, 221.

31. Green, Review of *The Theological Imagination*, 221.

32. This is a paraphrase of a great line in Falcetano, "Confession as Narrative

As I said, an impasse.

Green wasn't the only one concerned. Similar critiques were taken up by David J. Bryant in *Faith and the Play of Imagination*, which in many ways is a book-length criticism of Kaufman's project as a whole. In that text, Bryant also laments that Kaufman has only acknowledged the constructive aspects of imagination and failed to recognize its receptive capacities. Importantly, Bryant is *not* trying to invert Kaufman's claims and say that theology is never constructive and should only be certain and descriptive. He recognized that "there is no way for us to arrive at an extralinguistic point of view,"[33] so isn't arguing for a theology that somehow pierces the mystery and gets all the details correct. Instead, he wants Kaufman to recognize that imagination is inherently tied to "the ongoing stream of tradition"[34] and should result in a dialogue between tradition and construction, not a monologue of innovation.

Bryant was clear that he wasn't attempting to argue that theology can accurately and totally render the transcendent truth of God, but neither is he willing to cede that we are totally cut off from it, as Kaufman suggests.[35] Bryant's path forward heavily features Ricœur alongside another major hermeneutics scholar, Hans-Georg Gadamer. Bryant's work develops a view of imagination as the means of connecting newness and traditions of interpretation, yielding an "interplay between horizons."[36] Look for a bit at the world disclosed in traditional understanding, then to newer imagined interpretations, then back, seeing between them some new way that holds both in tension. Bryant identifies imagination as "the power of taking something as something by means of meaningful forms, which are rooted in our history and have the power to disclose truths about life in the world."[37] He emphasizes that "taking something as something" is what "enables one to be open to the play of dialogue."[38] This dialogue consequently results in "the imaginative production of meaning (that is, its redescription of the world)."[39] The words of Jewish philosopher Martin Buber are apt here.

> I have occasionally described my standpoint to my friends as the "narrow ridge." I wanted by this to express that I did

---

Contemplation."

33. Bryant, *Faith and the Play of Imagination*, 102.

34. Bryant, *Faith and the Play of Imagination*, 126.

35. Bryant, *Faith and the Play of Imagination*, 126.

36. Bryant, *Faith and the Play of Imagination*, 149.

37. Bryant, *Faith and the Play of Imagination*, 5.

38. Bryant, *Faith and the Play of Imagination*, 5.

39. Bryant, *Faith and the Play of Imagination*, 148.

not rest on the broad upland of a system that includes a series of sure statements about the absolute, but on a narrow rocky ridge between the upland and the gulf where there is no sureness of expressible knowledge.[40]

Like Buber, Bryant wants to encourage us to walk on the narrow ridge, picking a precarious path between the twin abysses of foundationless relativism and legalistic dogmatism.

Green has the paradigmatic imagination be the means by which God's impressed image, "embodied in Jesus Christ" comes to shape us via reflection on Scripture.[41] It forms the basis for how we can describe and understand God communally. Bryant's argument is that the imagination is not so much paradigmatic as it is how a swirling interaction takes place between the Bible, historical tradition, the reader, and the reader's situatedness in the contemporary world. The circular diagram of Ricœur's "hermeneutic spiral" on page 82 is largely applicable to Bryant's interpretation of imagination.

One of the things that Bryant made clear is that one of the core questions that separates Kaufman from others is a question of faith. For Bryant, "faith precedes theology," a position he took in opposition to Kaufman, who seems to think that theology gives rise to faith, "giving narratives, symbols and metaphors out of which it lives."[42] There is an interesting tension here because Kaufman makes quite a big deal of the importance of faith, but for him, it is the faith of continuing in the face of unknowing. For Bryant, it is faith as confidence in the affirmation of God. As Green sees the tension, it is because while Kaufman is interested in imagination, he doesn't seem to work with images much:

> To put the matter squarely, Kaufman does not really like imagery at all. Most particularly, he dislikes religious imagery; one gets the impression that he finds the language of piety embarrassing. When he uses it at all, he puts it in quotation marks. He seems, in fact, to want to put all our first-order language of worship, prayer, and praise in quotation marks. . . . In the end, this theology of imagination impoverishes theology by replacing the richness of its imagery with an impersonal conceptuality.[43]

---

40. Buber, *Between Man and Man*, 184.

41. Green, *Imagining God*, 106.

42. Bryant, *Faith and the Play of Imagination*, 211.

43. Green, Review of *The Theological Imagination*, 221.

Especially at the end of Kaufman's career, when he begins to refer to the work of Christ as "Jesus Trajectory$_2$," (yes, the little subscript "2" is part of how Kaufman refers to Christ), it is easy to see some merit in Green's accusation. There does seem to be some loss of the visceral power of particularity in Kaufman's work. It is certainly imaginative, but it is not particularly poetic.

All that being said, Kaufman was quite aware of this critique, and while his writing may well have veered into abstraction, his vision for its *consequences* was certainly not abstract. Kaufman wrote a specific reply to those critical of his theology, especially those wondering if he could believe the things he believes and still be a faithful Christian.

> True faith in God is not living with a conviction that everything is going to be okay in the end because we know that our heavenly father is taking care of us. It is, rather, acknowledging and accepting the ultimate mystery of things and, precisely in face of that mystery, going out like Abraham not really knowing where we are going, but nevertheless moving forward creatively and with confidence in the serendipitous creativity that has brought our trajectory and us into being, has continued to sustain the human project with the web of life that surrounds and nurtures us, and has given us a measure of hope for that project here on planet Earth. Since we now see that we are to love and give ourselves and our lives not only to our human neighbors and enemies, but also to the wider orders of life in which we find ourselves, this perspective deepens and widens the radicality of the Christian ethic, and thus the radicality of Christian faith.[44]

Kaufman's grounding of his work in the world's material needs is a central part of his claims. While he may be less concrete in his imagery, he nonetheless remained concrete in his ethical concerns and the importance of valuing a community's needs. What is interesting to note is that other theologians contemporary to Kaufman made very similar observations, similarly grounded their work in a concern for "human neighbors," but ended up in significantly different places.

Yoked to Memory

While Bryant and Green specifically took on Kaufman and centered imagination as an area of concern in their work, other approaches have similar convictions and offer significant insight even though they only address

44. Green, Review of *The Theological Imagination*, 221.

imagination peripherally. For example, in 1999, the Catholic theologian Peter Phan turned to the development of Asian American theology with a clear affirmation of the role that imagination must play. However, he did so by yoking it to memory.

Phan was a native of Vietnam who emigrated as a refugee to the US in 1975. He wrote that doing theology, especially as an immigrant, necessitates an orientation of being "betwixt and between."[45] Doing theology this way is a recognition that marginalization pushes some to the periphery so that they are caught between centers of power and tradition. With increasingly greater acknowledgements of diversity in the global church, "there is the need of developing a theological method that can take into account expressions of God's message that are different from those that have grown out of one's own philosophical, religious, political, and ethical traditions."[46] Phan argued that the development of interpretive humility will help to ease "the dangers of prejudice, racism, colonialism, and ethnocentrism"; at the same time it lifts up the possibilities and vitality of historically marginalized ways of knowing and being.

> Theology betwixt and between is theology done with both memory and imagination; it is contemplating the past and creating the future at the same time. Memory anchors the theologian in the ocean of history and tradition, the Church's and one's own; but the stability and security it affords is impermanent and illusory. Remembering is not re-producing reality exactly as it happened . . . but re-creating it imaginatively; it is re-membering disparate fragments of the past together and forming them into a new pattern under the pressure of present experiences, with a view to shaping a possible future. . . . Like a pair of wings, memory and imagination carry the theologian aloft in the work of linking past and future, east and west, north and south, earth and heaven.[47]

Here there are resonances with Kaufman's emphasis on imagination in method but done in a way that thinks "a new pattern" is possible without abandoning the value of tradition. Memory plays a crucial role in imagination, and certainly in our very definition of sacraments: "Do this in memory of me" (Luke 22:19).

Though only in passing, Phan offers his own critique of Kaufman in *Being Religious Interreligiously.* In his view, the problem with Kaufman's

45. Phan, "Betwixt and Between," 114–15.
46. Phan, "Betwixt and Between," 114.
47. Phan, "Betwixt and Between," 114.

position is that it misunderstands the viable responses to mystery. Kaufman seems to think that because the fullness of God will always be beyond our grasp, the only conceivable way forward is to accept that all the imaginative building we do must be done as if it stood on its own. Following Aquinas, Phan affirms that it is possible to accept the viability of theological claims about God at the same time that we recognize how those claims are made will be "necessarily inadequate."[48]

Interestingly, David Tracy makes a similar point in his articulation of the analogical imagination. He notes the importance of a "curiously overlooked passage in the documents of Vatican I," that set out an understanding of Catholic theology as appropriately partial and incomplete.[49] Recognizing theology to be unfinished but nevertheless real is freeing and powerful. As Tracy says:

> The key to understanding how liberating this model for theology was in its time is to note that theology is clearly distanced from any attempt at deductive proof of mysteries (so favored by the Cartesian scholastics of the day). Instead, after proper tributes to Anselm and Aquinas, theology is described as consisting of analogous but real understanding of those mysteries.[50]

Both Phan and Tracy might agree with Kaufman that theological reflection does not result in certainty, but they would challenge the idea that the results of imaginative construction have no foundation outside imagination.

Phan suggests Kaufman's error arises because he has too narrow a view of what counts as knowledge. If we admit that the category of "things that can be known" includes more than just logical propositions, then we can know things even if the details are not precise and the resolution is grainy.

> We have at our disposal modes of knowing that are not purely rational, that appeal to the imagination and the heart, that do not make grandiose claims to absolute validity and universal normativeness, that do not produce an infallible certainty but anchor the mind and the soul in an unshakable certitude, the kind of knowledge that is proper to interpersonal relationships, different from that of mathematical equations and physical laws, the sort of knowing that leads to decision and action.[51]

48. Phan, *Being Religious Interreligiously*, 87.
49. Tracy and Cobb, *Talking About God*, 42.
50. Tracy and Cobb, *Talking About God*, 42.
51. Tracy and Cobb, *Talking About God*, xx.

Rejecting rationally "infallible certainty" but affirming the experience of "soulful certitude" allows Phan to root himself equally between tradition and innovation. As he says, "both memory and imagination in their mutual interaction are indispensable tools for theology. Without memory, theology would be empty; without imagination, it would be blind."[52] This pairing of imagination and memory is a correlational approach also affirmed by the Scottish Anglican theologian, David Brown. As with Phan, there is an affirmation of the centrality of constructive imaginative work without jettisoning the importance of memory. How Brown arrives at this point is quite different, however.

Brown's *Tradition and Imagination* is a project of historical and constructed theology written to show how theological and cultural claims based on a "just what the Bible says" mentality are built upon a false premise. Given that the interpretation of Scripture is a fundamentally imaginative interpretive endeavor, we must recognize that how it is that we imagine has been influenced by numerous streams of historically and socially contingent factors.

> Certain truths can only come naturally to consciousness as a result of specific historical pressures. We can be absolutely certain that Jesus' idealism would have taken a very different form had he been born in a different century or place.[53]

The social context of imagination shapes not only what can be imagined by an individual but also the receptivity of a community to accept the new vision and begin to use it as their own.

The imagining person is not a socially detached Subject with a faculty of imagination that is somehow able to generate novel interpretations and visions that arrive from nothing. Instead, Brown thinks about the imagining individual as a "traditioned individual" that has come to see the world and God in it, as a function, yes, of "the Scriptures themselves," but also how they've heard those Scriptures preached, knowledge of the church through the centuries, Sunday school lessons about them, movies that reference them, businesses that capitalize on them, etc. Imagination and interpretation pulled away from tradition are superficial and have little power. Likewise, tradition without the ability to be constantly reinterpreted falls away from being experienced as relevant.

> Not only can truth be more powerful in its effect when mediated through the imagination, imaginative rewriting can convey

52. Phan, "Betwixt and Between," 115.
53. Brown, *Tradition and Imagination*, 319.

aspects of truth which might otherwise be neglected in a purely
factual account.[54]

Imaginative interpretations of tradition can make handholds and offer
clearer invitations for those looking to make meaning and orient themselves
toward something greater.

Brown is envisioning an affirmation of imaginative interpretation
of tradition as a form of authoritative revelation. "Tradition, so far from
being something secondary or reactionary, is the motor that sustains revelation both within Scripture and beyond."[55] Brown argues that it is an
error to think about Scripture as the fullness of revelation and tradition as
somehow supplemental to that. Instead, he pushes for an understanding
of Christian tradition as itself revelatory as well. The practice of reading
Scripture and valuing it as authoritative is a tradition that can continue to
be imaginatively reinterpreted.

What Brown shows is that imagination's action in the individual em-
ploys the images, stories, feelings, and structures in which the person is
imagining and has previously imagined. Tradition is one of the essential
components needed for imagination to operate; as such, it both allows for
the exercise of the imagination and delimits the kinds of things that can
be arrived at through that exercise. Imagination, he claims, "is absolutely
integral to the flourishing of any religion, Christianity included,"[56] because
it can "open up new perspectives undreamed of in the first century."[57] To
accept that tradition is itself part of revelation is to accept that to the degree
that the actions of the present influence the traditions of the future, we can
participate in the unfolding revelation of God's truth.

According to Brown, contemporary interpretations of tradition are
more likely to influence future tradition when they have greater "imaginative
density" and better "imaginative fit."[58] Leaders become more effective and
theologically engaged when they are able to braid together symbols and traditions of the past with current concerns and imagined future possibilities.

> Followers are most inspired by the leader whose vision is such
> that a different world seems just around the corner. The alter-
> native reality is allowed to "come alive" for them in the here
> and now.[59]

54. Brown, *Tradition and Imagination*, 282–83.
55. Brown, *Tradition and Imagination*, 1.
56. Brown, *Tradition and Imagination*, 366.
57. Brown, *Tradition and Imagination*, 25.
58. Brown, *Tradition and Imagination*, 7.
59. Brown, *Tradition and Imagination*, 310–11.

The more connected the vision for the future is with current interpretations of tradition, the more a sense of possibility for change "comes alive" and "the future becomes present."[60] What this "aliveness" means to Brown is value neutral. Just because something is imaginative doesn't mean it is good.

> Far from the imagination always being liberating, it too can sometimes stultify. To my mind, therefore, rather than playing imagination and ontology off against one another, they should be seen as generating similar challenges and similar problems.[61]

Rather than setting up the theories and abstraction of metaphysics and ontology as the "bad guy" and "imagination" as the story's hero, Brown encourages us to ask what work they might do together. He also points out that imagination is not always the knight in shining armor. If it is utilizing our imagination that we can play off of tradition to envision and live into the future, then it must also be the case that when things turn sinister, our imagination has a part in that as well.

In either event, and however it is that imagination plays a function in the method of writing academic theology, that is not its only role. Considering the methodological questions of *how* imagination is part of thinking about God is interesting, but eventually, theologians get to the actual practice of writing about God. How has imagination played a role in this work? How have scholars considered imagination in the context of classical areas of doctrinal reflection? These are the questions of the next chapter.

Questions for Reflection

1. Kaufman argues that theology is to be assessed "strictly in terms of our present needs and our present moral insight." He also says that theological work should be informed by past experience and tradition secondarily, prioritizing present pragmatic and ethical concerns. What are the possible benefits and challenges of this approach?

2. What do you think about Kaufman's argument that it is precisely *because* theology is an imaginative construction that it is so important that we study and work on it?

3. Kaufman, Green, and Bryant differ significantly on whether or not what we imagine can ever *directly* touch the divine and revelation. Which, if any, thinker do you find yourself more drawn towards? Why?

60. Brown, *Tradition and Imagination*, 312.
61. Brown, *Tradition and Imagination*, 288.

4. Phan argues that imagination plays a significant part in memory and remembering, suggesting that even how we think about concrete, material conditions is shaped by imagination. Do you agree with this claim? Why or why not?

5. Brown emphasizes that not only is all tradition the result of prior imaginative action, but that we need tradition to imagine well. What do you think about this and his idea that imagination that ties together past and present can help change in the future seem more possible?

Related Readings

Brown, David. *Tradition and Imagination: Revelation and Change*. Oxford: Oxford University Press, 1999.
Bryant, David J. *Faith and the Play of Imagination: On the Role of Imagination in Religion*. Macon, GA: Mercer University Press, 1989.
Kaufman, Gordon. *In the Beginning . . . Creativity*. Minneapolis: Fortress, 2004.
———. *The Theological Imagination: Constructing the Concept of God*. Philadelphia: Westminster, 1981.
McFague, Sallie. *Metaphorical Theology: Models of God in Religious Language*. Philadelphia: Fortress, 1982.
Thiel, John. *Imagination and Authority: Theological Authorship in the Modern Tradition*. Minneapolis: Fortress, 1991.

6

Imagination in Doctrine

AN ACADEMIC I FOLLOW on Twitter recently posted a couple of questions, presumably looking for some responses and a thread of interaction. The post read, "What first sparked your theological imagination? What sparks it now?"[1] Unsurprisingly, I followed the thread with some interest. I wondered what people would send in response. What did they think "theological imagination" was? How did it come about? There were dozens of replies. In general, people shared about topics or events that got them interested in studying theology or asking theological questions. Some folks shared Scripture passages. Others offered a story (in under 280 characters) about a loved one who used to pray with them. Narnia came up a few times. Art in general had a strong showing. So did nature. *Jesus Christ Superstar* showed up more than I expected and so did quite a few versions of "arguing with my youth pastor." Then came a reply which grabbed me enough that I copied it into my notes for this book: "I'm not sure if theological *imagination* applies to me, although I have studied theology formally and informally since 1975 and am now writing a PhD in theology thesis."

This raised a great set of questions for me.

Is it the case that imagination is inherently part of all theological work? I've argued that the answer is "yes," but I also recognize that may not be the general consensus. I think whenever someone (academic theologian or not) is doing constructive work and trying to think and explain the work of God imagination is at play. Last chapter was all about that. But what if we're not talking about theological imagination in a general sense as method, but something more specific? Are there particular doctrinal statements that reference imagination? Are there folks writing about traditional theological categories and how imagination connects to them? Not many, but yes.

So far in this book, we've explored each of the following:

1. Felker Jones, "What First Sparked . . . ," https://twitter.com/bethfelkerjones/status/1526959912181551105.

- ways of thinking about how imagination functions, particularly as part of interpretation

- ways in which imagination is sometimes considered problematic, especially for a person of faith

- what some folks have done to address the problematic issues, mostly in regard to interpretation

- how imagination is related to various methods and approaches to doing theology

Much of the sustained usage of imagination in academic theological writing is connected to one of the above topics. However, some writers have considered imagination as a subject of theological reflection itself.

Mostly these are short declarations like "the Body of Christ is at its core imaginative," made in the context of another argument in which imagination does not take a central role. Similarly, imagination often makes an appearance via some version of the phrase "the _____ imagination," where the blank is filled by some doctrinal or theological adjective (ecclesial, eschatological, pastoral, paschal, missional, sacramental, etc.). These references rarely focus long on the role of imagination itself, functionally using the phrase to mean "how we think about _____." Thus, the phrase "we really need to be concerned with the current state of our ecclesial imagination" is another way of saying, "we ought to rethink how we talk about church." Likewise, "theological imagination" ends up being interpreted as "how we think about theology." However, occasionally the topic of imagination is given a more substantive exploration. This chapter is a survey of the scholarship that engages imagination and its intersection with theology in more direct ways. How are God and imagination connected? What is the connection between the Holy Spirit and imaginative inspiration? Is imagination part of what it means to be human?

One of the basic assumptions of attempting to develop a full "systematic theology" is that various doctrines are connected. How we understand the nature of God is related to how we discuss Creation, Jesus, the Holy Spirit, humanity, sin, salvation, the church, and the end of days. To show the connections and bridges between them all is part of the work of developing a complete systematic. Gordon Kaufman is the scholar we've looked at so far that came the closest to creating a complete systematic with imagination as a central theme. In his later books, 2004's *In the Beginning . . . Creativity* and 2006's *Jesus and Creativity*, Kaufman began to develop constructive proposals regarding how we might think about Creation and Christ. While not wanting to dismiss these constructive theological contributions, it is nonetheless true that Kaufman's impact on theology was far more pronounced in the area of theological *method*.

Other than the later Kaufman, the Scottish theologian John McIntyre is the person whose body of work comes closest to developing a complete systematic theology that involves imagination as a central category. Most others who have engaged imagination doctrinally have done so as related to only one or two areas of doctrine. Because of this, rather than proceed thinker by thinker, I've opted to group the discussion by topic, splitting the sections into "Revelation and Knowledge of God," "Doctrine of God and The Holy Spirit," "Creation and Human Being," and "Christian Hope." There are some small asides about ecclesiology (study of the church) and soteriology (study of salvation), but these emerge in the context of other topics, so I have tucked them inside the relevant sections below rather than split them out into their own sections.

Revelation

As was discussed in chapters 1 and 2, imagination is usually acknowledged to have a central role in the human capacities of perception, interpretation, and knowing. In theological terms, discussion about revelation and how we know God is often categorized into "natural (or general) revelation" and "special revelation," referring to how God is revealed in the observable world (natural) and in inspired Scriptures (special). Relatedly, theologians will use the broader phrase "theological epistemology" to refer to the study of how knowledge of God is developed. All of these areas are ones in which scholars have employed explorations of imagination to build their arguments.

Perhaps most commonly, imagination is invoked when wrestling with the transcendent nature of interpreting Scripture and understanding God. For example, James Fowler wrote that imagination "is the principal human organ for knowing and responding to disclosures of transcendent Truth."[2] If God's ways are beyond our ways (Isa 55:8-9) and grace is so abundant as to be overwhelming to consider, how are we to write and think about the divine? American Catholic theologian Christopher Pramuk offers a keen perspective. He suggests that

> The sacramental imagination spirals around two elemental ex-
> periences: first, the wordless but vivid sense of God's presence
> in the conscience, memory, "true self," or seat of the soul, an ex-
> perience presumed available to all; and second, the experience

2. Fowler, "Future Christians and Church Education," 103.

of God's love and mercy poured out in history in the person of
Jesus Christ. These two experiences, both personal and communal at once, spring forth in and from a polyphonic range of
social forms, languages, and practices that make up Christian
ecclesial life.[3]

Given this spiral, Pramuk thinks that an aesthetic approach to the development of theology can be helpful. Expecting a "polyphonic range" of responses
means that instead of presuming theology will get closer and closer to some
fixed and accurate single vision, it will instead open more deeply into mystery and exploration of God. Many (*poly-*) voices and sounds (*-phonic*) will
emerge that attest to the experience of God. This opening can be powerfully
communicated in a similarly expansive and evocative register.

In his view, "a poetic approach to epistemology . . . offers an insight
into modern construals of reality that remain impoverished without it."[4]
This doesn't have to mean that theologians should only write poetry, or that
theology should be limited to the genre of poetry, but that there ought to
be emotional, embodied, aesthetic considerations given to the assessment
of theology, not only rational and historical-critical rubrics. We know God
not just through propositional knowledge, but through experience and
sensation as well. Imagination, as a faculty of perception and the senses is
uniquely suited to theological exploration. Paul Avis makes a similar point,
arguing that the Bible ought to be understood poetically because poetry
"is how the profoundest living truths are best communicated."[5] This is a
position shared by scholars of theopoetics as well.[6]

Amos Wilder was an American Congregationalist minister and Bible
scholar whose 1976 publication *Theopoetic: Theology and the Religious
Imagination* is the first book-length text focused on the topic. Wilder was
an intellectual explorer, brushing up against ideas that would become more
formally known as "social imaginaries" decades before that term came into
regular use in theology. Wilder was insistent that historical-critical innovations in biblical scholarship were important but should not come to dic-
tate the field's work. He argued that it was vital to consider the emotional
and imaginative consequences of Scripture: what we read and what we say
shapes how we interpret and experience the world.

> The language of a people is its fate. Thus the poets or seers who
> purify the language of the tribe are truly world-makers and the

3. Pramuk, *Sophia*, 53.
4. Pramuk, *Sophia*, 24.
5. Avis, *God and the Creative Imagination*, 66.
6. See my book *Way to Water* for more on the scholarship of theopoetics.

"unacknowledged legislators of the world." Perhaps one can say that nothing affects the significance of human existence more than the range and resources of our articulation, vocabulary, syntax, and discourse. Men [sic] awaken to a greater plenitude of being as they operate with more signs and names and media of communication, and so find themselves more aware of their world and its interrelationships.[7]

Wilder served as president of the Society of Biblical Literature, and in his 1956 presidential address, he encouraged his peers to remember that Scripture operates in a manner larger than can be addressed by deductive reason or rationality alone. He wrote that "on the one hand we take [Scripture] too literally and ignore the poetical mentality of the race and the age. On the other hand we make a mistake if we think of them as merely symbol and poetry as a modern would understand them."[8] It was important to Wilder that religious texts—especially apocalyptic ones—not be flattened and read as if they were manuals, journalistic accounts, or predictions, but as works with imaginative, poetic, and mythic registers. This kind of thinking is also found throughout the work of Rubem Alves.

Alves was a Brazilian Presbyterian minister and theologian that studied in the US while in political exile during the 1960s. He is one of the oft-forgotten fathers of liberation theology, writing about the concept years before Gustavo Gutiérrez's scholarship. For Alves, imagination is a central theme and tied up with work for justice and social change.

> I know nothing about God—I am not a theologian! I know nothing about the world—I am not a scientist. I know only this little space which is my body—and even my body I only see as a dim reflection in a dark mirror.
>
> Confessions.
>
> Not theology. Poetry.
>
> The poet is the person who speaks words which are not to be understood; they are to be eaten. And his [sic] stove is his own body lit with the fire of imagination.[9]

Especially in his later work, Alves does not follow the "appropriate form" for theological argumentation, developing his ideas in fits and spurts splattered with poetry, citations, and tangential asides that are compelling but

---

7. Wilder, *Early Christian Rhetoric*, 5–6.
8. Wilder, "Relation of Eschatology to Ethics," 7.
9. Alves, "Theopoetics: Longing and Liberation," 159–60.

rarely like academic writing. I'm not sure if Alves ever read the work of John Henry Newman, but if he did, I'm fairly certain he would have agreed that "the heart is commonly reached, not through the reason, but through the imagination, by means of direct impressions."[10] Alves's decisions about how to make theology were themselves imaginative and sensual. Rather than make arguments and rely primarily on reason, Alves decided his work should be evocative, encouraging readers to reflect on their own "direct impressions" of the sacred.

For Alves, knowledge of God can emerge from play, pleasure, and stern scholarship. He wrote, "theology is not a net woven to capture God in its meshes, for God is not a fish, but Wind that no one can hold. . . . Theology is a net which we weave for ourselves, so that we might stretch out our body in it."[11] Playing with language, form, and metaphor is all part of trying to find ways to articulate some aspect of the divine in language that will never be accurate enough to capture the whole experience. Instead of striving for a complete system, some strive to evoke some experience of the divine through language. This position is also resonant with the work of Sallie McFague.

An American Anglican and feminist theologian, McFague's scholarship was greatly influenced by Gordon Kaufman. She argued, "we construct the worlds we inhabit, but also we forget we have done so."[12] She extended this idea to how we ought to think about Scripture and how it is we come to know God.

> One does not say "Jesus is Lord" except through an act of the imagination. Likewise, one does not grasp the perversions in ordinary life or its potential re-orientation except through an exercise of the imagination which projects another possibility for human life by providing a critical perspective on the conventional view. The active imagination is necessary both for the question of who Jesus is and for the question of the nature of human existence as Jesus projected it.[13]

Faithful use of Christian symbols, stories, and practice require cognitive assent and a willingness to see in a new way. Part of following Christ means exploring how to practice perceiving and interpreting the world in such a way as to recognize that God may work in all things.

10. Newman, *Discussions and Arguments on Various Subjects*, 293.

11. Linhares, "Nevertheless I Am Continually with You," 237.

12. McFague, *Models of God*, 6.

13. McFague, "Imaginary Gardens with Real Toads," 251.

> Both who Jesus is and his re-description of reality demand . . .
> an imaginative (rather than a literalistic) mentality to overcome
> the distance between the story and its significance. Jesus is Lord
> through an act of the imagination; the kingdom of God is an
> imaginary garden, a future (and present) reality set over against
> the conventional view of reality.[14]

From an experiential perspective, the affirmation of Christ's lordship is less a statement of fact and more an act of interpretation. This isn't to deny Christ's lordship but to suggest that proclaiming it without reframing how one sees others means the proclamation is incomplete. Affirming allegiance to the reign of God is simultaneously a commitment to interpreting experience in a particular way. What our senses reveal to us will be seen as part of the larger story of God's work. In this way, McFague's position is similar to one of the earliest voices engaging imagination and theology in the modern era, Calvinist poet and theologian George MacDonald.

MacDonald wrote in Scotland at the end of the 1800s and argued that it is through the "operation of the imagination" that we go about "choosing, gathering, and vitally combining the material of a new revelation."[15] A poetic view of theology is needed to capture the sense—even if poorly—of the vibrancy and vitality of God.

> All words, then, belonging to the inner world of the mind,
> are of the imagination, are originally poetic words. The better,
> however, any such word is fitted for the needs of humanity,
> the sooner it loses its poetic aspect by commonness of use. It
> ceases to be heard as a symbol, and appears only as a sign. Thus
> thousands of words which were originally poetic words ow-
> ing their existence to the imagination, lose their vitality, and
> harden into mummies of prose.[16]

The theologian's task is to attempt to revivify "mummies of prose" and develop a vision of God that imaginatively captures some of God's dynamic and life-giving movement in the world.

MacDonald argues that given God's own dynamism, developing such a theology is best done imaginatively. Knowledge of God can emerge from any creative poetic spaces: not just Scripture, but any transcendent experience, including art. Once again, the task becomes to discern how to rightly interpret transcendent experiences in terms of their theological significance.

---

14. McFague, "Imaginary Gardens with Real Toads," 251.
15. MacDonald, Dish of Orts, 22.
16. MacDonald, Dish of Orts, 9.

Imaginative approaches to theology come with a paralleled need for sensitivity and discernment. This parallel is addressed by several scholars.

Gerald Bednar argues that imagination "bears all the freedom, as well as all the responsibility, of love."[17] It is connective and can bridge two ideas (or people!) but must be tended to with care. Michael Murphy, an American Catholic Balthasar scholar, makes a similar connection, writing that

> imagination is co-natural with the author of love, with the Creator, and therefore reaches out in relationality so as to invite creativity and participation. . . . Imagination connects love and truth; imagination provides for the very ontology of love.[18]

We often come to love someone before we know them in their entirety, only able to imagine how a life with them will be. Similarly, discovering that something important is true sometimes requires we reevaluate many facets of life. Imagining what comes next is a vital process in both of these accounts. As Murphy wrote, "imagination connects love and truth."[19] Imagination can be freeing and make connective bonds. The "ontology of love," or the nature of love's origin, is deeply connected to the ability to envision a shared future. I've seen this play out in my own life.

As an undergraduate student in Rochester, New York I was very interested in urban planning and community-building initiatives. I can remember a time when I was part of a group of folks working with the mayor's office who were tasked with collaborating with local business owners to help them fill out the paperwork that would give them access to grants from the city they could use for improvements to their facades and signage. The city was literally giving away money to small business owners and no one seemed interested. After some failures in door knocking, I had a very enlightening conversation with a friend who had grown up in the same neighborhood I was working in. Rochester had been declining for years and so many promises of a "turnaround" had failed that people just couldn't believe it would be worth it to trust the city again. It wasn't until a neighborhood block meeting when lots of folks could get in the same room, ask us questions, and talk *to each other* that any movement was made. People didn't trust any possibility of a different future until they had each other's vision and presence as a platform on which to build. The work we do of meaning-making with each other helps each of us to be able to consider more. The body of Christ is far better at envisioning the kingdom of God than any one of us is individually.

17. Bednar, *Faith as Imagination*, 169.

18. Murphy, *Theology of Criticism*, 157.

19. Murphy, *Theology of Criticism*, 157.

John McIntyre took this one step further, arguing that not only does imagination provide a vital category for reflection *on* God, but that God *is* inherently imaginative.[20] Interpreting (and writing) language about God ought to give greater attention to imagination because imagination is a central category of reflection for understanding the Divine.

God and the Holy Spirit

Throughout the course of several books in the late 1980s and 1990s, John McIntyre developed a nuanced articulation of the centrality of imagination to the project of reflecting on God and God's action.[21] In resonance with the first two chapters of this book, McIntyre emphasized how empathy, care, and concern for another requires the imagination.

For McIntyre, God's availability in the present is a result of the "projection by God of himself into the state and condition of the other who is the sinner," an action which is "an imaginative activity based upon a deep understanding of, and sympathy for, the other."[22] For McIntyre, "imagination is the medium" through which God's love for the world enters into the lives of those who need change and hope.[23] This perspective leads McIntyre to write, "I know of no better argument for placing imagination at the heart of God's dealings with us than the single, unique, unpredicted and unpredictable event of the Incarnation."[24] The ability for humanity to encounter God requires an imaginative act. In the incarnation it was God's action in Christ that was imaginative. Today it happens via a combination of God's action in the Holy Spirit and some responding imaginative interpretation on our part.

In both circumstances, imagination is one of the means by which there is some human capacity to articulate and comprehend transcendence. Theologians who write on theology, imagination, and the arts do an excellent job of framing how it is that the arts are one place where an encounter with transcendence is possible,[25] but the idea can be extended beyond the formal examination of the artistic into *all* areas of imaginative exploration.

20. Graber, "Shape of Imagination."

21. The work of Evan Graber is incredibly useful here. See his 2019 dissertation, "The Shape of Imagination in the Theology of John McIntyre."

22. McIntyre, *Faith, Theology, and Imagination*, 45.

23. McIntyre, *Faith, Theology, and Imagination*, 48.

24. McIntyre, *Faith, Theology, and Imagination*, 55.

25. Studzinski, "Tutoring the Religious Imagination," 29.

Though he was primarily a scholar of literature, American Jesuit J. Robert Barth also thought about the role of the imagination and theology.

> Deeper and more comprehensive than the understanding, the imagination is in fact a faculty of the transcendent, capable of perceiving and in some degree articulating transcendent reality—the reality of higher realms of being, including the divine. . . . It is by such language—poetic language—that the chasm between the immanent and the transcendent can be bridged.[26]

We'll look more closely at the consideration of imagination as a human "faculty" in the next section, but first it is worth noting that the categories Barth emphasizes are "perceiving" and "articulating."

What is articulated is our human sense of God's function and activity in the world. The activity of God is what we perceive and as a result of imaginative perception, there are moments in which the immanent and transcendent are not opposite but are both—perhaps just for a moment—fully present. Imagination helps to reconcile and hold together concepts that seem to oppose one another.

> Perhaps there can be a divine "leading of the Spirit" without loss of what we perceive as our freedom to choose, since the divine knowledge and the human action would be two "forces" of a single "power," which has its origin in God—the human action being a repetition in the finite mind of the eternal act of creation in the infinite I AM.[27]

One of the regularly recognized functions of imagination is holding together concepts with apparent tension. In some ways, this can also be seen in Christ.

For example, consider the incarnation and the two natures of Christ. The technical theological term "hypostatic union" is a declaration of his nature as fully human and divine. Athanasius has a good line about this: "at one and the same time—this is the wonder—as man He was living a human life, and as Word he was sustaining the life of the universe, and as Son he was in constant union with the Father."[28] There's a useful parallel to consider between the idea that in imagination there is the means to bridge our internal realities to those of others, and that Christ is also a bridge between Creation and God.

---

26. Barth, "Theological Implications of Coleridge's Theory," 29.

27. Barth, "Theological Implications of Coleridge's Theory," 27–28.

28. Athanasius, *On the Incarnation*, 3.

We regularly see references to imagination as the means by which seeming paradoxes or tensions are held together. A good illustration of this comes from one of the earliest theologians to produce a sustained text on imagination, American Baptist hymn writer Elias Henry Johnson. In Johnson's 1901 book, *The Religious Use of Imagination*, he argued that imagination is what allows humanity to hold together the seemingly opposing concepts of free will and the sovereignty of God.[29]

> I do not say that the religious imagination solves this problem, but that to religious imagination no such problem can exist. . . . Imagination finds no difficulty of any sort. Its picture must necessarily include all essentials, and it insists on these categorically without allowing one of them to be compromised in the smallest degree by puzzles which vex the understanding.[30]

Imagination allows us to fruitfully gain from reflecting on things that seem at first pass to be logically irreconcilable. Jesus is understood to have been fully human and fully divine. God as Trinity is simultaneously God, Jesus, and the Holy Spirit. Holding those ideas together is part of the Christian imagination. Indeed, explorations of the Holy Spirit (pneumatology) are one of the areas of rich work on theology and imagination.

Above I noted that one way to think about imagination and God is to say that the incarnation was an imaginative act and that today what we perceive directly is God's action in the Holy Spirit. This notion is one of the more common ones among theologians writing on imagination. For example, McIntyre says explicitly that "the Holy Spirit is God's imagination let loose in the world and working with all the freedom of God in the world, and in the lives, the words and actions, of the men and women of our time."[31] The motion of Spirit as God's imagination then resonates within us and it is by "working through our imagination, [that] the Spirit communicates interior knowledge of Christ and sparks love for him and his way of life."[32] The "resonance" between the movement of the Holy Spirit and our imagination is a theme found across Catholic and Protestant scholars.

Australian Catholic Ormond Rush has written about a "reception pneumatology" that lifts up a "God-given responsibility of being active, creative, imaginative receivers of revelation—for God's sake."[33] This kind of receptivity makes it easier for the Holy Spirit to work in us, "igniting imaginative

29. Johnson, *Religious Use of Imagination*, 101–6.

30. Johnson, *Religious Use of Imagination*, 101–2.

31. McIntyre, *Faith, Theology, and Imagination*, 64.

32. Brackley, *Call to Discernment*, 75–76.

33. Rush, *Still Interpreting Vatican II*, 79.

receptions of the tradition in the light of contemporary events."[34] Spirit works in our imagination, helping us to see tradition in new ways and then envision new ways of acting and thinking grounded in that vision.

American Catholic theologian John Thiel suggests one must turn to Spirit when discussing how we ought to understand the job of theologians and by what authority they work. He argued that a "pneumatology of the imagination true to its task would sketch the often surprising, coincidental, and even mysterious ways that consciousness builds creative associations," and that "the imaginative insights of the theological author can legitimately be understood as the yield of divine grace," suggesting that intellectual inspiration is "a charismatic gift of the Holy Spirit."[35] For Thiel, creative new work from theologians should be seen as inspired by Spirit. Even in terms of academic thought, making a way where there is no way is part of where we can see Spirit at work. The ability to grow in perception and approach problems (and people!) in more generative ways is often attributed to the movement of Spirit in imagination.

Resonantly, American Presbyterian theologian Kerry Dearborn has written that "the renewing grace of the Holy Spirit finds a route via the imagination past the intellectual and psychological constructs that can isolate us from God and others"[36] Her claim is that Spirit leads people who follow it from bondage, alienation, and falsehood to freedom, community, and truth. According to Dearborn, this leading and following results from Spirit using human imagination to empower us to perceive God's presence in a world where we might not notice it were it not for Spirit. Basing her argument on the story of Saul's conversion in Acts 9, she specifically suggests three ways in which Spirit uses imagination.[37]

First, the Holy Spirit "uses the imagination as a solvent to dissolve false notions of God, of Christ, and of Christ's followers."[38] Second, Spirit creates new understandings, providing "creative facility to receive and offer a new vision of life."[39] The third is the use of the imagination as the "process through which the Spirit's gifts of creativity, hope, and love can propel us forward."[40] Spirit—via the imagination—changes how we see and act. Like

---

34. Rush, *Still Interpreting Vatican II*, 80.

35. Thiel, *Imagination and Authority*, 213–14.

36. Dearborn, *Drinking from the Wells*, 117.

37. The three-part categorization of imagination's function is something she borrows directly from James Fowler's "Future Christians and Church Education," which, in turn, is a riff on Coleridge.

38. Dearborn, *Drinking from the Wells*, 85.

39. Dearborn, *Drinking from the Wells*, 69.

40. Dearborn, *Drinking from the Wells*, 70.

others, Dearborn sees in Spirit's use of imagination the capacity to hold to-gether tensions and see in the holding new possibilities.

> The Holy Spirit is the creative source of new beginnings, of a third way that miraculously creates a bridge between polar reali-ties and seemingly antithetical entities, like Peter and Cornelius, and Saul and the followers of Jesus. The Spirit also inspires the imagination to be a vehicle through which a bridge is perceived and practiced, to enable people to hear God's voice and to move with the Spirit across that bridge.[41]

Once again, we see the metaphor of imagination as a means or vehicle through which Spirit can travel. Justin Bailey, an American Reformed pas-tor, and theologian, has written on this particular theme with great clarity.

By my account, Bailey has done the best summative work on the topic of imagination and pneumatology. His three-part model for cat-egorizing how imagination is used is excellent and provides a superb way of considering the academic literature. He suggests that in regard to how imagination is discussed in theology there are three general categories into which work can be sorted.[42]

Within the "constructive imagination," imagination is understood to operate independently of the Spirit. The products of imagination may be at-tributed to Spirit interpretively but are not understood to arise from Spirit as an independent, actual entity with agency. Gordon Kaufman is perhaps the most notable scholar we've discussed that fits here, though Sallie McFague arguably could be categorized this way as well.

Within the "cooperative imagination," imagination is understood as a medium through which Spirit can work. Without air, there is no sound, but air does not create sound. Imagination is the medium in which Spirit travels and gains access to individual hopes and sight. Spirit and imagination work simultaneously, but Spirit needs to act first for the imagination to receive its inspiration and direction. Here we could put Dearborn and David Brown as well as Peter Phan and David Bryant.

---

41. Dearborn, *Drinking from the Wells*, 88–89.
42. Bailey, "Theodramatic Imagination," 459–62.

Three Models of Imagination and the Holy Spirit

Invention ←		→ Reflection
Constructive Imagination: Initiative is with the imagination	*Cooperative Imagination*: Imagination and Spirit cooperate	*Responsive Imagination*: Initiative is with the Holy Spirit
Gordon Kaufman: Imagination replaces revelation	Paul Avis: Imagination is revelation	David Brown: Imagination may be revelation	Garrett Green: Imagination is responsive to revelation

Figure 6.1: Bailey's "Models of Imagination and the Holy Spirit."[43]

Finally, in the "responsive" form, imagination plays less of a simultaneous role and participates in more of a call-and-response. Yes, imagination is essential to engage in subsequent theological reflection, but God has actually and definitively acted first: in creation, the incarnation, and the production of revelation. Imagination in this model is always a *response* to God's activity rather than simultaneous with it or interpreted as identical to it. Here we should think about Garrett Green's work.

However it is categorized, theological reflection on Spirit and imagination usually comes to consider the role that humanity plays in the process of imagination. To what extent is imagination an inherent God-given and essential quality of human being? If we are less imaginative, are we less human? Trevor Hart, a British Episcopal theologian, is one of the most lucid and poignant writers on this topic.[44]

> It is above all by laying hold of our imaginative life . . . that God's Spirit regenerates our humanity from the inside out. . . . Imagination lies at the heart of our humanity, and in many ways drives and directs who and what we are and are becoming. It's what makes us capable of the very best and the very worst of human behaviors. There's nothing more imaginative than a torture chamber. But at the same time, there's nothing more imaginative than the sort of self-giving love that actively seeks the best for others, even at its own expense.[45]

43. Bailey, "Theodramatic Imagination," 461.

44. Hart is also an important figure in that he was the co-founder of the Institute for Theology, Imagination and the Arts at St. Andrew's in Scotland.

45. Hart, "Interview," para. 3.

What does it mean if at the "heart of our humanity" is the imagination? What does that tell us about ourselves and God? These are the questions of theological anthropology.

Human Being

Theological anthropology is the technical name for the study of humanity and our relationship to God. Alongside doctrines of revelation, pneumatology, and theology proper, theological anthropology is the other most significant area of doctrinal reflection connected to imagination. It is the doctrinal area most written on thus far. A number of scholars (going back as far as Thomas Aquinas in the 1200s!) have considered imagination especially as it might relate to the *imago dei*, or, the image of God in humanity.

One of the long-standing questions regarding theological anthropology is a question of interpretation regarding Gen 1:26–27 and other passages that refer back to what is set forth there.

> Then God said, "Let us make humankind in our image, according to our likeness; and let them have dominion over the fish of the sea, and over the birds of the air, and over the cattle, and over all the wild animals of the earth, and over every creeping thing that creeps upon the earth." So God created humankind in his image, in the image of God he created them; male and female he created them.

In what ways does humanity have the image and likeness of God? How is that shown? There are some additional reference points in Scripture, but they are not entirely conclusive. If all the related passages that theologians delve into to reflect on anthropology are considered as a whole, there seem to be three kinds of things that get referred to as *imago dei*.

First, as in Genesis above, God makes humanity in the image and likeness of God. Second, Jesus is himself described as the *imago dei* by Paul (Col 1:15; 2 Cor 4:4; Rom 8:29, et al.). Finally, the new life in Christ that Christians find seems to be connected as well. For example, in 2 Cor 3:18 we read that "All of us, with unveiled faces, seeing the glory of the Lord as though reflected in a mirror, are being transformed into the same image from one degree of glory to another; for this comes from the Lord, the Spirit." This suggests that the *imago dei* is a dynamic quality that can shift from one degree of glory to another.

Part of the work of theologians that study theological anthropology has been to ask what about human nature is the *imago dei*. What fits the description given in Scripture and is something we could point to as the most like God in humanity? The lack of clear answer to this in the Bible itself has meant that we are left with trying to think about what is both inherent to humanity, reflective of God, and something that can grow and change. Historically, theology has seen several possible candidates considered, including imagination. Noting that complex thought, language, and the ability to make seem to be markers of difference between humanity and other created creatures, much attention has been given to these capacities or faculties as possible locations of the *imago*.

When Augustine began writing in the fifth century, he was building on earlier thinking and Greek philosophy to suggest a model in resonance with the Trinity.[46] As God is Father, Son, and Holy Spirit, so too is the *imago dei* memory, intellect, and will.[47] In the medieval period, Thomas Aquinas further developed this line of thinking, arguing that while the body itself cannot be an image of God, we can find a trace in the soul.[48] Within the soul and intellect, the *imago dei* was identified as human reason. However, while Aquinas argued it was a faculty of humanity, his idea was that the image was not in its fullness unless that intellect and rationality was being used to come to know and love God ever more deeply.[49] This connection between human action, knowing God, and what it means to be made in the image of God emerges through theological thinking about the imagination and anthropology as well.

MacDonald argued that imagination and faith are mutually related, suggesting that imagination is the manifestation of faith in the context of uncertainty. For him, imagination was a human faculty that "gives form to thought" and is most similar to "the power of God."[50] Thus, in its similarity, imagination is the likeness of God's creative capacities.

> The imagination of man [*sic*] is made in the image of the imagination of God. Everything of man must have been of God first; and it will help much towards our understanding of the imagination and its functions in man if we first succeed in regarding aright the imagination of God, in which the imagination of man lives and moves and has its being.[51]

---

46. Middleton, *Liberating Image*, 19.

47. Augustine, *Trin.*, esp. 13.20.

48. Aquinas, *Summa Theologiae*, IA.Q93.6.

49. Aquinas, *Summa Theologiae*, IA.Q93.4.

50. MacDonald, *Dish of Orts*, 2.

51. MacDonald, *Dish of Orts*, 3.

There is a connective hierarchy here between the doctrines of God, Creation, and Humanity. As MacDonald had it, the "imagination of man is made in the image of imagination of God."[52] Creation is the result of the imagination of God, and in a technical sense, only God ever truly creates from nothing since everything humanity imagines has emerged from something.

Humans might be imaginative and creative, but all that is—or ever will be—imagined and created is a consequence of God's imagination and creation. This connective hierarchy is a recurring theme. God made creation and humanity, then humanity, made in the image of a maker, continues to make.

> Imagination liberates the person from the confines of the self.
> Through acts of creative imagination, a person becomes real.
> It is there that a person "imitates" God, or participates in the divine, most closely.[53]

We see resonant claims from Avis that "the creative human imagination is one of the closest analogies to the being of God"[54] and "human freedom coincides with our capacity to imagine."[55] While Avis affirms the imagination, as we have seen before, this connection has not always been interpreted positively.

In the medieval period, it was commonly believed that congenital disabilities developed in babies due to parental sexual sin or "the mother's misuse of her imagination during pregnancy."[56] The belief was that "if the mother were to imagine something unusual either during conception or pregnancy, her child would bear a resemblance to that which she had imagined."[57] This interpretation had staying power: there's evidence that the philosopher Rene Descartes still advocated for this idea in the early 1600s.[58] While bizarre by modern Western perspectives, it is interesting to note how much power the imagination was presumed to have: what occurred in the mind could have direct physical implications. Thankfully, this position is not being advocated by philosophers and theologians today, but the real power of the imagination is still worth considering.

---

52. MacDonald, *Dish of Orts*," 8–9.
53. Bednar, *Faith as Imagination*, 166.
54. Avis, *God and the Creative Imagination*, ix.
55. Avis, *God and the Creative Imagination*, 26.
56. Frost, "Medieval Aristotelians on Congenital Disabilities," 51.
57. Resnick, *Marks of Distinction*, 296–300.
58. Smith, *Problem of Animal Generation*, 80–99.

Pope John Paul II wrote that God "created the human being to whom he subjected the visible world as a vast field in which human inventiveness might assert itself."[59] The assertion of inventiveness is a way for humanity to transform itself and the world. That is, through "creativity man appears more than ever 'in the image of God,' and he accomplishes this task above all in shaping the wondrous 'material' of his own humanity."[60] Our capacity to engage in reflection and making shapes us and the world in which we live. Given that Scripture tells us that the *imago dei* can go "from one degree of glory to another," the claim that through creativity, humanity appears "more than ever" in the *imago dei* is interesting to consider. It suggests that while imagination and creativity might not *be* the *imago dei*, somehow *using* them is a part of being human as God intended.[61]

The consideration of the central role of imagination in the human experience is a topic of considerable interest beyond theologians as well. For example, the philosopher Richard Rorty argued that "imagination, rather than reason, is the central human faculty," and that "a talent for speaking differently, rather than for arguing well, is the chief instrument of cultural change."[62] There is also an interesting overlap between science and theology, with some biologists claiming that imagination and the capacity to make is one of the unique markers of the human creature.

> If there is one single thing that distinguishes humans from all other life forms, living or extinct, it is the capacity for symbolic thought: the ability to generate complex mental symbols and to manipulate them into new combinations. This is the very foundation of imagination and creativity: the unique ability of humans to create a world in the mind and re-create it in the real world outside themselves.[63]

The American Lutheran theologian Philip Hefner has explored this idea in terms of our status as being made in the image of a maker. He has suggested that "our symbolic capabilities are both an expression of our skills at making

---

59. John Paul II, *To Artists*, para. 5.

60. John Paul II, *To Artists*, para. 5.

61. There are significant concerns here that disability theologians have raised around any of the claims that cognitive faculties are the home of the *imago*. What does that mean for people who lack the cognitive capacity to engage in that kind of thought? Are they less human? Surely not, but then how are we to proceed? This is not the book to explore this issue, but it certainly is worth flagging. For those interested I particularly recommend Reinders, *Receiving the Gift of Friendship*.

62. Rorty, *Contingency, Irony, and Solidarity*, 6.

63. Tattersall, *Becoming Human*, 177.

and building but also a sign of our calling to imagine divine activity."[64] As he sees it, our faculties of imagination and creativity allow us to work in the image of God, crafting new worlds.

When we say the invention of the internet—or any other such creation—means it is "a whole new world" we recognize that the worlds we craft are a kind of faded echo of God's original creation. In imagining and making, we "become participants in the divine nature" (2 Pet 1:4). Hefner is particularly interested in the fact that human inventiveness yields new *things* and new *meaning*. We create objects and material goods but also new ways of relating to them and ways of thinking about them and their significance. He sees this capacity as one grounded in our God-given desire for transcendence and connection.

Hefner develops the idea of humanity as "created co-creator," which neatly names the importance of the imaginative and creative faculties as well as our status as being dependent on God.[65] J. Robert Barth wrote on this same theme.

> Creative acts are of their very nature united with the ongoing creative acts of God. Thus man [*sic*] is truly a creator, both through the perception (primary imagination) by which he actively unites himself to the created world around him, and through the higher degree of creation he exercises (secondary imagination) in expressing the unity of the world, aesthetically, in new shapes and creative forms.[66]

Having humanity's imagination "united with the ongoing creative acts of God," furthers the idea of humanity as a created co-creator. This notion is in Elizabeth Ursic's work as well. She writes that "the interior imaginative place . . . is also the indwelling of presence and infinite connection with the universe," and that in that space "we are both cradled in stillness and called to co-create."[67] In all these thinkers, the idea of co-creation, by virtue of being connected to the presence of God, is one that comes with some significant responsibility.

The imagination can be the source of new insight into how it is that humanity might more justly live on the earth. For example, Garrett Green argues that "one way to shed light on the present human condition is to imagine it as it ought to have been—or, expressed in the narrative terms of

64. Hefner, *Technology and Human Becoming*, 88.
65. Hefner, *Human Factor*, 255–76.
66. Barth, "Theological Implications of Coleridge's Theory," 25.
67. Ursic, "Imagination, Art, and Feminist Theology," 323–24.

the biblical account, as it once actually was."[68] We can look into Scripture, seeing the serenity of Eden and the encouragements of the Beatitudes, then try to imagine what those images offer for today. As Green has it, in reflecting in such a way, the "religious imagination is doing its characteristic work of providing a framework of meaning for human life by viewing it within a broader, an ultimate, imaginative context."[69] In this view, imagination isn't just a source of novelty and progress, but also of morality. That is, "creative imagination is the supreme faculty of moral humanity.... Moral thinking at its best must perceive values that do not yet exist and must bring them into being through productive act."[70] Finding new, more ethical, and just ways of being is something we must imagine before we enact. David Bryant writes about this as well, explicitly connecting imagination to the *imago dei* and human responsibility for ecological care.[71]

Bryant notes that the concept of the *imago dei* "comes from the ancient Near Eastern practice of setting up statues of rulers to indicate [control] over a realm."[72] Consequently, its use in Scripture is likely meant to convey both the relationship between God and humanity as well as humanity and the rest of Creation. He writes that the *imago* means "that humans have a representative function vis-a-vis the rest of creation, which gives them the responsibility to care for creation on behalf of the one who has placed them in this situation."[73] According to Bryant, this responsibility comes along with the need to envision how our present actions affect the future.

This means not only considering the spiritual implications of our actions regarding the possibility of the afterlife but also the material consequences of our activities on the earth.

> The plea to take imagination seriously is nothing less than a summons to reckon with something lying close to the core of what it is to be human, a feature of our humanity that shapes our essentially human responses to others, to the world and (we may reasonably suppose) to God.[74]

Part of what it means to be human is exploring the ways in which what we imagine informs how we think about others, Creation, and the Divine.

68. Green, *Imagining God*, 86.
69. Green, *Imagining God*, 86.
70. Happel and Walters, *Conversion and Discipleship*, 168.
71. Bryant, "Imago Dei," 35–50.
72. Bryant, "Imago Dei," 36.
73. Bryant, "Imago Dei," 47.
74. Hart, *Between the Image and the Word*, 5.

Paying attention to the power and consequences of your imagination is another way to be mindful and intentional about how you want to live in the world.

> Christian theology can hardly afford not to get to grips with and afford a proper place to imagination as it attempts to make sense of what it is to be human in the world God has made. For it seems that God has made us imaginative beings, and placed us in a world which calls forth from us responses of an imaginative sort if we are to indwell it meaningfully and well.[75]

To live in a way that is both meaningful and Christian requires that I find some way to see in my life some parallel or resonant themes to those that are part of my religious tradition. Sometimes this was hard for even the disciples to do, so approaching the situation with an open mind and a readiness to imaginatively respond seems entirely appropriate.

Earlier in this chapter I mentioned Sallie McFague's idea that "one does not say 'Jesus is Lord' except through an act of the imagination."[76] I think a similar perspective is present in both Bryant and Hart. Being in the world while affirming the lordship of Christ necessitates living in a way that sees past initial appearances and affirms a possible future that we can only take on faith. When Pilate interrogates Jesus (John 18:28–40) he is incapable—or unwilling—of allowing himself to recognize the truth of what is before him. He was not yet ready to imagine that the suffering servant before him would usher in a new way of being in the world.

Christ's kingdom is decidedly not just like other human kingdoms but with Jesus as Lord. The reign of God that Jesus embodies and preaches is not like other kingdoms, but better. It is of a radically new type and shape. It is of a kind that requires an act of imagination to picture. How we imagine ourselves and our relationship to God impacts how we imagine the future. Who we are and who we can be changes as we strive to live in the world that Christ invites us into. This is a theme not only in the literature about theological anthropology but also in eschatology.

Christian Hope

Eschatology is the technical name for the doctrine concerned with reflecting on the end times, the afterlife, and more broadly, how Christians understand (or imagine) the end of existence will be for themselves and the

---

75. Hart, *Between the Image and the Word*, 5.
76. McFague, "Imaginary Gardens with Real Toads," 251.

rest of creation. If we are talking about how to think about the apocalyptic texts and different ways of interpreting them to think about the *eschaton*, or end of it all, then we're really just talking again about the doctrine of revelation and how we interpret Scripture. This isn't the same as thinking about imagination and eschatology distinctly.

Similarly, though a number of people have written about the "eschatological imagination," those works are about how we imagine the *eschaton*, not what the imagination has to do with the doctrine itself.[77] This use of imagination was mentioned in the introduction to this chapter and is true for "ecclesial imagination," "pastoral imagination," and a host of other imaginations people write about. So why bring it up again here? Because I think that questions about eschatology are *inherently* imaginative in an even more intense way than other doctrinal concerns.

In a general sense, *whenever* we attempt to be predictive about a sense of the possible future, we are being imaginative, bringing into consciousness an idea of what is not yet present. This has been recognized for centuries. For example, Hobbes wrote that from "our conceptions past, we make a future"[78] and "the future [is] but a fiction of the mind."[79] The question for Christian theology is how to think about the end of days when we can't be rationally certain of the way things will play out. Hobbes called the future "a fiction." Might Christians be able to think of it as taking it on faith?

Piotr Zygulski has done some fascinating work in this regard, drawing on the philosophical work of Paul Ricœur and Richard Kearney and reading it through the theological scholarship of John Henry Newman, Michael Paul Gallageher, and Nicolas Steeves.[80] Zygulski suggests that a mystical approach to eschatology is viable and that comparative scholarship with Islamic conceptions of the eschaton are useful for Catholic thinking. Specifically, he advocates for a model informed by flame, a symbol found in numerous mystical texts from Christianity as well as in Islam. Recognizing that some versions of the popular eschatological imagination contain images and assumptions that are problematic for Catholic thought, Zygulski notes that critique is insufficient. New models and metaphors must be provided, or nothing can change.

The act of imagining the future has practical consequences. It confers an intense awareness to our decision-making process in

77. For example, Rausch, *Eschatology, Liturgy, and Christology*, or Shields, *Eschatological Imagination*.

78. Hobbes, *Elements*, 4.7.

79. Hobbes, *Leviathan*, 42–44.

80. Zygulski, "Catholic Eschatological Imagination," 219–42.

a broader context where the true meaning of things comes to light, but also instills in us a constant openness to "something else than the present" and "new possibilities for action" in it. . . . We can only do away with faulty imaginaries by creating alternative ones which correspond to our bodily affective experiences, as the mystics of fire revealed.[81]

Thinking about the purifying nature of flame and the way it is ignited by mere sparks suggests a new way of viewing not only what is to come, but how to engage in the present. How we imagine the future to be shapes our contemporary experience and activity. Interestingly, Portuguese theologian João Manuel Duque considers the inverse.[82]

Exploring Ricœur's idea that new imagination can unfold into new ways of being, Duque considers that Christ's words about the coming kingdom of God, given in parables, had within them an unfolding possibility of the future. Noting how the contemporary church is also the body of Christ and the rapidly developing realities of internet-based worship and virtual congregations, Duque wonders if the unfolding imagination of what the future is to be is still being imagined within Christ. The church, as the body of Christ, may still be imagining what is to come.

In a less technologically oriented vein, Trevor Hart has also written about imagination and eschatology, arguing that imagination is "a vital category in eschatology as in theology more generally."[83] Hart defines hope as a function of imagination, writing that it is the capacity "to imagine a future which, in broad terms, furnishes an object of hope for us in the present."[84]

> What the imagination does in hope . . . is thus twofold. First it leaps over the limits and perceived discontinuities which lie between present reality and the Utopian future, even though it cannot yet see clearly the route from here to there—it intuits it as a Real-Possible. Second, through setting this vision before us and enabling us to "look forward" to it, hope drives us forward, empowering and guiding ways of being in the world in the present which themselves serve to create the conditions in which the object of hope becomes possible.[85]

Given Hart's framing, when he writes that "Christianity is above all a tradition characterized by hope," there is a parallel and implicit claim that

81. Zygulski, "Catholic Eschatological Imagination," 235.
82. Duque, "Para uma Teologia," 343–76.
83. Hart, "Imagination for the Kingdom," 75.
84. Hart, "Imagination for the Kingdom," 56.
85. Hart, "Imagination for the Kingdom," 61.

Christianity is a tradition of imagination.[86] While this is essential to recognize regarding reflection on the future in general, it is even more so when the future being considered is the *eschaton*.

> Only God is in a position actually to know of those things lying beyond the horizons of human history, and therefore only by an act of divine revealing could historical beings ever come to know of them. Again, to insist upon the imaginative form such knowing takes is not in any way to undercut or contradict this claim, unless we suppose that all divine revealing occurs in and through epistemic forms of one particular (unimaginative) type.[87]

Hart decidedly does *not* think all divine revealing is unimaginative. Quite to the contrary, Hart argues the inverse is true: God's revelation is intended to stoke imagination and evoke responses rather than confirm facts and figures.

> God makes himself and his purposes and promises known not by downloading a body of digitized factual data, but by taking our imagination captive, lifting us up through Spirit-filled reading to "see" and "taste" the substance of things lying way beyond our natural purview, and calling us responsibly to imagine further.[88]

What this "imagining further" looks like is a vital question. Especially if when God "calls us" it is not just a broad call to all Christians as individuals, but also to the church as a whole. In either instance, I think it is valuable to recognize the sensorial and embodied quality of the "seeing" and feeling that comes with this kind of imagination. There can be a distinct difference between the kinds of vision that comes with embodied imagining and that which is guided by argument and reason.

Phil Wyman, a friend of mine, used to pastor in a church in Salem, Massachusetts, that my wife and I used to attend with some regularity. Salem is famous for having been the site of the witch trials and during the month of October tens of thousands of tourists come to the small city to be part of raucous Halloween festivities every weekend. Along with the costumed—and often inebriated—revelers there were also often "fire and brimstone" preachers who would travel to Salem to set up street-corner preaching to let all the visitors know they were going to hell. These preachers usually came with a support team, large amounts of signage, and bullhorns

86. Hart, "Imagination for the Kingdom," 75.
87. Hart, "Eschatology," 264.
88. Hart, "Eschatology," 264.

to inform those passing by that they needed to repent from the Halloween-themed sinfulness and turn to Jesus. The preaching was always aggressive, and much of it focused on the supposed connection between "witchcraft" and homosexuality. While most of the costumed tourists ignored the street preachers, the fact is that they were loud, hateful, and a poor representation of what it was that Christianity could be about.

My friend's church had a regular October weekend ministry in which teams of people would go out to take posts near the corners where the street preachers were, there to connect with people in a loving way, offering water if needed and inviting people into the church if they needed a break. Sometimes this ministry of outreach would catch the attention of the bullhorn preachers and there would be a kind of public theology preaching session in which there would be a crowd of people listening to two visions of what Christianity could be. One year when I was volunteering as part of a team doing this, my ministry partner noticed a young woman who was standing near us. She was listening to the preacher but seemed on the verge of tears.

We approached her and let her know that the Christ we knew was a God of love. As we came near, she just broke down. We stayed for a while with her, just being present while she cried, gave her a bottle of water, and told her that there would be people to talk to in the church if she wanted. She was grateful, looked back at the preacher, shook her head sadly, asked for a hug, and went her way. We hoped it was enough.

Later that evening, as we were passing back through the area, we saw her again. This time she was with the preacher from before. Concerned, we approached only to learn that she was his daughter and was there as a member of his ministry support team. As we walked by, she gave us a look I'll never forget. It was sad and resigned. She shrugged slowly and mouthed "thank you" to us before turning back to helping the team disassemble a ten-foot-tall sign listing all the kinds of people headed to hell when judgement came.

Part of what I now see in this story is the disconnect between different ways of knowing. There, on a raised platform, a man drew on particular passages to argue in a very "logical" way, proving his point by knowing particular pieces of Scripture and putting them together like they were equations to be solved. Meanwhile, his daughter was there, literally at his feet, crying and struggling with something. Now, I have no way of knowing what she was going through, but I know that sometimes I am better served by quieting down some and seeing what can be learned by attending to those around me. I do not have to orient to the world as if it is just a series of arguments to be won.

The way I see it, it isn't just that there are multiple ways of knowing, but that these different ways of knowing impact what can be imagined about the future. How it is that we envision the future is related to how it is that we engage the present. If God is indeed, "calling us responsibly to imagine further,"[89] part of that work has to be about recognizing that attention to the full range of human feeling and expression provides a fuller picture than point and counterpoint argumentation alone. Imagination draws on experience and sensation as well as reason. What God calls us to isn't just an imagined future when everything works out well for us, but also a reminder of ways in which the present can be transformed. New ways of seeing, of feeling, of being in the world.

Importantly, I think that we should recognize that God isn't just calling to each of us as individuals, but to the church as a whole. How can we think about the imagination not just as an individual faculty but something that a whole people share? What are the *communal* qualities of imagination and how do they operate? These are questions about social imaginaries or "the Christian imagination." They are the topic for our next chapter.

Questions for Reflection

1. In terms of thinking about knowledge of God, the suggestion is made that because of God's transcendent nature we necessarily must be imaginative and metaphoric in terms of how we talk about knowing God. What do you think about this claim? Do you think there is a way to be entirely metaphor free and only factual and speak of God?

2. What did you think about Bailey's model for thinking about the different ways spirit and imagination are considered? Do you feel like it clarified anything? Was it helpful? If yes, how so?

3. How do you assess the claims that the imagination might be the site of the *imago dei*? Does it seem to you like our capacity for imagination is made in the image of God? How so?

4. The chapter closes with an argument that eschatology is especially connected to imagination because it is a consideration of something in the future that can only be imagined. How does this sit with you? Do you think eschatology is more resonant with imagination than other doctrines? Why or why not?

89. Hart, "Eschatology," 264.

Related Readings

Bailey, Justin. *Reimagining Apologetics: The Beauty of Faith in a Secular Age.* Downers Grove, IL: IVP Academic, 2020.

Bednar, Gerald. *Faith as Imagination: The Contribution of William Lynch SJ.* New York: Sheed and Ward, 1996.

Dearborn, Kerry. *Drinking from the Wells of New Creation: The Holy Spirit and the Imagination in Reconciliation.* Eugene, OR: Cascade, 2014.

Keefe-Perry, Callid. *Way to Water: A Theopoetics Primer.* Eugene, OR: Cascade, 2014.

McFague, Sallie. *Models of God: Theology for an Ecological, Nuclear Age.* Philadelphia: Fortress, 1987.

McIntyre, John. *Faith, Theology, and Imagination.* Edinburgh: Dunedin Academic Press, 1987.

Part III: Imaginaries and Imaginative Practices

7

Imaginary Worlds

IMAGINATION CAN BE THE source of life and deepening faithfulness. It can also be a stumbling block and source of confusion. Though there is no unity about all the details of faithfully considering imagination, nearly every scholar agrees that the imaginative capacity of individuals is affected by other individuals, other interpretations, and media. While each person has their own imagination, much of the material that imaginations use is shared in common.

Whether or not someone thinks an individual's imagination can brush against the truth of the Divine, the fact is that a person and their "individual imagination" is inherently knitted into the hopes, dreams, fears, and stories of a community. Even without the imagination being divinely placed in each person as the site of the *imago dei*, there is still something about the imagination that is broadly shared across humanity. The imagination has individual and social aspects. This chapter first explores the concept of a "social imaginary," and then considers how Christian thinkers have used that idea. It closes with some reflection on how it is that imaginaries can change for a community and what leaders might do to help imaginations change.

What Is a Social "Imaginary"?

The idea of "an imaginary" as it is used contemporarily in theology has its roots in sociology and philosophy from the mid-1900s. In 1948, Jean-Paul Sartre, a French philosopher and playwright, wrote *The Psychology of Imagination*. There he claimed that,

> For a consciousness to be able to imagine, it must be able to escape from the world by its very nature, it must be able by its own efforts to withdraw from the world. In a word, it must be free.[1]

1. Sartre, "Psychology of Imagination," 99.

145

The context here is complicated and pertains to Sartre wrestling with the German philosopher Heidegger's claim that "nothingness is the constitutive structure of existence."[2] The basic idea is that to be able to imagine that the world might be different than how you currently perceive it requires the capacity to conceptually negate "the world" as you've come to understand it.

Even if you've realized that much of what you have learned about societal norms, individual freedom, and the possibility of change is the result of a social construct, you still often operate within those values, and they shape how you interpret your perceptions and actions. To "get out" of this and provide a "place" for your imagination to consider alternatives requires at least some capacity to deny that your present experience has to be that way. This negation of the perceived present opens up an interpretive space in which your consciousness can imagine possibilities that present norms preclude. The realization of the new possibility can be both liberating and painful.

I remember very clearly late one summer day when my wife—then my fiancé—and I were driving somewhere and having a conversation about our upcoming wedding. We were talking about some logistics, including what the ceremony would look like, what food would be there, and the general feel we wanted guests to have during the service. As part of that conversation, we talked about our efforts to ethically source the gold for our rings and clothing for the day. As we were having that conversation, my wife began to cry. So much so that we pulled over and stopped in a mostly empty Circuit City parking lot. When I asked what was wrong, she replied that she realized we weren't going to have a big wedding cake, she wasn't going to have a big white wedding dress, and we weren't going to "end up with a white picket fence and 2.4 children." Confused, I remember telling her I hadn't known she wanted those things. "I don't," she said, "but I'm *supposed* to want them, and I somehow feel sad that I won't get them." The conversation wasn't rational, but it was real: the vision of what weddings and married life was supposed to be like was so strong for her that even though she cognitively dismissed it, there were deeper ways in which her vision had been formed. Negating a vision with strong social precedent can cause a sense of freedom and grief.

A decade after Sartre, the American sociologist C. Wright Mills published *The Sociological Imagination*. There he described the mentality and orientation needed for a sociologist to do their work. Early in the history of the discipline of sociology, Mills wanted to articulate how to look at large patterns of social data and work out what that might mean

2. Sartre, "Psychology of Imagination," 99.

for individuals. For Mills, the sociological imagination is the capacity to shift between perspectives and scales, learning from what seems to be different when new perspectives are taken. What changes when I think about this from the perspective of a person with a different background from mine? What about from the standpoint of a policy-writer thinking about a large group? What about from international economic perspectives? From theological traditions?

As Mills had it, the sociological imagination "is the capacity to range from the most impersonal and remote transformations to the most intimate features of the human self—and to see the relations between the two." Doing this allows people to "grasp what is going on in the world, and to understand what is happening in themselves as minute points of the intersections of biography and history within society."[3] What developed next was increasing consideration of the ways in which individual imaginations could be seen to arise as a result of a "social imaginary." How an individual imagined things was related to how others imagined. This next contribution came with the scholarship of the French-trained, Greek, post-Marxist political philosopher Cornelius Castoriadis. For decades, his work was the go-to theory for social imaginaries, so it is worth exploring in some detail.

Castoriadis first began to develop the idea of "social imaginary" in the 1960s, but his seminal work, *The Imaginary Institution of Society*, was published in 1975.[4] In that piece, he communicated his dissatisfaction with what he had come to see as the overly deterministic outlook of Marxist thought. Core to much of the Marxist discussion of those days was a sense that the power of economic forces was so profound that they inevitably shaped, or determined, *all* aspects of a society from politics and culture to education, art, and law. Economic and material conditions determined everything.

In response to this view, Castoriadis centered his theory on the presence of the creative force of imagination, an open-endedness through which individuals can envision, embody, and change society. He wanted to think about ways in which change might be possible *within* a given economic system, blazing a trail to what might come next *prior* to an economic and political revolution. For Castoriadis, imagination was important because it is "in its essence, rebellious against determinacy."[5] Maintaining this indeterminacy is a central theme for Castoriadis, who frames not only social dynamics as uncertain, but also the individual psyche. Castoriadis's

3. Mills, *Sociological Imagination*, 14.

4. Castoriadis published under the pseudonym "Cardan" for *Modern Capitalism and Revolution,* which was first published in three parts, in the French journal *Socialisme ou Barbarie* during 1960–1961.

5. Castoriadis, *World in Fragments*, 214.

model is complex, and I'll skip some technical details, but given that it is the first full-fledged theory of the "social imaginary" it is worth making some of his vocabulary accessible.

Castoriadis was quite prolific, and his theory of imagination ended up with lots of nuance. For example, he used the terms "radical imagination," "secondary imagination," and "social imagination," each of which is related but separate. He then also identified different ways of naming the qualities of structures that imagination produces, contracting "instituting imaginaries" from "instituted imaginaries" and "heteronomous" imaginaries from "autonomous" ones. I'll provide summaries of each of these terms below because together they provide a good sense of his project.

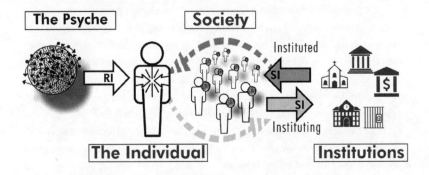

Figure 7.1: A diagram of Castoriadis's Theory of Imagination

Like some of the earlier definitions of imagination considered in chapter 1, Castoriadis distinguishes between a "secondary imagination" that copies or combines existing imaginings and a "radical imagination" from which novelty arises. What the radical imagination produces is "prior to the distinction between 'real' and 'fictitious.' To put it bluntly: it is because radical imagination exists that 'reality' exists for us."[6] The root of all perception and interpretation, the imagination is the ground upon which incoming sense data is sorted and made into sense. This imagination can be seen at work in two places: in the individual psyche and at the social-historical level.

At the level of the individual psyche, the radical imagination is an endless swirl of change. Imagination is so central to Castoriadis's ideas that he says from a psychological perspective, what we call "a person" is the collision between (a) the infinite possibility and chaos of the individual's radical

6. Castoriadis, "Radical Imagination," 138.

imagination and (b) society's institutions, patterns of interpretation, and normative values. Within an individual, the radical imagination exists as an unending capacity for new vision and change. However, the unbridled chaotic nature of that possibility has to be tempered with social norms, habits of language, and cultural patterns or the person will be disconnected from others and unable to communicate or change anything.

The "radical imagination" is like a geyser in the psyche that is the source of newness within the individual. The crash of this imagination as it comes into contact with society's institutions is the beginning of a "socialized soul," or a person. According to Castoriadis, socially speaking, who we are is the result of the collision between the infinite possibility of our radical imagination and society's patterns, structures, and habits. Each of us operates within society and interacts with other people who have also been formed by a similar collision. It is here that Castoriadis says we find the "radical social imaginary" or the "instituting social imaginary."[7]

Part of what Castoriadis argued is that it is problematic to think about an "individual's imagination" as an entirely internal capacity or a cognitive faculty because this neglects the ways in which how we imagine is also shaped by social and historical factors. His model is meant to make the connection between the individual and the social more evident. His theory is that as each person develops, they simultaneously (a) learn about who they are in relationship to others and to shared social norms and (b) further establish or solidify those norms because they are being used to shape the development of a person.

The social imaginary is simultaneously institut*ing* and institut*ed*. It is instituting in the sense that it is what assigns importance and value to the meaning of institutions. It is instituted because the meaning and value of those institutions always exist prior to an individual and are what the individual's psyche "crashes against" in the formation of a person. How others have imagined society shapes how we imagine ourselves. We make society as we are made by society.

Even though the psyche's radical imagination may be infinitely inventive and lacking all tethers, as it is expressed through individuals as instituting social imagination and reflected back to us in institutions. Imagination "leans on what is given, which conditions and limits it but does not totally determine it."[8] The basis of novelty emerges from that which has already come and its interaction with the radical imaginary. While able to produce newness, the psyche's radical imagination is nevertheless conditioned by

7. Castoriadis, *Imaginary Institution of Society*, 369.
8. Castoriadis, "Radical Imagination," 321.

the current moment because it must emerge through subjects who are always already socialized. Castoriadis thinks that a person without socialization (or access to the social imaginary) could not make sense of the world in a way that would allow them to participate in society. Everyone able to engage socially with others in a meaningful way has inherently been influenced by the social imaginary.

Consequently, Castoriadis identified institutions more technically as "social imaginary institutions" because he sees them all as "a socially sanctioned, symbolic network in which a functional component and an imaginary component are combined."[9] The buildings and material "stuff" of society matter to us because of the imaginary attributions we have assigned to those material things and actions. Institutions have meaning and value because people have assigned them meaning and value. These values push into society and are experienced by individuals in that society as the social imaginary. An example may help to clarify.

When I reflect on my own religious denomination of the Religious Society of Friends, I generally think of it fondly and recognize that I value our practices and social norms, which have enormous importance to me. I know that as a religious tradition it is relatively new, having only come into being in the 1650s. This relative newness doesn't seem to lessen its ability to shape my life and provide me with hopes, values, and symbols that I find meaningful. Partly this is because it is a Christian tradition and therefore has a history tied to older practices and contexts. It is also the case, though, that references are made to "early Quakers" and what they thought as if there is some greater authority in their perspective because they were there at the beginning of the tradition. I think the importance of my religious tradition to me doesn't result from external factors pertaining to how long it has been around but because of the members of my community who are attempting to faithfully live in our tradition *today*.

Even though there was a point when Quakerism didn't even exist, hundreds of years of practice and growth by Friends communities has led the tradition to where it is today. As a breakaway tradition from the Church of England, there was a point in the first generation of the Quaker tradition when everyone involved was born into Anglicanism and left it for the new Religious Society of Friends movement. Given that it was a new, emerging form of Christianity in the seventeenth century, the importance of a "Quaker way" of thinking and doing things was *assigned* value by those who were part of its early growth. While they had preexisting Christian norms in general to inform them, particular Quakery things—for example, our

9. Castoriadis, *Imaginary Institution of Society*, 132.

silent waiting worship with no preplanned liturgy—were new practices and had to have value and importance placed on them by the early practitioners. Those people, their descendants, and others who have joined the tradition have influenced the stories that are told, the practices we maintain, and the values we hold. Those stories, practices, and values—though they were new and imagined to be valuable—profoundly shape my life. Institutions have meaning and value because people have assigned them meaning and value. These values then echo back into society and are experienced by individuals in that society as the social imaginary.

When the meaning of a social institution—whether it be a denomination, the practice of schooling, or the concept of paper money having value—carries within it a self-reflective quality that recognizes it is an imagined construct, Castoriadis names this a situation of an institut-*ing* social imaginary with "autonomous" qualities. Conversely, when the meaning of a social institution carries within it a presumption of the finality of that institutional meaning being eternal (as opposed to being collectively constructed), he refers to this as an institut*ed* social imaginary with "heteronomous" qualities.

A social imaginary that is heteronomous is one that communicates that the images, stories, hopes, and aesthetics of that imaginary arose through a process somehow other than the social-historical. This is the reason to call it "hetero-nymous," from the Greek *heteros* meaning "the other, different" and *nomos* meaning "law." Castoriadis called a society "heteronomous" whenever the stories that society tells itself are framed as somehow extra-social and affirmed as arriving from outside of a social-historical framework. This form of social imaginary leads people to insist that what has been imagined before is actually extra-social and nurtures the belief that the social imaginary has some wholly exterior "reality" or "naturalness" that was not constructed but is simply a part of the way things are.[10] Within heteronomous social imaginaries, the story that society tells itself about itself obscures the fact that society has been co-author of that story.

For example, a literal interpretation of the story of Moses and the tablets of the Ten Commandments supports a view that those laws have a nonhuman, nonsocial origin. God (as entirely separate from humans) gave humans the law directly. It didn't come from us, and human interpretation wasn't part of us getting it. This is a heteronomous view for Castoriadis. A more "autonomous" one would question the objective reality of God-written laws and argue that even if God's finger did do the scribing at Mount

---

10. Castoriadis, "Socialism and Autonomous Society."

Sinai, there are nonetheless human fingerprints all over the interpretations of those texts since they were received.

When social norms are legitimated by claiming those norms have a divine (or nonhuman) origin, they are often treated differently. From Castoriadis's view, positive social change is much easier to achieve when people recognize that institutions, their values, norms, and laws result from historical human acts. Thus, one of the goals for those trying to change society ought to be to shift how we imagine society, working to help folks realize that norms and social structures need not be permanent.

From the 1970s until the early 2000s, Castoriadis's work was one of the dominant theories of social imagination. Other scholars were referenced, but for years Castoriadis's framing was one of the most significant when thinking about how imagination shapes a society. This changed profoundly beginning with the work of Canadian Catholic philosopher Charles Taylor. Starting in 2003 with the publication of his book *Modern Social Imaginaries,* Taylor's work has become far more widely engaged by theologians.

Before publishing his first book on the subject, Taylor was a part of the Center for Transcultural Studies, a Chicago-based nonprofit research network that published an entire issue of the journal *Public Culture* devoted to engaging with Castoriadis.[11] For Taylor, a social imaginary refers to "the ways people imagine their social existence, how they fit together with others, how things go on between them and their fellows, the expectations that are normally met, and the deeper normative notions and images that underlie these expectations."[12] Whereas Castoriadis developed the idea that society itself has an imagination, Taylor uses "social imaginary" in a way more similar to Sartre and Mills, clarifying that the concept isn't about the imagination of society but how individuals imagine society.

> I adopt the term imaginary (i) because my focus is on the way ordinary people "imagine" their social surroundings, and this is often not expressed in theoretical terms, but is carried in images, stories, and legends. It is also the case that (ii) theory is often the possession of a small minority, whereas what is interesting in the social imaginary is that it is shared by large groups of people, if not the whole society. Which leads to a third difference: (iii) the social imaginary is that common understanding that makes possible common practices and a widely shared sense of legitimacy.[13]

11. Gaonkar, "Toward New Imaginaries," 1–19.
12. Taylor, *Modern Social Imaginaries*, 23.
13. Taylor, *Modern Social Imaginaries*, 23.

For Taylor, a social imaginary includes the normative expectations individuals have of one another and the shared sense of what to expect of the world. A social imaginary makes the norms of interpersonal communication and shared life possible, both public and private.[14]

As Taylor sees it, the social imaginary is "not a set of ideas; rather, it is what enables, through making sense of, the practices of a society."[15] An imaginary is carried through the media of shared "images, stories and legends," that provide the raw reference material in which meaning and social norms are grounded. The development and maintenance of these meanings and norms is done through practice. People develop a sense of communal belonging by drawing on shared narratives, Scripture, and embodied practices.

From a Christian theological perspective, most folks who find attending church meaningful to them rarely feel this way due to technical details of doctrine. Instead, it is due to a mix of a sense of belonging and the practice of seeing oneself as part of a larger story and community. While Castoriadis would have likely agreed that a social imaginary is "that common understanding that makes possible common practices," he would probably have balked at how Taylor seems to understand it as inherently leaning toward heteronomy.

Consider that Taylor claims that "once we are well installed in the modern social imaginary, it seems the only possible one, the only one that makes sense,"[16] and understands that an imaginary "constitutes a horizon we are virtually incapable of thinking beyond."[17] This is a claim that Castoriadis would assign to a *heteronomous* social imaginary, not a social imaginary in general. As I see it, this difference occurs because for Castoriadis, the radical imagination *precedes* society. For a social imaginary to shift, the force acting on it must also have an imaginary quality. With Taylor, while imagination is an important and constitutive component of society, it does not have the same priority. I think it is reasonable to conjecture that Castoriadis's framing of the radical imagination seems too wildly free for Taylor and that is why this part of his work has not been carried forward as much.

Whether imagination is considered to have as much power as Castoriadis assigns to it or toned down some as in Taylor, discussion about a social imaginary necessarily entails a kind of "intersubjectivity," a sense that who we are is deeply connected to who other people are. How others have

---

14. Taylor, *Modern Social Imaginaries*, 23.
15. Taylor, *Modern Social Imaginaries*, 1.
16. Taylor, *Modern Social Imaginaries*, 17.
17. Taylor, *Modern Social Imaginaries*, 185.

imagined society shapes how we imagine ourselves. As previously noted, we make society as we are made by society. An individual's imagination has some tools, tropes, and hopes that are shared with other people. These shared imaginative instruments form a kind of interior tool kit for interpretation and construction. They can be used to build various sets and scenery.

When groups of people use similar tools to build similar sets that stay standing for a while, these get called "imaginaries" or "imagined worlds." Used this way, an "imaginary world" is decidedly *not* a stand-in for "a pretend world" or "a make-believe fantasy." The world envisioned through the creative imagination is a collective opening into what might yet be.

> Social imaginaries, then, are constellations of imaginary understandings of the world which directly arise from embodied experience and which are shared with other bodies that have similar experiences of the world. . . . These imaginaries may circulate through texts and images, institutions and regimes, which, in their sensory interrelation with bodies, contribute to the ongoing production of imaginaries. Texts and other objects are imagined differently by different bodies, whose histories produce different subjectivities. They are continually produced as constantly changing constellations of embodied experiences.[18]

These "constellations" are not certain or permanent, but insofar as an imaginary is a network of stories, symbols, and significance that some folks feel is cohesive and actively articulate as related, they do have some staying power or social momentum.

"Imaginaries" are "imaginaries" and not just ideas because they begin to be carried in shared and inherited generations of images, stories, legends, and hopes that collectively lead to shared practices. We'll talk more about practices in the following two chapters, but the point to focus on here is that the concept of an "imaginary" does not just refer to a set of symbols and stories that a group feels is coherent: it includes that web of images *and* how people feel about them and relate to them.

> The imaginary is the affectively laden patterns/images/forms, by means of which we experience the world, other people and ourselves. This contemporary usage is distinguished most importantly by its constitutive linkage of imagery with affect, the emotions, feelings and desires which mark our engagement with the world. The images are the vehicles for such affect, the way in which it is given form. By means of these images the emotional

18. Dawney, "Social Imaginaries and Therapeutic Self-Work," 542.

contours of the subject's world are revealed. They are the way in which we not only think, but also feel our way around.[19]

The imaginative capacity of individuals leads to shared social imaginaries, which yield practices that give meaning to symbols, goods, and institutions. Our shared imaginaries are not perceived as systems outside of us, but as part of how it is we make sense of the world.

I said above that from Castoriadis's perspective, one of the goals for those trying to change society ought to be to shift how we imagine society, working to help folks realize the ways in which norms and social structures need not be permanent. Does an emphasis on a social imaginary implicitly suggest a strong type of imaginative constructivism like Kaufman? How would that work for a Christian thinker unwilling to cede the importance of history and tradition? It is to these questions we turn next.

Christian Imaginaries

The concept of "an imaginary" is related to the ways in which patterns of imagination are shared between people in a community. As Castoriadis scholar Marcela Tovar-Restrepo argues, "whoever wants to become free must be necessarily interested in the freedom of others, must be interested in the collective dimension of politics."[20] Freedom to be oneself and to shape society comes from the realization that the self is inherently bound up with other people. In this sense, theologians often refer to particular imaginaries and the need to shift them to lessen oppression and injustice. Thinking back to the discussion of Valerie Saiving and Robert Allen Warrior in chapter 3, we can see that part of the work they were doing had to do with shifting theological imaginaries. Indeed, a large part of the work that Christian feminist and de-colonial theologians were doing in the twentieth century was asking about the consequences of the decidedly male and colonially centered religious imaginaries.

For example, Mary Daly had already made waves with her rallying cry that "if God is male, then the male is God," when she published *Beyond God the Father* in 1973. There she pushed the idea even further. There are imaginative consequences regarding how people think about women that are developed and sustained when religion diminishes women's voice, agency, and centrality.

---

19. Lennon, *Imagination and the Imaginary*, 1.
20. Tovar-Restrepo, *Castoriadis, Foucault, and Autonomy*, 62.

We already suggested that if God is male, then the male is God. The divine patriarch castrates women as long as he is allowed to live in the human imagination. The process of cutting away the Supreme phallus can hardly be a "rational" affair. The problem is one of transforming the collective imagination.[21]

With a vivid and explicit appeal to change the "collective imagination," Daly called for a shift in the Christian imaginary. In fact, feminist theologians have consistently been clear that one of the areas of their focus must be the imagination.

In a chapter for *The Oxford Handbook of Feminist Theology*, the American theologian Serene Jones suggests that imagination continues to be a central category of concern for feminist scholarship. In her definition of feminist theology Jones claims it is "an endeavor undertaken by women who understand themselves to be part of a broad social movement devoted to improving the lives of women everywhere."[22] This endeavor is about commitments to fostering a principle of equality and concrete actions that will help bring about transformation, especially in religious communities.

> Changing society requires both changing laws and practices and challenging the categories and processes we use to think about life and to make sense of our world. I find it useful to think of this dimension of transformative practice as the recrafting of "imagination," using the term not just to refer to our fantasies or dream lives—things imagined but not real—but also and more broadly to that vast interior landscape of thought within which our experiences are crafted and receive order and significance.[23]

As Jones sees it, it is vital to pair material and policy change together with work that reorders and renovates inward patterns.

Jones recognizes that imagination's "vast interior landscape" is where "experiences are crafted and receive order and significance." This is vital as she argues that feminist theologians are committed to changing society and that their primary contribution to that process is the "work of reshaping religious imaginations and the practices they engender."[24] Here I think Jones has hit upon one of the central reasons to consider the imagination as a critical theological category. I think practices are a key means of interacting with

21. Daly, *Beyond God the Father*, 19.
22. Jones, "Feminist Theology," 24.
23. Jones, "Feminist Theology," 25.
24. Jones, "Feminist Theology," 31.

imaginaries. As I use the term, a practice is a pattern of action that (among other things) maintains, creates, and/or disrupts a social imaginary.[25]

Practices can be seen as patterns of action that build upon shared images and reference common institutions and stories, working to maintain, create, or disrupt social imaginaries. Christian practices like communal worship or taking communion arise from a shared Christian imaginary and help to form the inward life of practitioners. Imagination both provides the material for meaningful religious practice and can be shifted by changes in practice. In Castoriadis's terms, practice has both instituting and instituted qualities. Once we recognize that another way of imagining is possible, we also begin making new ways of acting and being available. New patterns of acting and being further establish new ways of seeing. This view is powerfully developed in the scholarship of American Baptist ethicist Emilie Townes.

In her 2006 book, *Womanist Ethics and the Cultural Production of Evil*, Townes makes explicit the connection between imagination and evil.[26] Part of her argument in that book is that one of the means of changing systems of thought is to interrogate the concept of memory, recognizing that it is not simply a recitation of historical facts, but is heavily influenced by imagination. Drawing on the work of Michel Foucault and Antonio Gramsci, she explores how the "fantastic hegemonic imagination" operates to "play with history and memory to spawn caricatures and stereotypes."[27] Townes notes how the contributions of people of color—especially black women—have been erased from most history and art, a tragedy made worse by the weight of the burdens those same folks have had to endure in the form of violence and trauma.

Part of a movement toward justice in the present is renarrating the truth of history, more fully capturing the stories that have been suppressed. Historical narratives have to shift because they usually function from within the "fantastic hegemonic imagination," which

> conjures up worlds and their social structures that are not based on supernatural events and phantoms but on the ordinariness of evil. It is this imagination, I argue, that helps to hold systematic,

25. As I understand it, a practice is "a pattern of action that is situational, strategic, embedded in misrecognition, and maintains, creates, and/or disrupts a social imaginary." This is a modification of ritual scholar Catherine Bell's definition in *Ritual: Perspectives and Dimensions*. The middle bits of this are not as important for this conversation, but if you are interested you can see my work in *Schooling the Imagination* for more on this.

26. Townes, *Womanist Ethics*.

27. Townes, *Womanist Ethics*, 7.

structural evil, in place. The fantastic hegemonic imagination uses a politicized sense of history and memory to create and shape its worldview.[28]

The idea here is to recognize that evil doesn't gain purchase on society via central villainous figures nearly as much as it does in small daily ways, constantly seeping into our souls and shaping our imagination.

Townes is building off the Italian political theorist Antonio Gramsci, who differentiated between "rule" and "hegemony" as two ways societies are changed. Rule is an explicit coercion, often by the threat of violence or intimidation through physical force, military or otherwise.[29] On the other hand, hegemony is a movement of power in which the threat comes indirectly through manipulating a society's values and norms.

> [Hegemonic control] is a whole body of practices and expectations, over the whole of living; our senses and assignments of energy, our shaping perceptions of ourselves and our world. It is a lived system of meanings and values—constitutive and constituting—which as they are experienced as practices appear as reciprocally confirming. It thus constitutes a sense of reality for most people in the society, a sense of absolute because experienced reality beyond which it is very difficult for most members of the society to move, in most areas of their lives.[30]

A crucial development in Gramsci is his attempt to explain that hegemony exerts not only material control, but *experiential* control as well. Under hegemonic control, oppressed groups themselves feel as if the systems that marginalize them are simply "the way things are" and often do not act to change the dynamics of the system.

In *The Prison Notebooks*, Gramsci moved beyond a sense of earlier Marxist thought in which the economic conditions of production were seen as the only relevant site of analysis and everything else followed from that. This is the same kind of determinism that Castoriadis was pushing against. Instead, Gramsci argued that

> The way in which "civil society" represents itself to itself determines the overall cast of mind of any given culture—the system of images, myths and moral values a people identifies with—both publicly at the level of national self-representation and privately at the level of personal or family self-presentation.

28. Townes, *Womanist Ethics*, 21.

29. Williams, *Marxism and Literature*, 108.

30. Williams, *Marxism and Literature*, 110.

The idioms of power extend beyond the state apparatus to the
general "ethos" of the national community which imbues every
area of our social experience from church to school to family.[31]

I suggest that the "general ethos" in which a "society represents itself to itself" is a social imaginary. As such, it cannot be addressed via only material
changes. To disrupt the status quo requires interior imaginative, interpretive, and spiritual work alongside social imaginary changes and exterior
political and material concerns.

Following Gramsci's ideas of hegemony and counter-hegemony,
Townes forwards Michel Foucault's idea of "countermemory" as an act "to
disrupt ignorance and invisibility" by looking "to the past for microhistories
to force a reconsideration of flawed (incomplete or vastly circumscribed)
histories."[32] What is needed is a disruption of storytelling that suppresses,
ignores, or does violence to the voices and actions of black women. She
suggests that for countermemory to succeed, the re-narrations and countermemories produced have to both meaningfully reframe history *and* resonate with those who have been marginalized.

Townes has written that countermemory "must address the collective
memory—however partial and incomplete and socially constructed—of
those who have experienced real historical oppressions and memories."[33]
The work of surfacing and elevating suppressed stories is not an easy one. It
is pragmatically difficult and time-consuming to learn the resistance narratives that have been pushed to the side under the presence of dominant ones.
It is also the case that there is hefty psychological labor this work demands.

> Rather than content ourselves with the belief that the fantastic
> hegemonic imagination, the motive force behind the cultural
> production of evil, is a force that sits outside of us, we must an-
> swer remembering that we are in a world that we have helped
> make. The fantastic hegemonic imagination is deep within us
> and none of us can escape its influence by simply wishing to do
> so or thinking that our ontological perch exempts us from its
> spuming oppressive hierarchies.[34]

Similar to the work of Phan discussed in chapter 5, Townes recognizes
that "as we engage in the process of collective memory, we are in dynamic

---

31. Kearney, *Modern Movements in European Philosophy*, 174.

32. Townes, *Womanist Ethics*, 22–23.

33. Townes, *Womanist Ethics*, 24.

34. Townes, *Womanist Ethics*, 159.

tension between the past, the present, and the future."[35] How we choose to discuss history shapes present imagination and future possibility. An example may help to clarify this point.

My friend and colleague, Michael Woolf, is the senior pastor at Lake Street Church in Evanston, Illinois. It is a fairly wealthy American Baptist church that is predominantly white and "striving to address its legacy of white supremacy."[36] Formerly named the "First Baptist" church of Evanston, it was the church that led to the start of "Second Baptist" when black members left to found a new congregation that wouldn't enforce segregated seating. The name of "First Church" was replaced with "Lake Street" in the 1980s, but the realities of the history of exclusion and racism don't disappear with a name change.

Today Lake Street and Second Baptist are in regular conversation about what reparations might look like. Is it possible to repair a relationship between two communities that is generations old? What might that look like? Part of it began with making sure that the story of Nathan Branch was known. Branch was the leader of the group that felt the need to leave and found Second Baptist. Recognizing the undeniable presence of racial animus behind that decision is an important part of proceeding into the future. Discussions are underway between Woolf and the pastor of Second Baptist, Michael Nabors, regarding Lake Street restoring the legal ownership of their building to Second Baptist. By naming complex histories that those in power might prefer to overlook, they also restory the past to allow for a different way forward.

Being honest about the past and whose voices have been absent from dominant narratives is essential to the task of seeking liberation. The imaginative retrieval and development of these countermemories is part of the work of pursuing justice and equity. The power of naming isn't just about truth and connection in the present but also about reshaping the materials available for imagining the future. Related themes are explored in the work of several contemporary theologians. For example, the American feminist, postcolonial, and Anglican theologian Kwok Pui-lan has substantially worked with these ideas, most notably in her 2005 book, *Postcolonial Imagination and Feminist Theology*.

In that text she wrote, "memory is a powerful tool in resisting institutionally sanctioned forgetfulness."[37] Renarrating shared history can help to counteract some of the erasures that have removed voice and agency from

35. Townes, *Womanist Ethics*, 17.
36. Woolf, "What Reparations Is Costing," para. 1.
37. Kwok, *Postcolonial Imagination and Feminist Theology*, 37.

so many in the past *and* present. Kwok recognizes that "all the voices are not equal and some cultures dominate center stage, with the power to push the rest to the periphery."[38] Her development of a "postcolonial imagination" is related to her desire to explore how things might be different if the stage was not so monopolized.

For Kwok, the pursuit of postcoloniality is "a determination, and a process of disengagement with the whole colonial syndrome which takes many forms and guises."[39] In this vein, Kwok understands the postcolonial imagination as "discerning something that is not fitting, to search for new images, and to arrive at new patterns of meaning and interpretation."[40] This imaginative work may be an inherent part of any theological work, but it is imperative to do when confronting legacies of colonial violence and exclusion. A similar argument is made by the American Baptist theologian Willie James Jennings.

In his 2010 book, *The Christian Imagination: Theology and the Origins of Race*, Jennings discussed ways dominant Western Christianity operates within an imperial mindset and has a "diseased social imagination."[41] Jennings' historical narrative shows how the modern Christian imagination grew hand in hand with colonial socialization from late medieval times. The result is that there are deeply embedded racial categories in dominant Western society that the church is complicit in creating. Jennings argues that this is a direct outcome of the European Christians who arrived on African and American soil and began to imagine the land and the people as possessions. An example will help show the connection between imagination and action, in this case, law. Let's consider the 1823 United States Supreme Court case *Johnson & Graham's Lessee v. McIntosh*.[42]

This case was about a dispute between two descendants of colonial settlers who both felt they had a legitimate claim to ownership of a plot of land in the state of Virginia. One person claimed to have inherited the land from his father, who had purchased it from the Piankeshaw Indian tribe in 1763. The other person said he had purchased the same land from the US government in 1818. Totally ignoring the question of unjust colonization and possibly coerced sales from the tribe, the court case was a fight over whose colonial claim to the property had authority.

38. Kwok, *Postcolonial Imagination and Feminist Theology*, 42.

39. Kwok, *Postcolonial Imagination and Feminist Theology*, 3.

40. Kwok, *Postcolonial Imagination and Feminist Theology*, 30.

41. Jennings, *Christian Imagination*, 6–7.

42. See "Johnson & Graham's Lessee v. McIntosh."

In a unanimous decision, the court established that the federal government had the sole right of negotiation and that Native Americans themselves did not have the right to sell the property. The basis for this decision emerged at least partly because of the scholarship of seventeenth-century English political philosopher John Locke. He had a theory of ownership that said when you mix your labor with something that is unowned, you come to own the whole thing. Initial claims of ownership arise once substantial labor has been done on a piece of property. However, since the Native Americans didn't construct European-style buildings with the same intended permanence as colonists, it was concluded they had not done enough labor to warrant a claim to own the land.

Chief Justice John Marshall wrote the opinion, central passages of which are excerpted below, with some paraphrasing to help make the legalese more understandable.[43]

> Upon "the discovery of this immense continent, the great nations of Europe were eager" to claim as much of it as they could. "Its vast extent offered an ample field to the ambition and enterprise of all." Because "the character and religion of its inhabitants" was what it was, there was a clear argument to be made "for considering them as a people over whom the superior genius of Europe might claim an ascendency."
>
> Colonial leaders "found no difficulty in convincing themselves that they made ample compensation to the inhabitants of the new, by bestowing on them civilization and Christianity, in exchange for unlimited independence."
>
> "Humanity demands, and a wise policy requires, that the rights of the conquered to property should remain unimpaired; that the new subjects should be governed as equitably as the old. . . . But the tribes of Indians inhabiting this country were fierce savages, whose occupation was war, and whose subsistence was drawn chiefly from the forest. To leave them in possession of their country, was to leave the country a wilderness."
>
> Thus, "the Indian inhabitants are to be considered merely as occupants . . . to be deemed incapable of transferring the absolute title to others." The government's claim to the land via discovery and acquisition supersedes the inhabitants' claim of occupancy.

Because of "the character and religion" of the tribes, the "superior genius of Europe might claim an ascendency." The trade here is the idea that "in exchange for unlimited independence" and growth on this "newly discovered"

43. All quoted text is from the decision above.

continent, the colonists provided "ample compensation" to the Native popu-
lation by "bestowing on them civilization and Christianity." In this mindset,
getting access to Christianity and European culture is framed as sufficient
compensation for the loss of land and native way of life.

Jennings suggests this kind of use of Christianity for colonization and
commodification has left the Christian imaginary marked and marred. Part
of the colonial project included the practice of referring to Native peoples
"as Amalekites and Canaanites—in other words, people who, if they would
not be converted, were worthy of annihilation."[44] The consequences of
weaponizing Scripture against a people are told throughout the bloody and
unjust history of European colonization.

As Jennings argued, colonization has left a trail of Christianity being used for nation-building and conquering, rather than as an ethic of
neighborliness and love that could have been Christianity's gift to history.
Colonization has taken root in the Western Christian mind and spirit.
Jennings states:

> Christian social imagination is diseased and disfigured. . . . This
> loss points not only to deep psychic cuts and gashes in the social
> imaginary of western peoples, but also to an abiding mutilation
> of a Christian vision of creation and our own creatureliness. . . .
> I want Christians to recognize the grotesque nature of a social
> performance of Christianity that imagines Christian identity
> floating above land, landscape, animals, place, and space.[45]

Western Christianity has now been "diseased" so long that while Christians
can still imagine "new things" and forms of justice, the visions and hopes
that they arrive at as "new" have been built upon—and from—a sickened
imagination. The result of this is that it is improbable for a Christian to
imagine actual justice that is equitable without first reimagining deeply
rooted colonial ideas, images, and stories that have become braided into the
Christian imagination. In Towne's terms, we might say that countermemory
is needed before new flourishing memories can be made.

Jennings' approach is to distance "Christianity" as something distinct
from the "Christian imagination," allowing for a reformation, healing, and
decolonization of the Christian imagination so that it might more fully reflect the original goals of Christ's striving for justice and intimacy between
all peoples. For example, Jennings is explicit that if we endeavor to craft a
"new optic" by which we learn to see Christianity—that is, to develop a re-
vised and revising Christian imagination—it is possible to more successfully

44. Warrior, "Canaanites, Cowboys, and Indians," 261.

45. Jennings, *Christian Imagination*, 293.

renounce empire, supersessionism, and human objectification. The aim of such an optic would be nothing short of imagining reconfigurations of living spaces that would promote more just societies.[46]

Even given all of the above, consideration of how to shift imaginaries still requires some fleshing out. While both "countermemory" and the concept of a "new optic" are compelling, how are they accomplished? Is there a step-by-step method by which new imaginaries can be encouraged? Is there a process? Principles to follow? These are the questions inspiring the next section.

Transforming Imaginaries

American Methodist biblical scholar Richard Hays suggests that in several places, what is usually translated as a "renewing of minds" in Rom 12:2 or being "united in the same mind" in 1 Cor 1:10 is actually better understood as a "conversion of imagination."[47] For Hays, Scripture ought not be seen as a to-do list or manual against which to check experiences to see if they are Christian enough or properly adhere to a "biblical worldview." Instead, it is "an eschatological community-forming word."[48] The literature about social imaginary provides a way to see that part of what makes this community a community is a shared imaginary carried in stories, hopes, and symbols.

Consider the basic definition of imagination I gave in chapter 1: imagination is the human capacity to bring into consciousness things that are not observably present. At the level of the social imaginary, I think this becomes something like the capacity to bring into social consciousness things that are not observably present. This means community members discuss together and practice together things that are not present in service to deepening a sense of the world they hope to live into. They do things in remembrance of Christ and unite themselves with a vision of the world as they understand it.

For some Christians, the consequences of an "eschatological community-forming word" draws their imagination, energy, and activity to a consideration of the world as the eschaton approaches. Focus is placed on the eternal reality that will unfold as the kingdom of God arrives and the apocalyptic visions of the book of Revelation come to pass. Sufferings in the present world are not as important to tend to because they are temporary, but our heavenly rewards will be eternal when they come

46. Jennings, *Christian Imagination*, 293.

47. Hays, "Conversion of the Imagination," 391–412.

48. Hays, "Conversion of the Imagination," 401.

later. For others, the shaping vision of Christianity pushes attention to the present and how good might be done for those currently oppressed and marginalized. Some traditions have a "realized eschatology," which says that though the reign of God has not been fully manifested, there are sometimes moments in which it breaks into the present, exposing us to glimpses of what may yet come. In each of those instances, people will be eager to help people shift current imaginaries.

In the work of many scholars considered in this chapter, the desire to interrogate the visions amplified in the "Christian imaginary" comes from a sense that our traditions have been marred by unexamined social practices, biases, and violence done in the name of faith. For Christians who feel that there are oppressive constructs and interpretations of faith but don't want to leave the church, the work is about helping others shift how they imagine the community formed by the word of God. This will likely include reconsidering how we tell past stories, reflecting on whose voices are excluded in the present and whose flourishing will be attended to in visions of the future. Working to shape the Christian imaginary means working with what images, stories, and practices are lifted up and valued. Just arguing for people to change how they think and see the world rarely works.[49]

The work of shifting social imaginaries is iterative. A wholesale rejection and reformation of symbols, stories, and visions is far more likely to be rejected than one with its roots in history. And yet . . . for those who see impending global ecological disruption or those whose communities have suffered under the weight of racism and coopted colonial Christianity, speed feels imperative. There is notable tension between wanting change and recognizing that change might be best served by reinterpreting the past. This tension is a similar kind of dynamic as the one captured in the idea of an "Overton window" from chapter 2.

The Overton window is a model to help understand how social norms change over time and influence politics. The idea is that if a politician is interested in remaining in office, they are limited in what policy they can support: it is safest to only pursue policies based on ideas that are widely accepted throughout society. These "acceptable policies" are *within* the Overton window. Other possible policies exist that theoretically *could* be advocated for, but politicians are less inclined to support them because they

---

49. The psychologist Richard Beck has done some fascinating work in brain science suggesting that how we orient ourselves to the world may be impacted by biology and neurology. Consequently, just words are insufficient to change our opinions and we have to engage in some actions that contribute to the ability to rewire mental habits and perspectives. See, for example, *Unclean: Meditations on Purity, Hospitality, and Mortality*.

would likely lose the popular support they need to remain in power. To some degree, *any* movement away from the norm makes support harder to find. The window can move, widen, or shrink, but it is rare that any single individual can markedly push the window in size or position. In chapter 2, I suggested that this is similar to how the hermeneutic function of imagination works in relation to individuals and society. We can now see that this is a question of the social imaginary.

Interpretation of perception happens within the context of both a personal and societal history. Interpretations of texts and experiences in the present gain social purchase when they are digestible by others. "Digestibility," as such, is determined by a combination of the idiosyncratic inclinations and openness of individuals as well as social norms and mores that influence what counts as acceptable behavior or thinking. Imagination, as the capacity to bring into consciousness things that are not observably present, can bring new ideas and interpretations into being. However, for them to remain in the world outside of an individual, those new ideas and interpretations must be brought into circulation among others. This is true beyond religious perspectives as well.

The geographer David C. Eisenhauer is concerned with how we communicate ecological science and the looming effects of global climate change. He suggests that how most people imagine the future is far off the mark of what the science says is actually coming. Our shared social imaginary of what is and what will be is obscuring a vision of what is far more likely to actually be the case. As such, he is trying to think about how to help shift environmental imaginaries to contribute to changes in practice. As a scholar of imaginaries, Eisenhauer has very helpfully written about how shifting ecological imaginaries requires a dance between "imaginative fit" and "imaginative interplay."

Imaginative fit refers to how claims gain value and consideration within a community's present shared imagining of life and the future. Imaginative interplay describes how those claims resonate with alternative imaginaries that do not yet have as much influence in shaping community visions, identity, and practice.[50] These two constructs exist in inherent tension with one another. On one side, "increasing imaginative fit seeks resonance within existing . . . imaginaries in order to gain sociocultural traction." Conversely, "increasing imaginative interplay aims to disrupt the given distribution of things and produce something new." This means that an emphasis on fit might unintentionally reinforce unsustainable or unjust systems. A focus on interplay might result in "a failure to gain a

50. Eisenhauer, "Up in the Air," 224.

foothold in prevailing practices and narratives."[51] The work of shifting imaginaries requires finding—and finding again—a viable equilibrium point in a system that is always in flux.

To think about social imaginaries is an exercise in reflecting on community and the symbols, stories, and practices that shape visions of the world as it is and will be. As I see it, attention given to transforming imaginaries in a community requires a consideration of each of the following questions.

Questions to Help with Imagination Shifting

- What is the extent of the community you are considering? Where are its borders, physically, socially, and otherwise?
- What values are held by the community?
- What stories are told that enforce those values?
- What symbols emerge from those stories that are rich with meaning and referenced often?
- What symbols, characters, or portions of stories are left out when people share?
- What practices exist that refer to a community's shared symbols and stories?
- What visions of the world are sustained and encouraged in those stories, symbols, and practices?
- How do those visions shape activities in the present and views of possibility for the future?
- How do individual community members experience, understand, and feel about all of the above?
- Given the above, what desired changes might be possible that would still "fit" with the community's sense of itself and what it wants to be?

Within theological scholarship, a number of these individual questions are taken up by constructive theologians, ethicists, sociologists of religion, and Biblical scholars. However, the collection of questions above taken as a whole is probably most closely attended to by those specializing in "practical theology."

51. Eisenhauer, "Up in the Air," 224.

For practical theology, the study of practices often presumes that the activities a community teaches are inherently "theory-laden." That is, they have embedded within them some—often unacknowledged—values and views.[52] The practice of taking communion is important not just as a distinct activity but because it carries within it some cultural norms about community, hope, and sacrifice. Considered via a lens informed by the concept of social imaginaries, I think practices can be seen as "imaginary laden" just as much as "theory laden." How practices might shape imaginaries and what work has been done on developing practices that explicitly engage the imagination is the subject of the next chapter.

Questions for Reflection

1. Castoriadis insisted on the centrality of the "radical imagination" because he wanted to make sure there was some accounting for the possibility of newness that couldn't be constrained by material, political, or economic forces. How do you feel about this position? Is this "radical imagination" something Christian thinkers could use?

2. One of the criticisms of Castoriadis is that his theory suggests that social imagination isn't just how people imagine society, but that society itself has an imagination. What do you think of this idea?

3. Taylor is particularly interested in thinking about imaginaries because he thinks that how people conceive of the world around them is far more about stories, symbols, and practices than about theories. Do you agree with him? Why or why not?

4. Townes suggests the "fantastic hegemonic imagination," is both (a) the motive force behind the cultural production of evil and (b) is deep within us. Why does she think this is the case? How do you feel about this argument? Does it seem accurate? Is there anything more it makes you want to ask questions about?

5. One of the common threads throughout the theologians in this chapter is that they differentiate between how we *currently* imagine Christianity to be and what it could become in the future. They all suggest that working to change how we imagine it might materially yield greater flourishing and equity. Do you think this is viable? How would that happen if so? What is the relationship between imaginaries and the material stuff of daily life?

52. This is especially true of those following in scholarship of Don Browning and his work in *A Fundamental Practical Theology*.

Related Readings

Adams, Suzi. *Cornelius Castoriadis: Key Concepts*. London: Bloomsbury Academic, 2014.

Jennings, Willie James. *The Christian Imagination: Theology and the Origins of Race*. New Haven: Yale University Press, 2010.

Lennon, Kathleen. *Imagination and the Imaginary*. Abingdon, UK: Routledge, 2015.

Pui-lan, Kwok. *Postcolonial Imagination and Feminist Theology*. Louisville: Westminster John Knox, 2005.

Taylor, Charles. *Modern Social Imaginaries*. London: Duke University Press, 2007.

Townes, Emilie M. *Womanist Ethics and the Cultural Production of Evil*. New York: Palgrave Macmillan, 2006.

8

Prayer, Preaching, and Worship

"IMAGINARIES" ARE "IMAGINARIES" AND not just ideas about the world when they begin to be carried in images, stories, symbols, and hopes that lead to shared practices. The imaginative capacity of individuals leads to shared social imaginaries, which yield practices that give meaning to symbols, goods, and institutions. Practices, in turn, can be seen as patterns of action that build upon shared symbols and reference common institutions and stories, working to maintain, create, or disrupt social imaginaries.

Whatever else we do when we pray together in worship that God's will be done on earth as it is in heaven, we are also forming bonds with others in worship, affirming that our God is a God with a will, and that somehow things on earth can change. What exactly is meant by those bonds, affirmations, and hopes is separate from the fact that they animate connection, grounding, and our shared vocabulary of meaning. When we say that we have faith in God we are also saying that how we imagine the future is influenced by the promises and hopes of our tradition.

Because imagination is such a key part of the human experience, Christian people should think about what practices we encourage and participate in. What values and imagined futures project out from how we practice in the present? What attention are we giving to the ways we imagine how the world is and will be? Walter Brueggemann says it well:

> Obedience follows imagination. Our obedience will not venture
> far beyond or run risks beyond our imagined world. If we wish
> to have transformed obedience . . . then we must be summoned
> to an alternative imagination.[1]

James K. A. Smith concurs, writing that "it is not primarily our minds that are captivated but rather our imaginations that are captured, and when

---

1. Brueggemann, *Finally Comes the Poet*, 85.

our imagination is hooked, we're hooked."[2] The language of "obedience" in Brueggemann and "captured" in Smith is paired here intentionally. As the last chapter showed, not only does imagination have a profound impact on what images, stories, and hopes we use, but also our capacity to envision ourselves, our history, and possibilities for the future. Consequently, when religious practices provide an alternative version of the future, they enable the possibility of living into that future. Imagination, associated with obedience and capture, implies analogy to conquest and dominance, but imagination can also be framed as accompanying waymaking and invitation. How we communicate the consequences of imagination and our practice is significant.

As I understand it, *all* meaningful practices are imaginative practices. By this, I mean that valued practices are valued in part because they sustain, disrupt, or develop imaginaries. Practice sows seeds of the possible in the present. Christian practices have embedded in them the roots of a world vision. For example, how we see and act shifts when we practice worship that encourages us to ignore pains of the present because of promises of what is to come. Likewise, a vision of the reign of God that understands it as something that can break into our daily life can lend depth to our daily experience of faithfulness.

This being said, some practices have been crafted with an explicit awareness of how they draw on the capacity for imagination. Last chapter I discussed how Castoriadis thought that "heteronomous imaginaries" allowed for a more significant opportunity to positively impact society because they promoted self-reflective awareness of the ways in which the institutions that structure our experiences of community are "a socially sanctioned, symbolic network in which a functional component and an imaginary component are combined."[3] I think practices work this way as well. They always already shape how we imagine the world to be, but when they intentionally do so, they can provide additional leverage for change. This chapter considers the work of scholars and practitioners who have advocated for practices that are explicitly—and self-reflectively—tied to the imagination.

Prayer and Engaging Scripture

In terms of imagination and Christian religious practice, one of the topics that has received the most attention is prayer. Partly I think this is due to the central role that prayer plays in faith and its nature as a practice that

2. Smith, *Desiring the Kingdom*, 54.
3. Castoriadis, *Imaginary Institution of Society*, 132.

spans inward exploration and communal expression. It is also the case that imagination and prayer is something that Jesuits discuss quite often, and as a consequence, their scholarship has greatly informed this area.

Imagination is a vital component of the "Spiritual Exercises" of Ignatian practice that Jesuits teach. In fact, Ignatius of Loyola himself first converted to Christianity as a result of a prolonged period of bed rest (after a cannonball wound!), during which time he regularly read and daydreamed about the lives of saints and what it might be like to be one.[4] As he came to envision what that life might be like, he was gradually transformed.

Ultimately, Ignatius would come to see "the products of the imagination as vehicles that transport us to an understanding and experience of higher realities in ways that linear discourse cannot carry us."[5] In the prayer retreat called Ignatius' "Spiritual Exercises," retreatants are asked to engage in a prayerful experience of Scripture called "Gospel Imagination" in which they read a piece of Scripture and allow themselves to "become onlooker-participants and give full rein to the imagination."[6] Rather than reading about Jesus, this is an invitation to imagine the embodied fullness of the story. Ignatius

> chooses scenes of Jesus acting rather than Jesus teaching or telling parables. He wants us to see Jesus interacting with others, Jesus making decisions, Jesus moving about, Jesus ministering. He doesn't want us to think about Jesus. He wants us to experience him. He wants Jesus to fill our senses. He wants us to meet him.[7]

Ignatius does not go so far as to say that what the imagination produces in gospel imagination is actually (historically speaking) what happened. However, he thinks that faithful and true formation can result by immersing ourselves in that narrative and allowing the Spirit to help guide our imaginative journey.

The Jesuits suggest that "this type of imagining helps us . . . take on God's qualities of love, compassion, and understanding.[8] These qualities are important to note because one of the Ignatian "rules for discernment" is that we ought to test the consequences of our imagining. If the results of our imaginative work are joy, harmony, and growth, chances are they result as a gift from God. If our imagining yields sadness, despair, or fragmentation, it

---

4. Ignatius, *Autobiography of St. Ignatius*, 24.

5. Lucas, "Grandeur of God," 18.

6. Fleming, *What Is Ignatian Spirituality?*, 57.

7. Fleming, *What Is Ignatian Spirituality?*, 58.

8. Fleming, *What Is Ignatian Spirituality?*, 57.

may be as a result of "a temptation of the evil spirit."[9] The key thing to note in Ignatian spirituality is that imagination, while important, is not an end in itself. It provides for types of reflection which can enable an experiential encounter with God and *that* is the goal.

The Ignatian perspectives on imagination have spread beyond the prayer practices of the Jesuits. In another example of how imagination can bridge divides across Christianity, there are several prominent evangelical authors whose language entirely aligns with the Ignatian perspective. In Richard Foster's *Celebration of Discipline*, he writes about a way to pray based on reflection of Christ as in Matt 9:20–22. We can immerse ourselves and "apply all our senses to our task." As we pray, we are invited to

> Smell the sea. Hear the lap of the water against the shore. See the crowd. Feel the sun on your head and the hunger in your stomach. Taste the salt in the air. Touch the hem of his garment.[10]

Foster explicitly names that he is drawing inspiration from Ignatian spirituality. This is significant to note because, in addition to the hundreds or thousands of Catholic parishes and retreat centers that teach Ignatius's *Spiritual Exercises* and prayer, Foster's book has sold more than two million copies and is widely used across mainline and evangelical churches in the US and globally; it has been translated in more than twenty-five languages! Many people who would be unlikely to pray with Jesuits have been exposed to Ignatian prayer practice through Foster. The evangelical vineyard pastor Ken Wilson makes a similar comment in a reflection on praying with the 23rd Psalm. He writes that sometimes, "words are useless without the imagination."[11] For prayer to be as inwardly transformative as possible, we need to not just say the words but also engage our inward senses. This is especially true of the practices of *lectio divina* and *visio divina*.

In *lectio divina*, one selects a passage of Scripture for a period of slow, contemplative reading, attempting to savor the text and get drawn into it. This is not reading for comprehension only but reading for immersion. Thomas Merton suggests that before you practice *lectio* with a passage, it is wise to do pre-prayer work and make sure you understand it and its context. Attempting to prayerfully engage the imagination with Scripture without first reading it for comprehension is an error. He says that "to jump over the intermediate steps and try to pray immediately may end in self-deception and waste of

---

9. Ignatius, *Spiritual Exercises*, 316–17.

10. Foster, *Celebration of Discipline*, 29–30.

11. Wilson, *Mystically Wired*, 106.

time."[12] However, first reading for comprehension and context provides the grounds for allowing for prayer to guide you deeper than that.

If, at some point, a word, phrase, or sentence has a particularly strong pull, the invitation is to remain there, seeing what other connections emerge or what insight God might have for you in those moments. Often the passage is read through in this reflective way several times, seeing if anything new emerges. The pausing and deepening reflection is a kind of savoring, of resting in the word until it thickens. This practice of prayer, though grounded in the reading of Scripture, is not about comprehension and analysis, but the experience of dwelling in the word of God.

The practice of "*visio divina*" is similar, though the object of reflection in this case is an image rather than a text. Often the image selected is of Scripture, for example, an illumination from the *Book of Kells*. However, it is also the case that many kinds of artwork could be used. Allowing your gaze to slide over the image and appreciate small portions, sometimes minute things take on a larger sense: a particular brushstroke or line might seem to carry weight.

If God's ways and thoughts are more than humans can fully comprehend with reason alone,[13] our only option is an imaginative and faithful act. As Jesuit J. Robert Barth wrote, "it is only the imagination that can bring us . . . to the full encounter with religious reality, because it is only the symbolic language of imagination that can resist the human drive for simple clarity and determinateness."[14] For both *lectio* and *visio divina*, the task isn't to decipher the experience and try to figure out exactly what "it means" that you felt drawn to a particular part of the image or passage. Instead, it is a practice of noticing, of allowing yourself the time to slow down and enter into a period of contemplation, inviting Spirit to help guide your sight and reflection.

Not all traditions agree on the appropriateness of imagination for prayer, however. Some streams of the North American evangelical tradition are very suspicious of imagination, as are several theologians from the Orthodox Christian community. Russian Orthodox theologian Dmitry Alexandrovich Brianchaninov is clear of the dangers of imagination in prayer.

> If during your prayer there appears to your senses or spontaneously in your mind an image of Christ, or of an Angel, or of any Saint—in other words, any image whatsoever—do not accept this apparition as true in any way, do not pay any attention to

12. Merton, "Lectio Divina," 15.

13. E.g. Isa 55:8–9; Job 26:14; Eph 3:20, et al.

14. Barth, *Romanticism and Transcendence*, 7.

it, and do not enter into a conversation with it. Otherwise, you
will surely suffer deceit and most serious damage to your soul,
which has happened to many.[15]

For those familiar with the Orthodox usage of icons and images for prayer
and reflection, the fact that there is significant opposition to imagination
might come as a surprise. How could a tradition that is so rich in imagery
and embodied practice be so opposed and suspicious of imagination? Because Orthodox thinkers do not think icons have merit because of their
artistry or self-expression.

> The discipline of icon painting as a sacred art is often con-
> trasted to the modernist notion of "self-expression," since what
> is to guide the hand and determine the composition is not the
> painter's ego, but rather the Holy Spirit and Tradition. The
> painter is to supply only his skill, his craftsmanship. He must
> get out of the way.[16]

This distancing between self, creative powers, and God is present not only in
the writing of icons, but in the use of them as well.

> Holy icons are accepted by the Holy Church for the purpose of
> arousing pious memories and feelings, but not at all for arous-
> ing imagination. Standing before an icon of the Savior, stand as
> if before the Lord Jesus Christ himself, Who is invisibly every-
> where present and by His icon is in that place, where the icon is;
> standing before an icon of the Mother of God, stand as if before
> the Most-Holy Virgin Herself; but keep your mind without im-
> ages: there is a great difference between being in the presence of
> the Lord or standing before the Lord and imagining the Lord.[17]

As I mentioned earlier, I am not a scholar of Orthodox spirituality. However,
it seems that the distinction here between actually standing "as if before the
Lord" and "imagining the Lord" is nebulous. I wonder how we are to tell,
experientially, the difference between these experiences. My sense is that
underneath this distinction is a particular understanding of how God's presence functions and how it has been articulated narrows the understanding
of imagination to a smaller category than I usually take. In any event, these
cautions might be valuable even if you think visualization prayer *can* be done
faithfully: we must be aware that humans are wildly good at self-deception.

15. Sveshnikov, *Imagine That*, 29.

16. Justiano, "Imagination, Expression, Icon," para. 1.

17. Sveshnikov, *Imagine That*, 35.

This ought to be taken into account even when attempting to consider the imagination as a legitimate source of theological reflection.

Though grounded in a different basis, a warning of suspicion is issued from some evangelical thinkers as well. In his book, *Contemplative Mysticism*, David Cloud takes aim at what he sees as the insidious and problematic influence of all contemplative and mystical practices. He directly opposes all use of imagination and visualization in prayer.

> Visualization prayer is disobedience. The Bible contains everything we need for faith and practice. It is able to make the man of God "perfect, thoroughly furnished unto all good works" (2 Timothy 3:16–17). The Bible contains everything we need in order to learn how to pray correctly, and it says nothing whatsoever about imagination prayer. This is not the type of prayer that Jesus taught us to pray (Matthew 6:9–15). . . .

> Faith is not based on imagination; it is based on Scripture. "So then faith cometh by hearing, and hearing by the word of God" (Romans 10:17). God has given us everything we need in Scripture and our part is to believe what God says. "But these are written, that ye might believe that Jesus is the Christ, the Son of God; and that believing ye might have life through his name" (John 20:31). We have everything we need to know about Christ for the present dispensation in the Scripture, and we accept it by faith. "Whom HAVING NOT SEEN, ye love; in whom, THOUGH NOW YE SEE HIM NOT, yet believing, ye rejoice with joy unspeakable and full of glory" (1 Peter 1:8).[18]

Though Cloud's concerns arise from his version of biblical literalism, which is not at all the same as the position taken by Orthodox thinkers, what both have in common is the presumption of the possibility of a "pure" experience of God that a Christian can have which is entirely unsullied by any human thought or interpretation. My argument is that no such experience exists. The act of finding something meaningful is itself an imaginative act.

I think David Bryant's definition of imagination is useful here as he says that "imagining is the activity of taking something as something or of understanding things as having some sort of significance."[19] Both facets of this are operative in contemplative prayer. First, the practice presumes that the reflection, Scripture, or image can be seen as a means by which an encounter with God is accessible: the text or image is taken *as* a conduit to the divine. Second, and as a consequence of the first, experiences that arise from such

18. Cloud, *Contemplative Mysticism*, 53–54.
19. Bryant, "Imago Dei and Ecological Responsibility," 37.

contemplation are often felt to be profound or insightful. They are moments that seem fuller than usual. Regular practice of such prayer and reflection on Scripture can shape how you see the world, even when not specifically praying. A deep, consistent, and integrative reflection on Scripture is part of how one becomes acquainted and identified with the stories, symbols, and hopes of a Christian imaginary, as discussed in the last chapter.

American Catholic Biblical scholar Sandra Schneider talks about the "paschal imagination,"[20] as a way to have what we read in the Bible form how we think about and understand the world. What if we take some of Jesus' promises and encouragements as "possible worlds" and allow ourselves to act in ways that guide us there? She argues that Biblical interpretation should not be limited to historical contextualization and determining the precise meaning of the text within the frame of age in which it was written. There is also the work of "interpreting the text as the Church's normative source of revelation."[21] It is helpful to know what the texts of the Bible claim and information about the contexts in which they were written. It is also important to ask how those texts ought to speak to us today.

> The purpose of this kind of interpretation is not to extract historical information from the text but to understand what the Gospel testimony *means*—in other words, to allow the text to become the word of God in the community of believers. Here the question is not, for example, to establish factually: whether Mary Magdalene actually appears in John's Gospel as an apostle in the technical sense of the term but to understand what the Easter proclamation "I ascend to my Father and your Father, to my God any your God" (Jn 20:17) really means. What does the symbol "resurrection" convey?[22]

This does not mean that the fact-finding part of biblical scholarship ought to be dismissed. But it is insufficient if not yoked to asking about how it is shaping present meaning-making activities. Schneiders suggests that the task is to "create concretely, in the socio-historical context . . . a Gospel-based imaginative reality construction."[23] This creation is the human response, using our generative imagination in response to the divine invitation to acknowledge the reign of God. Both prayer and reading Scripture imaginatively can help us be receptive to the possible vision of the world.

---

20. Schneiders, "Paschal Imagination," 52–68.

21. Schneiders, "Paschal Imagination," 57.

22. Schneiders, "Paschal Imagination,"57.

23. Schneiders, "Women Religious in a Renewing Church," 24.

This is similar to Walter Brueggemann's argument in his classic book, *The Prophetic Imagination*.

Brueggemann, an American Presbyterian Bible scholar, attempts to understand the nature of the biblical prophets and what they were called to do, articulating it in a way that resonates with Christ's service and our current needs. Brueggemann argues that systems of power and oppression operate within a "royal consciousness" that shapes the vision and hope of people, whether they are "royal" or not. The prophet's work is to help people realize that how the powerful say the world is need not be how it remains. Prophets are catalysts of imaginary change.

For example, Brueggemann says that Moses' task was not just to lead the Israelites from enslavement under Pharaoh, but also—and perhaps more difficult—to first figure out how to help them believe that liberation was possible. Moses' "work is nothing less than an assault on the consciousness of the empire, aimed at nothing less than the dismantling of the empire both in its social practices and in its mythic pretensions."[24] Read in the context of chapter 7, it is clear that "royal consciousness" is an imaginary and the prophet's task is to shift it into one that has a greater vision of flourishing for God's people. Brueggemann writes that "it is the vocation of the prophet to keep alive the ministry of imagination, to keep on conjuring and proposing future alternatives to the single one the king wants to urge as the only thinkable one."[25] The royal consciousness operates as a kind of "totalism," that seeks to maintain the status quo as the only viable way of being.

Deeply engaging with the message of the prophets as related in Scripture helps us to remain attentive to the possibility of a new world. The development of a prophetic or paschal imagination helps Christian leaders be able to name oppressive structures of the present, seeing in them the marks of power and control from the past. Thinking about Robert Allen Warrior's call for great attention to the colonizing narrative of Canaan, it is likely worth additional interpretive labor to reckon with seeds of violence in the text itself, the results of which might well be an imagination that could provide rich resources, hope, and capacity to articulate a liberation that transcends such structures. This can be done in your own life through prayer and reflection, but it can also be proclaimed in word to others.

---

24. Brueggemann, *Prophetic Imagination*, 9.
25. Brueggemann, *Prophetic Imagination*, 40.

Preaching

Within theological education, the study and art of preaching is called "homiletics." Given the nature of preaching and the fact that new words are required from a preacher weekly, many homiletics books engage the imagination. However, few actually detail the particular role of imagination as its own area of exploration.

Several scholars have written about the connections between poets and preachers, noting how they each have to use language in a way that is evocative, transforming familiar sounds and ideas into moments of transcendence. Brueggemann provides an excellent example of this.

> The event of preaching is an event in transformed imagination. Poets, in the moment of preaching, are permitted to perceive and voice the world differently, to dare a new phrase, a new picture, a fresh juxtaposition of matters long known.[26]

As we've seen with many other areas, this broad appeal to imagination as a container or seedbed of hope is common. It is rarer to find consideration of specific challenges and opportunities resulting in reflection on imagination and theology. The same is true for writing on preaching as well. Where we see the most detailed and nuanced engagement with imagination among homiletics scholars comes from people associated with "the New Homiletic movement."

This school of thought (and practice) emerged as a response to concerns in the 1960s that traditional expository preaching was "discursive, deductive, and propositional," and therefore not as suited for connecting with contemporary Christians who were looking for more interactive and experiential reflection. The New Homiletic position was that instead of preaching being seen as a set of techniques to make clear the meaning of Scripture, it could be seen as an opportunity to use the content of Scripture to ground the creation of a transformative experience that works in the heart, mind, and spirit of a congregant.[27]

A common approach of those in the New Homiletics school is to emphasize the active role of those who listen to sermons. There is a move away from the focus being on the preacher, assuming that those listening will passively receive the content if the preacher is adequately skilled. Instead, attention is given to active reactions, responses, and acceptance (or not) of the message of a sermon. Rather than the preacher as a signal-sending

26. Brueggemann, *Finally Comes the Poet*, 109.
27. Eslinger, *New Hearing*, 11–12.

broadcaster and the listener as a signal-receiving antenna, both are framed as "co-participants" in an experience of the word of God.[28]

Many of the scholars and preachers associated with the New Homiletic discuss imagination at some level, but Paul Scott Wilson is the first to write a book on preaching that considers imagination in a prolonged and nuanced way.[29] In 1988 he published *Imagination of the Heart*,[30] taking his title from a colleague's passage that inspired him to consider imagination more deeply.

> The Bible does not push a dogma upon us; it lets us enter into events by imagination, until the story becomes our story and we are transformed by it. . . . Why turn God's love into a proposition, when in reality it is made up of two thousand years of actions? . . . Propositional and moralistic sermons both have one fault in common: They fail to mediate the actions of a saving Lord, because they fail to allow us to experience those actions for ourselves. They tell us about them; they never let us enter into them in the imaginations of our hearts.[31]

As Wilson sees it, preaching ought to be evocative and help provide people with an experiential vocabulary that can help them better notice God in the world. Imagination "gives us the ability both to see this world as it is, with Christ in the midst of our brokenness, and to imagine a world different from our own, a world already transfigured by Christ's love, already penetrated by the new order."[32] One of the compelling things about this book is that Wilson explains *how* it is that he thinks imagination does this.

In terms of the function of imagination, Wilson is very much in the vein of Coleridge, who I've discussed previously in a number of spots so far. Bottom line? Imagination allows for the reconciliation of opposites, or for things in tension to be held together generatively. As Wilson puts it, imagination is the medium in which we can have "two ideas brought together, each with its own identity, to create a third new identity by their union."[33] The preaching task requires engaging with Scripture and then finding

---

28. Bullock et al., "Preaching as the Creation of an Experience," 1.

29. I'm profoundly grateful for the work of Peter Henry, whose scholarship on imagination and homiletics was an essential part of contextualizing Wilson within preaching literature. See, for example, "Shared Imaginings: The Understanding and Role of Imagination in Contemporary Homiletics."

30. Wilson, *Imagination of the Heart*.

31. Achtemeier, *Creative Preaching*, 80.

32. Wilson, *Imagination of the Heart*, 16.

33. Wilson, *Imagination of the Heart*, 33.

contemporary contexts which can be brought together with scriptural insight to yield an experience that is formative and fulfilling.

Wilson suggests that before a preacher turns to expert technical knowledge like biblical commentaries, there should be some dedicated time for imaginative reflection on the text.[34]

> We want to hear the text laughing and angry, we want to see where it pauses and where it rushes, we want to smell and taste the air it breathes, we want to touch what it touches. More than this, we want to respond to it, resist it, question it, enjoy it, be bothered by it.[35]

One of the things that this passage makes immediately evident is that Wilson's understanding of imagination is of the broader type, encompassing all of the senses and not just "images." Another is that because the imagination is allowed to roam, it could find (or create!) connections that logical or deductive reasoning might miss. Because of this, Wilson is also clear that the imagination must be yoked to something since it is not inherently going to produce positive things. He writes that "like the relationship between head and heart, imagination is inspired by faith and faith is strengthened by imagination."[36] Imagination at the service of the Spirit of God can be a powerful part of beginning to reflect on a biblical text.

When crafting an imaginative sermon, exegesis ought only to come after allowing the imagination some time to roam.[37] Then, when turning to technical resources, one should check to ensure there are no contradictions between the imagined connections and what experts know about the text. The preacher's goal is to find some contemporary idea, story, or circumstance that feels like a good, high-tension, fit for reflection alongside Scripture, hoping that by bringing them together, she might create a "third new identity by their union." Exegesis is there to make sure that the "new identity" and new interpretation is resonant with Scripture and tradition.

Wilson's work led the way for additional scholars taking up extended reflection on imagination and homiletics, including Thomas Troeger's *Imagining a Sermon* in 1990 and more recently, Kate Bruce's *Igniting the Heart: Preaching and Imagination* from 2015.[38] Bruce goes so far as to dedicate a chapter of her book to developing a "theology of imagination," which

---

34. Wilson, *Imagination of the Heart*, 58–59.

35. Wilson, *Imagination of the Heart*, 61–62.

36. Wilson, *Imagination of the Heart*, 17.

37. Wilson, *Imagination of the Heart*, 77.

38. Bruce, *Igniting the Heart.*

she then uses to explore the context of preaching. Her building blocks are primarily ones we've discussed: Trevor Hart, Garrett Green, and John McIntyre. However, in addition to these now-familiar names, she has braided in some literature about play, arguing that preaching with some playfulness and give-and-take in it helps people to connect with it more.[39]

Via Mary Warnock, Bruce follows a Kantian perspective, affirming the role of imagination as part of all human perception.

> There is a power in the human mind which is at work in our everyday perception of the world, and is also at work in our thoughts about what is absent; which enables us to see the world, whether present or absent as significant, and also to present this vision to others, for them to share or reject. And this power . . . is not only intellectual. Its impetus comes from the emotions as much as from the reason, from the heart as much as from the head.[40]

From this, Bruce sorts the functions of the imagination into four different categories: the sensory, the intuitive, the affective, and the intellectual.[41] Giving greater emphasis to these gifts of the imagination can result in a kind of Spirit-inspired subversion that resists the status quo and extends the vision of the reign of God to the people of God through imaginative invitation.

> We can invite a congregation, in which some may be highly skeptical, to suppose in imagination that the resurrection—for example—occurred and imaginatively explore the possibilities of that supposition, even if their current experience is to doubt or deny such a possibility. In such suppositional engagement lies the invitation to faith, which is essentially rooted in the question "What if the gospel accounts of the nature of God are true? Were they to be true, then what?" This is fundamentally an imaginative question with the potential to affect our perception of reality. . . . What goes on in imagination affects who we are and how we live.[42]

Bruce develops a guide to crafting what she calls "preaching in the lyrical voice," a type of preaching full of emotion, sensorial references, and playful invitations.[43] The more vivid the scenes we invite our congregation to consider, the more possibility there is some on-ramp into change. Given

39. Bruce, *Igniting the Heart*, 49–54.
40. Warnock, *Imagination*, 196.
41. Bruce, *Igniting the Heart*, 3–28.
42. Bruce, *Igniting the Heart*, 19.
43. Bruce, *Igniting the Heart*, 55–62.

the sensorial and embodied qualities of imagination, the vividness helps to provide material for imaginative exploration.

This emphasis on transformation is part of why it is that Bruce also explores the "sacramental potential of preaching." She notes that "sacraments draw our attention to the 'more' present in the everyday" and "engage our imaginations, operating as windows, drawing us in to capture new vision." She then suggests that "if we recognize that there is a materiality about language that has the power to disclose the 'more', then we can begin to see that there is a profound sacramentality about preaching."[44] Experience of this "more" is a brush against transcendence within the immanent, a meeting of Spirit and imagination.

> The sermon is a potential bearer of disclosure that can help the hearer to reframe their view of themselves, their neighbor, and the world in the light of the self-revealing love of God. Seeing this disclosure, framing it, communicating it, receiving it and responding to it requires the active engagement of the imagination in all four functions. We notice and name grace through the sensory function; make connections between Scripture and the everyday in the intuitive function; feel the pain and dis-grace of the world, as well as the joy of life, in the affective function; shape ethical responses formulated around the "if then" model of the intellectual imagining.[45]

Note that the sermon is a "*potential* bearer" of disclosure. Bruce stops short of a full declaration that the sermon *is* a sacrament. Regardless, it is clear that she sees qualities that allow it to be thought of as deeply sacramental.

One of the things evident with both Bruce and Wilson is that the vital role of the imagination isn't just centered on the preacher. Listening to the sermon can itself be an imaginative act. In fact, developing a capacity for deep listening is useful throughout worship, not just within the period set aside for preaching.

Worship and Sacrament

Different Christian traditions practice sacraments differently, so there is no one way to write a chapter about sacramental activity and worship and have every tradition represented distinctly. Instead, I want to proceed by saying that the experience of participating in a sacrament is particularly imaginative

44. Bruce, *Igniting the Heart*, 85.
45. Bruce, *Igniting the Heart*, 85.

within the context of corporate worship. Worship and sacrament reinforce each other as part of the liturgical celebration of communities.

In a piece written to explain the connection between the sacraments and imagination, the American Catholic Alejandro García-Rivera suggests that one of their distinguishing characteristics is their relationship to imagination.

> The sacraments . . . are not things to be explained but acts that
> engage us in a very special kind of imagination, an imagination
> that flows from the origins of things. At the origins, there is only
> a special imagination, a primal imagination that can "imagine"
> us into being. . . . As such, I cannot tell you what sacraments are,
> but I can tell you why we must enter that primal imagination to
> be re-created, reimagined anew.[46]

God's "primal imagination" led to what we could call "primal creation," or as we usually refer to it, creation. What is being referenced here is the idea that only God, in creation, brought forth newness from nothing. The imagination and creation that humanity explores is not "primal" like God's, but follows after. García-Rivera suggests that engagement with the sacraments can be seen as a point of contact with the breath of God that swept over the face of the waters in Gen 1. We may not be able to create with the fullness that God did, but we can, in sacramentally rich moments, experience it.

Bob O'Gorman, a Catholic theologian and religious educator, writes that "ritual is crucial to our imaginative knowing. We have a dual consciousness—both an everyday and an altered one—present at the same time . . . we can live in the 'real world' and the mystical world simultaneously; we are citizens of both."[47] How it is that we understand these "citizenships" is profoundly shaped by the experience of sacraments and communal worship. Paul Avis, a British Anglican priest and theologian, has written about the ways in which imagination and liturgy are connected.

Avis is another scholar working in the vein of Coleridge, affirming that imagination has the capacity to stabilize ideas that are in tension. For Avis, this results in worship having an "integrative function."[48]

> It is the imagination that has the power to bind together many
> discordant and divergent elements into a unified whole. It does
> this through metaphor, symbol and myth. Only the truth of

46. García-Rivera, "Sacraments," 6–12.

47. O'Gorman, "Imagination Embodied," 34.

48. Avis, *God and the Creative Imagination*, 78.

imagination has this unifying power. Liturgy is arid and inept without it.[49]

Resonant with Peter Phan's idea of theology operating "betwixt and between" memory and an imagined future,[50] Avis insists that serious attention should be given to how liturgy must be simultaneously grounded in contemporary aesthetic responses and tradition. It is both the case that "imagination is the matrix of Christian faith"[51] *and* that worship must have its roots in what has come before to be faithful to a tradition.

> Like any artistic creation, liturgy results from the creative in-teraction between the imaginative vision of the artist and the disciplined energy of the tradition. The liturgist is above all the servant of the tradition and cannot make free with it. The liturgist is also the servant of the community and must respond to its pastoral needs. This requires a sensitivity to the religious affections of Christians in the Church today.[52]

Avis's idea of the liturgist as a simultaneous servant to tradition and community is instructive. Carried forth in worship, the pastoral needs of the community are met with an "imaginative vision" connected to a "disciplined" line of continuity with the past. The American philosopher and Reformed theologian James K. A. Smith also writes on this exact topic, though he ends up with different conclusions.

In his book, *Imagining the Kingdom: How Worship Works*, Smith argues that "we become a people who desire the kingdom insofar as we are a people who have been trained to imagine the kingdom in a certain way."[53] This "training" takes place most powerfully in communal practice or worship. The suggestion is not that worship ought to become a series of workshops or educational seminars, but that worship does the work of shaping how we imagine and act in the world. He goes so far as to suggest that worship itself is an "alternative imaginary, a way that the Spirit of God invites us into the Story of God in Christ."[54] Our practice of worship is one of the ways in which we "participate in the divine nature" (2 Pet 1:4) and engage with the story of God's work in the world. Taking part in that story is part of allowing

---

49. Avis, *God and the Creative Imagination*, 78.
50. Phan, "Betwixt and Between," 114.
51. Avis, *God and the Creative Imagination*, 73.
52. Avis, *God and the Creative Imagination*, 75.
53. Smith, *Imagining the Kingdom*, 125.
54. Smith, *Imagining the Kingdom*, 150.

God's vision to "capture our imagination."[55] It isn't just that in worship we hear Scripture, pray together, and (sometimes) partake in sacraments. It *is* those things, but it is also their aesthetic qualities that matter.

One of the centers of Smith's argument is a move to put poetry and worship in parallel. He suggests that "with liturgy, like poetry, we should beware of 'the heresy of paraphrase.'"[56] Borrowing the idea of this "heresy" from the poet Cleanth Brooks, Smith suggests we must be very cautious about attempting to split content and form.

> A poem's meaning . . . is not just a matter of its propositional content—as if the words and form and meter and all of those exquisite aspects of craft were just decorative flourishes that could be dispensed with once you got "the message." No . . . the meaning of the poem is ineluctably bound up with its form and is not reducible to what can be propositionalized or paraphrased. A poem is not just a vehicle for ideas; it means both more than that and differently than that.[57]

Smith suggests that this same dynamic is in play with worship, concluding that it is spiritually unwise to alter liturgical forms.

In Avis's terms, Smith heavily emphasizes that "the liturgist is above all the servant of the tradition" and any response to "pastoral needs" for adaptation ought not to fuss with the form of worship. He's particularly critical of attempts to make worship more appealing via changing the style or shape of a service or sanctuary.

> The forms of the mall or coffee shop are not just benign containers that can carry any content. . . . While we might think that reconfiguring worship to feel like the mall is a way of making Jesus relevant and accessible, in fact we are unwittingly teaching worshipers and seekers to treat Jesus like any other commodity they encounter in the mall, because the very form of the mall's ("secular") liturgy unconsciously trains us to relate to the world as consumers.[58]

For Smith, the aesthetics of the practice of worship are an essential part of worship itself. As he says, "it is not enough to convince our intellects; our imaginations need to be caught by—and caught up into—the Story of God's restorative, reconciling grace for all of creation. It won't be enough for us to

---

55. Smith, *Imagining the Kingdom*, 150.
56. Smith, *Imagining the Kingdom*, 171.
57. Smith, *Imagining the Kingdom*, 172.
58. Smith, *Imagining the Kingdom*, 168.

be convinced; we need to be moved."[59] The missional question that Smith doesn't quite answer is what to do about situations where people don't seem to be "moved" in this way by the liturgy as it is.

If Smith is right and form and function are so fused in worship that *how* we worship must keep to traditional forms. This raises questions for me. What is the proper response for a church leader when those forms seem ineffective in "catching people up" in God's Story? What is the basis by which we are to assess the rightness of worship? The philosopher and Free Church theologian Philip Kenneson has work that provides one compelling answer to this question.

Though Kenneson's work on imagination rests in just a single chapter within a multiauthor volume on Christian ethics, I've found his perspectives profoundly compelling. In the chapter, Kenneson is thinking through how worship can be seen as formative from the perspective of ethics. He sees imagination as one of the most important tools for examining this question. Especially given the discussion of imaginaries in chapter 7, Kenneson's work is powerful.

Influenced by Garrett Green and the idea of the "paradigmatic imagination" as discussed in chapter 4, Kenneson works from an understanding that imagination and reason are not opposed to one another but interconnected. As he says, "imagination cannot in any simple way be pitted against practical reason or judgment, since such judgments always assume and make use of prior imaginings.[60] One of Kenneson's most intriguing moves is to zoom out beyond Christian worship to think broadly about many of the ways—and reasons—people gather. In his words, "human gatherings powerfully shape the human social imagination, inevitably forming the horizon within which all human action—including worship—takes place.[61] Following this logic, he invites us to consider that "worship" might be a broader category than what faith communities do.

Kenneson notes that early uses of the word "worship" have to do with "the activity of ascribing worth."[62] Thinking this way results in a perspective that suggests we worship not only as a human response to God, but as an activity in which we assign value to different dispositions, pursuits, and relationships. He argues that human beings are inherently social beings and that whenever people gather, they cannot help but "presuppose and reinforce much about the shape, meaning, and purpose of the world that they

59. Smith, *Imagining the Kingdom*, 157.
60. Kenneson, "Gathering," 58.
61. Kenneson, "Gathering," 58.
62. Kenneson, "Gathering," 56.

understand themselves to inhabit."[63] He goes so far as to say that "to the extent
that they presuppose and reinforce certain ascriptions of worth ... *all* human
gatherings are a kind of worship."[64] Sports games in a stadium, massed bodies
in the streets for political protest, and thousands of people in line for the newest Apple cell phone are all expressions of what people value.

> For this reason, human gatherings are inevitably formative, not
> least because such gatherings construct an imaginative land-
> scape (a "world") within which all future action and reflection
> upon it will take place. . . . In short, every human life is "bent"
> toward something. Every human life is an act of worship.[65]

From Kenneson's perspective, the uniqueness of Christian worship is not
that it can form people particularly well, but *how* and *what* it forms people
toward.

That Kenneson is thinking about imagination and worship from the
perspective of ethics and ethical formation is crucial to keep in mind. It
helps him to more clearly see the ways in which how we imagine ourselves
and God to operate profoundly shapes our actions in the world.

> The reason the liturgy is given priority is not because offering
> praise and adoration to a deity is inherently more important than
> feeding the hungry or sheltering the homeless, but because learn-
> ing to praise and adore this God who was revealed most fully in
> the flesh and blood of a first-century carpenter from Nazareth
> has everything to do with the care we offer our neighbors.[66]

The shaping of a shared imagination is yoked to both identity formation
and a kind of emulation and patterning that arises from attention to Christ.

Smith cites Kenneson's chapter once in *Imagining the Kingdom*, so
he at least knows of it, but other than that, I don't know if they've engaged
one another's work on imagination and worship anywhere else in print.
I mention this because I think a conversation between the two would be
compelling. If Kenneson is correct that "every human life is 'bent' toward
something," and the measure of the power of worship has to do with the
degree to which it is pulled toward the kinds of things we understand
Christ to have done, then questions about the "right" form of worship have
more to do with *effects* of that practice than on whether or not they adhere
to the proper aesthetic form.

63. Kenneson, "Gathering," 57.
64. Kenneson, "Gathering," 57. Italics added for emphasis.
65. Kenneson, "Gathering," 57.
66. Kenneson, "Gathering," 61.

The community of disciples gathered for worship seeks to have its imagination so shaped by these formative liturgical actions that its entire life outside the liturgy will itself be a powerful expression of the worship of this God.[67]

In Smith's terms, how are we to think about "the heresy of paraphrase" given contexts where the form is "off," but the paraphrase seems to work at shaping imaginations?

For example, Smith includes a detailed mapping of "The Common Shape of the Liturgy," showing admittedly marked similarities between the shape of worship in the Catholic Church, Lutherans, Methodists, Presbyterians, and Anglicans.[68] In his reflection on this shared set of patterns, he offers the following:

> The logic of the practice cannot be paraphrased because there is an "imaginative coherence" that is undistillable and yet incredibly significant. . . . While it has been intentionally and communally crafted over time, the logic of historic Christian worship also means on a register that exceeds and eludes our conscious appropriation—which is precisely why worship isn't just something that we do; it does something to us.[69]

This leaves me with some questions. In my own denominational context of the Religious Society of Friends, our traditional liturgical and sacramental practices are far from the norm. With some mental gymnastics, I could attempt to argue that our form of silent waiting worship maps onto the liturgical chart Smith provides, but I think most liturgical theologians I know would be dubious at my claims to any outward "imaginative coherence" with other liturgical practices. Compared to Smith's yardstick, my tradition has "paraphrased" its liturgy quite a bit.

Quakers who have been part of our traditional form of silent worship have been shaped by a version of liturgy that doesn't much look like corporate Christian worship in any other tradition in the world. But we've also had a long history of being intensely "bent toward" the care we offer our neighbors, having impacted abolition, prison reform, and the development of nonviolent activism. How could our worship have "worked" if it doesn't adhere to the logic of the form? I raise this point not to praise Quakerism—Lord knows we have our own problems, just like all other traditions—but to surface an example that seems to call for more discussion. There is ambiguity

67. Kenneson, "Gathering," 60.
68. Smith, *Imagining the Kingdom*, 171.
69. Smith, *Imagining the Kingdom*, 173.

here that deserves further exploration. I think Smith is correct that the form of worship shapes the inward life of the worshiper, but what might it mean to recognize that *multiple* forms are viable and faithful?

Christian worship and the practice of sacraments clearly help to supply the materials from which our Christian imagination is built and maintained. However, to what extent that material determines the quality of faithfulness seems less clear. What *is* clear is that prayer, reading Scripture, preaching, and the form of worship are all things which can shape the values, stories, and symbols that help people to make meaning in their lives. Our imaginations are enriched by exposure to compelling content that allows for us to experience and explore faith in embodied ways. How we come to learn those stories and symbols in the first place is the question of the next chapter.

Questions for Reflection

1. Have you ever heard about or tried to pray in ways that are like the Ignatian form described? If so, what was your experience? If not, what do you think about attempting it? Does any resistance or excitement arise when you consider the possibility?

2. What do you think about the idea that one of the things that reading Scripture does is shape how it is we imagine the world? How is this different from saying we read Scripture to learn about how the world is? How is it similar?

3. This chapter describes a type of preaching that attempts to be more experiential, interactive, and connected to the senses. Have you ever experienced the kind of preaching described in this chapter? Do you think it is a useful way to consider preaching?

4. Smith says that worship itself is an "alternative imaginary, a way that the Spirit of God invites us into the Story of God in Christ." How does this claim sit with you? Any reflections on it?

5. Kenneson makes a claim that all human gatherings are formative in the sense that they "bend" people toward certain values and views on the world. If this is true, what (if anything) does this change about how you think of Christian worship?

Related Readings

Avis, Paul. *God and the Creative Imagination: Metaphor, Symbol, and Myth in Religion and Theology*. London: Routledge, 1999.

Bruce, Kate. *Igniting the Heart: Preaching and Imagination*. London: SCM, 2015.

Fleming, David L. *What Is Ignatian Spirituality?* Chicago: Loyola, 2008.

Schneiders, Sandra. *The Revelatory Text: Interpreting the New Testament as Sacred Scripture*. San Francisco: Harper, 1991.

Smith, James K. A. *Desiring the Kingdom: Worship, Worldview, and Cultural Formation*. Grand Rapids: Baker Academic, 2009.

Wilson, Paul Scott. *Imagination of the Heart: New Understandings in Preaching*. Nashville: Abingdon, 1988.

9

Education and Formation

THE WORLD VALUES SURVEY is a global network of social scientists studying changing values and their impact on social and political life. The survey consists of nationally representative surveys conducted in almost a hundred countries and includes interviews with almost 400,000 respondents. One of the portions of the survey asks respondents to consider possible qualities children can be encouraged to learn at home. The 2017–20 results below represent what percentage of those surveyed (globally and in the USA) felt each quality was "especially important."

Which qualities that children can be encouraged to learn at home are especially important?	% who consider it important (globally)	% who consider it important (USA)
Good Manners	78%	52%
Feeling of Responsibility	65%	59%
Tolerance and Respect for Others	62%	71%
Hard Work	53%	68%
Independence	42%	56%
Religious Faith	36%	32%
Determination and Perseverance	32%	39%
Obedience	32%	21%
Thrift: Saving Money and Things	30%	27%
Unselfishness	27%	28%
Imagination	21%	30%

Imagination was the least selected quality globally and ranked eighth out of eleven in the USA.[1]

Given this context, if imagination is a vital part of a life of faith, then there is significant work to be done. There is a consequent compounding effect as well: children raised in family systems with little emphasis on imagination usually become adults, often with their own children. Intervening at the level of religious education is one place where the intentional cultivation of imagination has been addressed with some regularity. In fact, several scholars talk about the task of religious education in ways that are very similar to Peter Phan's tensions between memory and an imagined future and David Brown's ideas about the imaginative interpretations of tradition. This chapter explores the explicit ways that education and formation have been written about as connected to imagination.

Religious Education

American Methodist practical theologian Mary Elizabeth Moore specializes in research on religious education. She understands the task of religious education to be about "educating for continuity and change." For her, continuity is about maintaining connective links from Christ and the early church until the present day. Affirming change means recognizing that continuity and connection can be maintained while still inviting conversion, transformation, and renewal.[2] The role of imagination is central to the process of healthy community growth.

> Imagination is not one thing; it is an action, indeed a medley of actions, exercised in relation to a context and in a singular effort or a collaborative effort with others. The purpose of imagination is finally to move creation through time and space. In the case of human educational systems, its purpose is to move the learning community and the communities with whom they relate into the future.[3]

Note that she places such a high value on imagination that it is associated directly with the movement of the community into the future. The ability to imaginatively adapt and transform forms the continuity itself.

---

1. Haerpfer et al., "World Values Survey."
2. Moore, *Educating for Continuity and Change*, 21–23.
3. Moore, "Imagination at the Center," 192–210.

For Moore, imagination is directly and distinctly tied to the capacity for people to make decisions to hope.[4] A more developed imagination yields a greater possibility for developing a critical hope. This is not pie-in-the-sky optimism but a self-reflective prayer that recognizes present conditions and considers what more might be possible.

> What is most needed now is a vision of flourishing, formed and continually reformed by a collaborative exercise of imagination. Imagination is needed first to discern the kinds of flourishing— past and present—that best contribute to the common good. It is further needed to envision alternative futures for local communities and beyond. These alternative futures will not likely be calmly chosen, easily implemented, or fully achieved visions. The very process of visioning can destabilize a community, and its instability can have salutary, negligible, or destructive consequences.[5]

The uncertainty present in imagination makes it potentially threatening to the status quo, including parts of the status quo people would rather *not* change.

Imagining that the future might be different from the present raises questions about how sufficient—or not—life is currently. Moore thinks this potential "destabilizing" is worth pursuing because "the closing of imagination and the failure to risk new ventures will likely destroy a community over time."[6] Lacking change, continuity becomes impossible because a community that cannot change cannot survive. Attempting to ignore the realities of the world changing around us, a community will yield a community that is increasingly disconnected from other communities and individuals that are open to transformation.

Our communities need to risk change because change is coming regardless, and we'd be better off doing it when we can be attentive and reflective rather than be forced into it. With attention given, change can be managed so that the community changing remains in continuity with tradition *and* experiments with forms that might yield greater flourishing. Similar themes are present in other religious education scholars' work as well.

For example, Mary C. Boys writes, "religious education is the making accessible of the traditions of the religious community and the making manifest of the intrinsic connection between tradition and transformation."[7]

4. Moore, "Youth Navigating Identities," 65–76.
5. Moore, "Imagination at the Center," 199.
6. Moore, "Imagination at the Center," 199.
7. Boys, *Educating in Faith*, 193.

Similarly, Maria Harris suggests that teaching, "when seen as an activity of religious imagination," is the "incarnation of subject matter in ways that lead to the revelation of subject matter."[8] Then, "having incarnated subject matter so that it leads to the revelation of subject matter, we discover that we (participating subjects) have received the grace of power in order to help re-create a world of communion, of justice, and of peace."[9] How, though, can religious educators encourage imagination's development and appreciation? What lessons or techniques can imaginatively support this deepening continuity, transformation, and justice? Especially for younger children, Jerome Berryman's work on "Godly Play" is often referenced.[10]

Godly Play is a form of Christian religious education and spiritual formation, created in the early 1990s and intended primarily for use with congregational youth up until the age of twelve. An American, Berryman was initially a Presbyterian pastor, though he later converted to the Episcopal Church and became a priest there. Deeply informed by the teaching and theory of Maria Montessori, Berryman's work in Godly Play understands religious practice as a kind of language or type of communication:

> We need to learn a particular religious language system well, such as Christianity, if we hope to understand another religion, such as Islam, or to make meaningful comments about religion in general. What follows is a description of a way to teach "how to speak Christian" that is wholly rooted in the creative process so that it includes both the rooting of orthodoxy and the openness needed to grow and to meet new challenges.[11]

In brief, a session of Godly Play proceeds as follows:

- Youth are welcomed into a prepared space and storytelling from the adult leader begins.

- Each story is based on a script that is provided with Godly Play literature. Each is a passage or theme from Scripture written in a developmentally appropriate way. Versions of the story are developed to match the age for the youth involved. The leader must follow the story but must not be reading it.

- Each story is paired with physical materials that represent relevant biblical characters, environments, and objects.

---

8. Harris, *Teaching and Religious Imagination*, xv.

9. Harris, *Teaching and Religious Imagination*, 77.

10. Berryman, *Godly Play*.

11. Berryman, "Playful Orthodoxy," 452.

- As the story unfolds, the materials are brought out and used to physically represent the narrative.

- After the story is complete, youth are invited to wonder about the story. The storyteller often initiates the wondering with prompts like "I wonder which part of the story felt the most important to you?" Or "I wonder what it felt like to be noticed by Jesus?" Responses to wondering are affirming.

- After wondering, the youth are asked to reflect on how they want to respond. Based on how they are feeling about the story they may choose to share a drawing, a movement, or another story that they were reminded of.

- Once the sharing is finished, all the materials are put away, drawings are set aside, and everyone settles for "the feast."

- The feast serves double duty as both "snack time," and an opportunity for community building in a manner that is preparative for taking communion.[12]

Participating in this process, youth become fluent in Christian values, stories, and symbols, learning how to use them through playful observation and experimentation rather than didactic instruction and repetition.

Berryman's work is both profoundly practical and philosophically well-developed. In addition to the many lessons and concrete instructions he has developed, he is clearly conversant with imagination and theology literature, citing Richard Kearney, Paul Ricœur, and Mary Warnock in the same book as the one from which the above list was drawn. His emphasis on play is significant as when he cites literature establishing that all mammals play and suggests that "play is much more important to religious education than either science or theology have led us to believe."[13] Youth should be encouraged to wonder and use their imagination throughout structured programs. As Berryman understands it, imagination can lead to two distinct forms of play.

> *What-if*, or wondering play, gives rise to creating new ways of doing things. *As-if*, or role play, helps form continuity by ritual and storytelling to induct children into adult roles. These two kinds of play suggest that they are grounded in the exploring (wondering play) and conserving (role play) aspects of the creative process. Religion's early function, then, was to

---

12. Berryman, *Godly Play*, 114–16.

13. Berryman, *Complete Guide to Godly Play*, 47.

cope creatively with existential trouble and to celebrate the miraculous by play, ritual, art, and storytelling. This was, perhaps, the beginning of the particular kind of discourse we now call "religious," which at its beginning was rooted in the creative process rather than in social power.[14]

In this pairing of exploration and conservation, we see again a braiding of what is and what might yet come. Play serves as a means not just to relieve tension or to provide amusement but also to try on possibilities, roles, and ways of relating. American Methodist practical theologian and religious education scholar Courtney Goto explores this point at length.

Goto's book, *The Grace of Playing*, emphasizes the importance of play in religious education. She distinguishes "playfulness" as a cheery kind of entertainment or fun from "playing," which has broader and potentially deeper resonances. Drawing on Berryman's work alongside the psychological scholarship of D. W. Winnicott and the theology of Jürgen Moltmann, Goto establishes several themes resonant with the discussions in this section. Though imagination literature isn't a significant part of her approach, she develops her arguments in ways that are clearly connected to the task of thinking about imagination and religious education.

For example, Goto develops the concept of "revelatory experiencing," identifying it as "on a continuum with revelation." She says that revelation focuses "on God's action in which God acts as the agent," whereas revelatory experiencing "draws attention to the human role in preparing for, receiving, and participating in processes of Spirit."[15] The book explores the kind of teaching environments that are more conducive to these kinds of revelatory experiences, suggesting that play can be vital in preparing people to be surprised and moved by Spirit.

Goto argues that "one need not wait for revelation to dawn or to fall from the sky. Rather, one can wisely shape pedagogies of playing that invite and prepare the faithful to welcome, experience, and fully participate."[16] She is clear that the "wise shaping of pedagogy" must be contextualized to communities because situations and needs differ from place to place. Consequently, she suggests that "facilitating revelatory experiencing requires becoming increasingly astute at imagining case by case the most conducive conditions for learners."[17] For our purposes, I think what Goto develops helps facilitators discern what imaginaries are most operative and how to work with them to

14. Berryman, "Playful Orthodoxy," 440. Italics added for emphasis.

15. Goto, *Grace of Playing*, 5.

16. Goto, *Grace of Playing*, 13.

17. Goto, *Grace of Playing*, 14.

allow for a greater chance that people are more responsive to Spirit. Though in different terms, she explores many of the same areas that are in chapter 7's list of "Questions to Help with Imagination Shifting."

At the core of her argument, she suggests that "when Christians are playing together, they are playing at/in God's new creation." This play can have profound implications because when "the faithful lose themselves in exploring a world of possibilities in Christ" they come away with the hope of being able to "live into them more fully."[18] As Goto develops it, play, while engaging, has less to do with recreation and games and far more to do with exploring what is possible.

> In playing at the new creation, Christian communities attempt to create the world to which Jesus' life, death, and resurrection point—a place where all of creation can live in justice, harmony, and authenticity. In this play world lit by the Gospel, Christians are called to engage in the creative act of seeing one another truly as brothers and sisters in Christ. In the Eucharist (a structure for playing), the faithful sense the reality to which Christians are called by believing "as if" and being reconciled to one another and to God in the sharing of Christ's body. . . . Over time Christians are formed by repeated experiences of playing together at/in the new creation.[19]

Goto does not arrive at her affirmation of the power of using "as-if" through the same scholarly sources, but there are significant similarities between her ideas of active imagining and Mary Warnock's imaginative "seeing-as."[20] Faced with the challenge of thinking through how to help people live into a promise that is "already" but "not yet," Goto turns to play as a tool to help people explore possibilities that seem currently beyond their reach. Annie Lockhart-Gilroy considers this same dynamic, specifically discussing the importance of imagination for urban youth.

Lockhart-Gilroy, another American Methodist practical theologian and religious education scholar, writes about the nurture and support youth need to thrive. One of the insights she provides is a recognition that youth in marginalized situations of economic and social dislocation aren't just impacted financially or socially. Their circumstances shape how they act in the present and imagine the future.

18. Goto, *Grace of Playing*, 33.

19. Goto, *Grace of Playing*, 33.

20. Warnock, *Imagination*, 202.

The idea of hope is not a foreign concept for these youth: They spoke of hope in God and all the things that God could do. They spoke of how God could make a way out of no way, but they spoke of this in an abstract or corporate sense. God could make a way for some people, just not for them. God could do things in the abstract, but not on a personal level. What they demonstrated was personal hopelessness. God could help other people; just not me.[21]

Lockhart-Gilroy suggests that one of the causes of this disconnect is a "crippling nostalgia that squelches the hope to explore new possibilities."[22] Especially in cities that had—and have since lost—economic stability, lots of jobs, and numerous models of success, there can be a lamentation of "the way things were," without any work for the way things could be. Getting stuck in the rear-looking position shrinks visions of what is possible. She suggests that the concept of "sankofa" can be a helpful guide, especially for communities and youth in these circumstances.[23]

Sankofa is a symbol and idea from the Akan peoples of West Africa. The concept of sankofa is that it is important to "go back and fetch" what is valuable *and* to stay facing the future. It is represented by a bird turned forward with its head reaching backwards for an egg. Lockhart-Gilroy suggests there are important lessons in this for youth and those who will work with them.

As the bird holds the egg, it holds the promise—the future. This can be seen as holding the youth, but it is important to remember that while youth are adults of the future, they are currently present in the here and now and are capable of joining in the work of imagining a way forward. For our purposes, imagine that the bird is the congregation in the urban community fighting against the work of communal crippling nostalgia. The act of moving forward is the work of youth and the imagination needed to fight personal hopelessness. The act of looking back reflects the wisdom needed from the elders. The delicate egg that is held is the theological imagination needed for the future.[24]

21. Lockhart-Gilroy, *Nurturing the Sanctified Imagination*, 26.
22. Lockhart-Gilroy, *Nurturing the Sanctified Imagination*, 18.
23. Lockhart-Gilroy, *Nurturing the Sanctified Imagination*, 34.
24. Lockhart-Gilroy, *Nurturing the Sanctified Imagination*, 35.

Figure 9.1: A sankofa symbol (Sankofa Global Project; public domain).

For Lockhart-Gilroy the idea of "joining in the work of imagining" is not abstract at all. She suggests that congregations consider programs of bidirectional mentoring in which youth and their elders enter into relationships with each other, carrying explicit intentions to learn from one another. She sees multigenerational connection as essential to nurturing a "sanctified imagination."[25]

A term often associated with African American preaching traditions, sanctified imagination is "the fertile creative space where the preacher-interpreter enters the text, particularly the spaces in the text, and fills them out with missing details: names, back stories, detailed descriptions of the scene and characters, and so on."[26] The way Lockhart-Gilroy thinks about it addresses an issue that has popped up several times in the previous chapters of this book. Numerous scholars have noted that imagination is not inherently good or bad but can become yoked to either or both kinds of intentions. Lockhart-Gilroy agrees.

The *sanctified* imagination is when imagination is discerningly yoked to service and flourishing. It is "an imagination gifted by God that enables us to be more like God and see the world through God-colored glasses so that we can participate in making the world."[27] One of the consequences of this kind of sight is a renewed capacity to envision the future differently, to

25. Lockhart-Gilroy, *Nurturing the Sanctified Imagination*, 66–80.

26. Gafney, *Womanish Midrash*, 3.

27. Lockhart-Gilroy, *Nurturing the Sanctified Imagination*, 46.

imagine that God's hope for us isn't just abstractly true, but something that can break into our own lives.

> Conditioned to construct a problematic reality, many youth have been stripped of the power of their imagination. . . . Having suffered the killing of one's ability to imagine a different life, one is left with the belief that one's perceived reality is not only an acceptable option, but the only true option. Therefore, to see a new vision, this imagination needs to be rekindled.[28]

Employing the concept of imaginaries from chapter 7, Lockhart-Gilroy's use of the phrase "stripped of the power of imagination" seems interchangeable with "coerced into accepting the dominant imaginary."

Consequently, rekindling becomes an act of refusal and a rejection of at least some part of the normative use of stories, symbols, and hopes. Lockhart-Gilroy cites the work of bell hooks to emphasize this point: "imagination is one of the most powerful modes of resistance that oppressed and exploited folk can and do use."[29] Helping youth to imagine the possibilities of the future differently can lead to them seeing themselves differently, as part of a community moving forward while reaching back for the wisdom that elders have already raised up. Then, together as a community, more pathways seem possible. A similar approach can be found in the work of Patrick Manning, an American Catholic pastoral theologian and religious education scholar.

Manning's book, *Converting the Imagination*,[30] develops a particular religious education method intended to support the growth of "post-critical meaning-making." Drawing on Charles Taylor's understanding of imaginaries (as discussed in chapter 7) and Paul Ricœur's work on symbolism and interpretation (as explored in chapter 4), Manning suggests that given contemporary culture, it is no longer viable for religious educators to try and instill in youth the same kind of faith that was possible generations ago. The truth of Christ's message can persist even as it adapts and grows with culture.

> If people are not finding meaning in the Christian tradition, it is not because there is no meaning to be found. The problem lies with the failure of Christian communities to adapt to new cultural challenges to faith. The problem is at root a problem of meaning, and meaning is always fundamentally a matter of the

28. Lockhart-Gilroy, *Nurturing the Sanctified Imagination*, 43.
29. hooks, *Teaching Critical Thinking*, 43.
30. Manning, *Converting the Imagination*.

imagination. Nostalgic appeals to the old Christian imaginary will not help such people insofar as that imaginary will never again enjoy the unquestioned acceptance it once did.[31]

In a way, Manning is pointing to the same problem as Lockhart-Gilroy's "crippling nostalgia." Religious educators should not think their charge is to nourish the faith of those in their care in such a way that it manifests just as it did when they were young. Moore would likely note that without change, continuity itself is threatened.

As Manning sees it, the appropriate task is to help youth develop their own, contextually relevant, contemporarily suited means of making meaning with the tradition. This is what he calls "post-critical meaning-making."

> The post-critical meaning-maker is more aware of the limits of her knowing and how her bodily experience, feelings and desires, relationships, social setting, and exposure to cultural productions (TV, social media, etc.) all subtly influence the way she thinks and experiences reality. Because she is more aware of these subtle forces, she is better able to modify her own desires and affective responses and to regulate her interactions with others and her consumption of media that she knows are day-by-day shaping her world view.[32]

Manning suggests this kind of reflection can encourage a deepening in faith and an experience of Christian practice as powerful. Given that the post-critical person of faith has an appreciation for embodied reflection and "extra-rational modes of thinking," it is easier to return to the stories, symbols, and practices of tradition, finding new resonances in them as well as new materials for identification and connection. This is not a "regression into naive immediacy or a repudiation of the achievements of critical consciousness," but a recovery of "the power and meaning of symbols with all their disclosive possibilities, now through interpretation instead of naive imaginings.[33] Manning offers a teaching method that he says supports this kind of learning.

Building on the philosophy of Taylor and Ricœur, Manning also braids in insights from social science, particularly from Robert Kegan. Drawing on psychological research, which shows that people grow best in social environments where they experience support *and* challenge, Kegan

---

31. Manning, *Converting the Imagination*, 10.
32. Manning, *Converting the Imagination*, 44.
33. Manning, *Converting the Imagination*, 45.

suggests we ought to be attentive to developing communities that can balance these dynamics.

> Environments that are weighted too heavily in the direction of challenge without adequate support are toxic; they promote defensiveness and constriction. Those weighted too heavily toward support without adequate challenge are ultimately boring; they promote devitalization. Both kinds of imbalance lead to withdrawal or dissociation from the context. In contrast, the balance of support and challenge leads to vital engagement.[34]

Manning sees in Kegan an affirmation of the very method Jesus used in his own teaching. From Manning's perspective, at the center of Christ's teaching was "a call to interior transformation or conversion—a transformation of what we love, how we look at reality, and, subsequently, our way of being in the world."[35] Biblically, Manning associates this most intensely with Christ's invitation in Mark 1:15 and Matt 4:17: "the kingdom of God has come near; repent [or be converted], and believe in the good news." However, Jesus didn't just say this and wait—rather, he had a method to draw people into the hope of what God's reign could be.

> In order to draw people into a vision and experience of God's reign, he told stories. Jesus' parables tend to follow a three-fold pattern: First, he activates the audience's imaginations (for example, in the parable of the good Samaritan, which begins on a familiar road that his audience could readily picture in their minds). Second, he disrupts and expands their accustomed way of seeing things (for example, by having the hated Samaritan rather than the priest or Levite come to the victim's aid). Finally, he invites them to embrace a new way of seeing (for example, by asking the audience which one was neighbor to the victim and inviting them to do likewise).[36]

Building on what he understands Christ's method to be, Manning builds out his system as the "SEE Process," graciously providing significant information about the method on his website, which also includes lesson plans and activities. The SEE approach consists of three movements:

34. Kegan, *In Over Our Heads*, 42.
35. Manning, "SEE Process."
36. Manning, "SEE Process."

1. Stimulating the imagination

2. Expanding the imagination

3. Embracing new ways of imagining[37]

In the first movement, the teacher or facilitator provides content or activities to encourage participants to consider how they experience the world, inviting them to represent their perspectives in imaginative ways. For example, the facilitator could share clips from films around the theme of "hope for the future" and invite participants to respond by sharing other clips, songs, artwork, or stories. If someone has a story to share that is their own connection, space is made for the group to listen to the individual and the connections they have made. The point of this movement is to provide a social container in which participants can further develop skills of concept-connection, meaning-making, and interest in the perspectives of others.[38]

In the second movement, the facilitator intends to broaden or deepen the possible connections that participants see as relevant to their contemporary setting. Here activities and questions "expose limits in learners' current manner of constructing meaning." The idea is to cultivate a sense that how meaning is made can always be deepened or expanded and that stories, symbols, and practices from the Christian tradition are helpful in making connections and making meaning. By being explicit about the possibility of using new sources for connection, participants hopefully develop a more profound sense of critical self-reflection, recognizing that the sources they draw on for connection and orientation can be examined critically *and* provide meaning.[39]

In the final movement, the facilitator invites participants to consider which new sources from the Christian traditions seem like they would be most helpful to continue exploring. Opportunities are provided for participants to make decisions about "whether or how they will pursue their new vision." For participants beginning to explore significantly new meaning-making, psychological and emotional support is provided. While often eventually positive, new spiritual growth can be turbulent at the moment.[40]

Ultimately, what Manning hopes the SEE method provides is a tool to help participants develop a kind of interior landscape that is intentionally populated with meaningful connections that provide a sense of self and stability in the midst of change.

37. Manning, *Converting the Imagination*, 133–34.
38. Manning, *Converting the Imagination*, 58–82.
39. Manning, *Converting the Imagination*, 83–110.
40. Manning, *Converting the Imagination*, 111–31.

Anchoring them are an image of God as Love incarnate in the person of Jesus Christ, an image of the world as the ground of the inbreaking of God's reign, and images of self and other alike as beloved children of God (or some variation thereof). . . Grounding themselves in these revealed symbols enables Christians to respond to life's challenges with greater adaptability and resilience and in a way that is authentically Christian.[41]

As Manning frames it, authenticity is more about adaptability than unchangeability. The vibrant and decisive thing isn't the human thought clung to without end but the grounding and ongoing hope for God's reign, the fullness of which we can only imagine.

Spiritual Formation and Direction

While the formal study and practice of religious education is a significant place where scholars and practitioners consider the impact of imagination on spiritual formation, it is not the only area in which this is an area of reflection. This is understandable in the sense that all spiritual formation is also imaginary formation. That is, helping people deepen in their spiritual lives will inherently entail changes in the stories, symbols, and experiences they reference to make meaning and find significance in their lives. However, more than in just a rhetorical way, imagination and formation have been written about quite a bit.

In addition to explicitly religious practices like prayer, worship, and partaking in sacraments, it is the case that a "secular" activity can be done in such a way to invite God into the space regardless. Two of the most common forms of this are reading and writing. For example, in his book *The Wounded Angel*, Paul Lakeland discusses how reading can be spiritually formative in positive ways.[42]

To the person of faith, fiction supports the love of the world as it is and contradicts the simplistic separation of the sacred and profane. To the searcher or the agnostic, fiction teases with intimations of a beyond that may be either unnerving or intriguing but cannot be ignored.[43]

---

41. Manning, *Converting the Imagination*, 138.
42. Lakeland, *Wounded Angel*.
43. Lakeland, *Wounded Angel*, ix–x.

Lakeland argues that faith practices and the act of reading "have much in common structurally."[44] What is this common structure? There are at least two clear connections.

First, imagination is used in both to apprehend and express a sense of mystery and a loving sense of the whole. Second, they both allow for someone to be "creatively engaged with transcendence, by whatever name."[45] As Lakeland has it, an "incapacity to grasp any sense of transcendence is simply a failure of imagination."[46] As such, activities that increase our capacity to sustain imaginative exploration can also develop our capacity to experience transcendence and thereby reflect on the divine.

> The creative artist, in particular but by no means exclusively the writer of prose fiction, sets out to tell a story that, if the author is successful, is somehow a conduit for the reader to grasp something that lies beyond the story. . . . When we turn to consider faith, there is no human "author" of the moment in which the believer makes the act of faith. God, we might reasonably say, is the author of the scenario, the created world, in which the act of faith necessarily takes place. But the act of faith itself is a free act of the will, informed by reason, in which the person says yes to a vision of the whole with which he or she has been presented.[47]

In terms of faith formation, "saying yes to a vision of the whole" is the central concern, far more than the specific content of the work being reflected upon. That isn't to say that the content of the novel being read doesn't matter at *all* to Lakeland, but the emphasis is clearly more on the degree to which a reader's vision is stretched and allowed to experience transcendence.

As an exercise in formation, this imaginative "saying yes" extends beyond the act of reading. The work of Eileen Daily and Robert Imbelli both suggest that there is a role for visual art to play in deepening one's faith through the experiential expansion of the imagination.[48] Experiencing art that is gripping to you can, in and of itself, be an opportunity for growth. The dynamic of concern is not which sense is used or which form of art is explored but the extent to which that exploration invites reflection and a sense of something more.

44. Lakeland, *Wounded Angel*, xii.
45. Lakeland, *Wounded Angel*, x.
46. Lakeland, *Wounded Angel*, 67.
47. Lakeland, *Wounded Angel*, 65–66.
48. E.g., Daily, "Theological Education," 116–29; Imbelli, *Rekindling the Christic Imagination*.

In sharp contrast to the Orthodox insistence on distancing an artist's self-expression and the spiritual value of an icon, others understand that self-reflectively *producing* artistic work can also be formative. Even if the result isn't the professional quality of a painter or novelist, the exploration may be of service. Kate Bruce, whose work on preaching and imagination we considered in chapter 8, has also written about how creative writing can be spiritually enriching.[49] She notes that "the point is not to produce a polished piece of art," but "to engage in a formative experience, bringing to the page the writer's lived experience of God and by grace discovering more of God through the process."[50] Intentionally allowing one's own work to be a place to encounter God suggests deepening skills of craft can support formation.

> Creative writing can take many forms: poems, stories, parables, letters, psalms, webs of associated words, vignettes, descriptive prose, and arguably journal entries which may weave together recollection and interpretation in creative ways. Such writing has the potential to become a conversation between our God-concepts, framed in the external world of liturgical engagement and theological reflection, and our God-images, formed in the internal world of early experience, question, doubt and desire. Understood in these terms, creative writing becomes the equivalent of praying with a pen in hand.[51]

Bruce's work has been more than theoretical. In research exploring the actual practice of creative writing for faith formation in communities she shows evidence that participants felt inspired and deepened by their writing, even if they didn't think of themselves as "writers" per se. She concludes that "the research bears out the idea that creative writing enables some people to explore their images of God, discovering what they already knew, but were not aware of knowing."[52] This same kind of discovery is possible in self-reflection and spiritual direction as well.

In brief, spiritual direction is "help given by one Christian to another which enables that person to pay attention to God's personal communication to him or her, to respond to this personally communicating God, to grow in intimacy with this God, and to live out the consequences of the relationship."[53] For years the tradition of Christian spiritual direction was mostly practiced in Catholic communities and retreats. However, the end

49. Bruce, "Praying with a Pen in Hand," 183–96.
50. Bruce, "Praying with a Pen in Hand," 185.
51. Bruce, "Praying with a Pen in Hand," 185.
52. Bruce, "Praying with a Pen in Hand," 195.
53. Barry and Connolly, *Practice of Spiritual Direction*, 21.

of the twentieth century saw its use expand significantly, being taken up in mainline, nondenominational, and evangelical spaces.

Richard Foster, the founder of the organization Renovaré, has been instrumental in expanding the practice. Among the things that Foster says of spiritual direction, three have direct bearing on the conversation about imagination and formation. Foster says that spiritual direction:

- Involves a process through which one person helps another person understand what God is doing and saying;

- Is characterized by a relationship in which there is absolutely no domination or control;

- Depends heavily on the use of discernment, both by the director and the directee.[54]

This presents a picture of spiritual direction in which the director is far more of a guide than a drill sergeant. By providing a space for a directee to be self-reflective, the question of how God can be seen at work becomes easier to consider. Imagining how God might be at work is more accessible when someone actively invites us into that reflection. Marlene Halpin, an American Catholic theologian, wrote about this same dynamic.

Halpin's book, *Imagine That!*, provides a basic description of imagination and its role in faith formation before rapidly moving on to specific ways spiritual directors can help their directees by calling on the imagination.[55] She reflected often on 1 Cor 2:9, noting that though "no eye has seen, nor ear heard, nor the human heart conceived, what God has prepared," we might be well served to imagine what may yet be possible. Halpin offers prompts to help guide people into discovery. One example is "The God Tree," which is "a quick, easy way to perceive how we are relating to God at a particular time in our life. It also shows us how we feel about ourselves."[56] She suggests that a director could offer this prompt to a directee when it would be useful to reflect on how they are relating to God. After helping the directee to relax, feeling grounded, prayerfully settled, and physically comfortable, this reflection could be used.

> Imagine yourself in summer, somewhere out-of-doors. It might be a place familiar to you, or it might not. But the weather is pleasant. You are alone . . . you like being there and alone. Find yourself in a pleasant, outdoor place in summer.

54. Foster, "What Is Spiritual Direction?," 30.
55. Halpin, *Imagine That!*
56. Halpin, *Imagine That!*, 63.

As you are enjoying being alone out-of-doors, you begin to realize something. (Anything is possible in imagination, you know.)
So, gently, you become aware that God is appearing to you as a
tree. A tree is God. Let that tree slowly come into focus for you.

What kind of tree is your God tree?

How does it look?[57]

With pauses between prompts and time allowed for participants to mentally explore, she also suggests possible follow-up questions. "As you are
noticing the God tree, you slowly and gently become aware that you are
a tree as well. What kind of tree are you? Let the answer come to you, let
it come into focus."[58] Once the imaginative and interior, sensorial experience is over she suggests that people can then engage their intellectual
capacities and reflect on the exploration.

What kind of tree was the God tree? What might that mean to
you? What kind of associations have you with that kind of tree?
What was the condition of the tree: healthy? barren? fruitful?
dead? Was it alone? far? near? Was it hospitable to birds? animals? people? aloof? What might these answers mean to you?

What kind of tree were you? What might that mean to you?
What kind of association have you with that kind of tree? What
was the condition of the "my" tree—healthy? barren? fruitful?
dead? Was it alone? near the God tree? near anything? Was it
hospitable to birds? animals? people? aloof? deserted? How did
you feel about seeing the "my" tree so situated?[59]

Halpin braids together the sensorial and imaginative with the analytic and
cognitive. Meaning-making can be done with the material uncovered during direction.

In all the examples in this section, imagination does not *replace* rea-
soned reflection but serves alongside it as a possible path toward discovering what we already knew but were unaware of. This is an expansion of
what is generally considered for counting as "knowledge" in the context of
Western, professional, academic spaces, including places like seminaries
and divinity schools. What might it mean if this expansion of knowing
became more accepted and present in theological education? This is the
question we now turn to.

57. Halpin, *Imagine That!*, 63.
58. Halpin, *Imagine That!*, 64.
59. Halpin, *Imagine That!*, 65.

Theological Education

Thinking about theological education as a Christian practice might first seem odd, but I think something significant is gained when we look at it this way. As I understand it, a practice is a pattern of action that (among other things) maintains, creates, and/or disrupts a social imaginary. I'm saying that attending a graduate program to get a seminary or divinity school degree does more than just provide an education. Participating in the practice of theological education doesn't just get you a degree; it is a formation of sorts as well. Paying attention to the vision of the world embedded in the practice of theological education can help us to see what else is going on in that activity other than just learning information about the church.

In this section, I explain why I think of theological education as a practice and consider what imaginaries that practice might interact with. Whenever thinking about large systems or interconnected organizations, I find it helpful to ask, "What were the circumstances in which this system began?" Answering this question for theological education is just as important. Having a sense of where theological educational systems came from provides some key insights into the imaginaries in which they are embedded. To start, we'll look at theological education's origins, returning to its roots in Europe.[60]

In the US, theological education started in the early seventeenth century, beginning with Protestant churches at Harvard and Yale. At that time, education was for young white men and was a program in which students intending to go into ministry would do their theological reading in the fourth year of what we would now call a bachelor's degree. After graduation from college, the hopeful minister-to-be would be taken into the care of an established pastor and serve as an apprentice. This model transformed in the early nineteenth century as seminaries were founded to function as institutionalized opportunities for apprenticeship. By the mid-1800s, things were already changing again. This nineteenth-century change resulted in the form of theological education that is still present today. American Christian Historian Edwin Aponte suggests that to understand this change, it is essential to look to Germany.[61]

The 1810 creation of the University of Berlin is a crucially important event in the history of theological education in the US. The founding of the university was the responsibility of William von Humboldt, the royal minister for "Ecclesiastical Affairs and Public Education" under the Prussian

---

60. My overall guide for this history is Justo González's *The History of Theological Education.*

61. Aponte, "Friedrich Schleiermacher."

king. The new university promoted by von Humboldt "was intended to set new standards for both teaching and research," and the theologian Friedrich Schleiermacher was a crucial part of the plan.[62]

> When Schleiermacher joined the new enterprise at Berlin, he brought with him the conviction that, as one embraced "modern" understandings of the world and human experience, theology could no longer be held to be the "queen of the sciences" in any self-respecting modern university, as it had been in the Middle Ages. However, he endorsed a twofold function for theology in the university, as a practical discipline for improving general pastoral care in a Christian society, and equally a general branch of scholarship, with as much potential as any hard science for research and analysis.[63]

Conceiving of theology as a science to be studied in the university setting had consequences. The "Berlin Model" of theological education became the dominant form of university-based theological education.

One of this form's major features was how it developed categories of thinking. Designed by Schleiermacher, the "fourfold curriculum" will be familiar to anyone who has studied in an institution of graduate theological education. Usually, this model manifests with departmental categories like the following:

1. Biblical studies and languages

2. Theology (fundamental/systematic/constructive)

3. History of Christianity or church history

4. Practical theology or pastoral studies

Sometimes "Christian ethics" is separated from theology as its fifth category, but even without this further split, a pattern can be discerned. Aponte points out that one of the painful consequences of this model is that Schleiermacher's original intent, "for all of it to be tied to practice, with the goal of improving general pastoral care in a Christian society," often has been forgotten and led to the fragmentation of learning. Furthermore, biblical studies, theology, and history are often "valued more highly" and taken more seriously as areas of study than practical or pastoral studies.[64] As someone trained as a practical theologian, I can personally attest to colleagues

---

62. Aponte, "Friedrich Schleiermacher," 107.

63. Aponte, "Friedrich Schleiermacher," 108–9.

64. Aponte, "Friedrich Schleiermacher," 108.

regularly making the "joke" that I work in "practical theology," and they do "real theology." This is precisely the dynamic Aponte is pointing toward.

> In addition to the issue of the dominance of these broad or-
> ganizing categories with their internal pecking order, there
> is the problem that the specific content within each category
> is increasingly fragmented, so that holistic integration across
> categories has become a burden. The four categories remain,
> even as the content of each category has become more discrete
> and disconnected.[65]

In an effort to standardize and legitimize graduate education in seminaries and divinity schools, theological disciplines became increasingly siloed. What are the implications of having the structure of theological education itself be segmented and siloed?

Aponte suggests that while this disconnection is likely problematic for Christians as a whole, it has had particular consequences for communities of color.

> Contemporary theological education, as the heir of the Uni
> versity of Berlin, is detrimental. . . . Whereas many communi
> ties of color value shared work and collaboration, its members
> who venture into theological education are confronted by
> a dominant context that fosters hyper-individualism and is
> predisposed to competition. . . . Those who perceive cultural
> insensitivities to different ways of learning and shared work are
> answered by admonitions to be more "academic" and adjust
> themselves to the "objective" standards.[66]

In the case of theological education, we see a concrete instance of what we discussed about imaginaries and institutions in chapter 7. Castoriadis suggested that institutions are "a socially sanctioned, symbolic network in which a functional component and an imaginary component are combined."[67] Our interactions with these institutions structure our experiences of community, shape our sense of self, and contribute to forming what we find valuable and imagining is possible. That theological education is pulled toward standardization *and* fragmentation has organizational consequences for the schools and spiritual significance for students. I've found some helpful reflections about this issue in the work of César Baldelomar.

65. Aponte, "Friedrich Schleiermacher," 109.
66. Aponte, "Friedrich Schleiermacher," 111.
67. Castoriadis, *Imaginary Institution of Society*, 132.

In Baldelomar's book, *Fragmented Theological Imaginings*, he considers an Aztec myth.[68] Riffing on a theme from Gloria Anzaldúa, he shares how Coyolxāuhqui was the grown daughter of Coatlicue, the Earth mother. Hearing of her mother's new pregnancy, Coyolxāuhqui felt ashamed and angered. She made plans to attack her mother but ultimately failed as Coatlicue's other children rushed in to defeat their sibling. In recalling this story, Baldelomar encourages us to realize that sometimes what we have given life to can, in fact, take life as well.

> Unlearning what one has learned in order to undo a perceived self requires a series of violent deaths: decapitations of one's epistemology, as learned from normative systems of knowledge organization, and of ontology, as scripted according to dominant disciplinary gazes (both external and internal).[69]

Following Anzaldúa, Baldelomar calls these "deaths" the "Coyolxauhqui imperative," an act of "calling back those pieces of the self/soul that have been dispersed or lost, the act of mourning the losses that haunt us."[70] He writes knowing that it can be painful to recognize that parts of the stories you have taken as your own are damaging to you and those you love.

> Teachers and writers, repeat after me: We are fractured. We are not neatly folded octavos. We are not chapters, clean breaks, limited pages, or word counts. We are not hero/ines or villains, with strictly good or bad dispositions. We are fragments beholden to cycles of death and rebirth. The myth of Coyolxauhqui also teaches us that imagination must always accompany memory on its way to reconstruction, recollection, and retelling.[71]

Trying to maintain being "neatly folded" despite our clay-footed-ness isn't just an impossible task; it also interferes with our recognition of what new ways of being might be ready to be birthed. As we imagine the future, let us not be fooled into thinking that as our organizations and institutions change, we will remain the same.

At first you could read Baldelomar and see in his advocacy for fragments and fracture some tacit support for the kind of siloing brought about by Schleiermacher. The "fourfold curriculum" certainly has fractured much of the sense of theological education's holism. Isn't this an affirmation of his call-and-response "we are fractured"? I don't think so.

68. Baldelomar, *Fragmented Theological Imaginings*, forthcoming.
69. Baldelomar, *Fragmented Theological Imaginings*, forthcoming.
70. Baldelomar, *Fragmented Theological Imaginings*, forthcoming.
71. Baldelomar, *Fragmented Theological Imaginings*, forthcoming.

Though the "fourfold curriculum" has resulted in a kind of fracturing, it came about as an attempt to show that theological studies in the Modern German university had "as much potential as any hard science for research and analysis." What I see Baldelomar pointing toward is not a fragmentation due to aiming at academic standardization and legitimacy but rather an acceptance that in our interior life, we will never be neatly folded into clearly segmented departments.

The study of theology and the study of self ought to be organic and interdisciplinary. We are both source and echo of our understandings of each other, sounding out as best we can what we think we hear God call us toward. Attention to the experiences, stories, and symbols we use to talk about seminaries and divinity schools can help us to be self-reflective about what it is we imagine these institutions are for and *who* they are for. Changing systems of theological education will change those of us who work in those systems and those who will be formed in them in the years to come.

The North American organization that oversees the accreditation of theological education programs is called the Association for Theological Schools. Dan Aleshire was the executive director of that organization from 1990 until 2017. In a recent book, he outlined what he sees as the looming horizon for the field as a whole.[72] His sense is that what comes next will be less preoccupied with technical requirements and preparation for religious leadership as a profession and more attentive to the holistic formation of the leader.

In Aleshire's words, the goal of theological education ought to be "the acquisition of a wisdom of God and the ways of God fashioned from intellectual, affective, and behavioral understanding and evidenced by spiritual and moral maturity, relational integrity, knowledge of the Scripture and tradition, and the capacity to exercise religious leadership."[73] A wordy mouthful, I nonetheless think he's on target. For the purposes of this book, I'd also note that intellect and affect both cross into imagination. I think that part of "spiritual maturity" and "religious leadership" has to do with discerning how to walk the path between continuity and change, between tradition and imagined transformation. At any level—from congregational Sunday school to national accrediting organizations—there is imaginative work to be done that can lead to greater faithful flourishing.

Since mine isn't a book about the reform of theological education systems, I won't go into great detail about what this "imaginative work" might be, but I want to point to at least one principle that might have a

72. Aleshire, *Beyond Profession.*
73. Aleshire, *Beyond Profession,* 109–10.

significant impact. As discussed throughout the book, imagination draws on what has come before, pulling from past experience, sensation, and memory, mixing it in new ways and allowing us to envision a possibility that has not yet come to be. Imaginative leadership *is* about new ways of leading, but the newness comes from affirming the importance of embodied experience and sensation as well as recognizing that how we tell stories about the past is influenced by power. Exercising religious leadership that values imaginative practice is leadership that recognizes we are not "neatly folded octavos, chapters, and clean breaks" and that it is alright for our education to reflect that.

Questions for Reflection

1. Consider the chart of values in the beginning of the chapter. Were you surprised by this information? Why or why not? What do you think about the fact that imagination seems to be valued so low? Is it because the other values are more important? Something else?

2. Moore argues that sometimes it is worth some organizational and communal destabilization if that is what is needed for change toward the better. How do you feel about this position? Have you ever experienced change in a community that was challenging but was ultimately worth it? What about change that damaged a community?

3. Lockhart-Gilroy talks about "crippling nostalgia" and the ways in which longing for the past limits our capacity to imagine the future. Is this something you have ever experienced for yourself or in a community/organization that you have been a part of?

4. Lakeland and Bruce both suggest that any creative engagement which leads to an experience of transcendence could potentially be useful for spiritual formation. How does this claim sit with you? Does it seem right? Problematic? Something else? If it *is* true, what might some of the implications of this be?

5. Did you know about the shifts in theological education and how they were influenced by the development of the modern university system? To what extent do you think that how our seminaries and divinities schools run affects our churches?

Related Readings

Berryman, Jerome. *Godly Play: An Imaginative Approach to Religious Education.* Minneapolis: Augsburg, 1995.

Halpin, Marlene. *Imagine That! Using Phantasy in Spiritual Direction.* Dubuque, IA: Religious Education Division, W. C. Brown, 1982.

Harris, Maria. *Teaching and Religious Imagination.* San Francisco: Harper & Row, 1987.

Jennings, Willie James. *After Whiteness: An Education in Belonging.* Grand Rapids: Eerdmans, 2020.

Lockhart-Gilroy, Annie. *Nurturing the Sanctified Imagination of Urban Youth.* Skyforest, CA: Urban Loft, 2020.

Manning, Patrick R. *Converting the Imagination: Teaching to Recover Jesus' Vision for Fullness of Life.* Eugene, OR: Pickwick, 2020.

Conclusion

AT A LOGISTICAL LEVEL, part of the reason I wrote this book is because I wanted an affordable and current resource that provided access to the work that has been done thus far regarding theology and imagination. I couldn't find a book out there that accomplished that, so I felt like I should work on making one myself. My hope is that you feel that I've done that. The question remains, though, beyond the surface of logistics, *why* does it matter that a book like this exists? I touched on some of this in a few spots throughout but given that most of the book was dedicated to sharing what *others* have done, I figured I owed it to you to at least tip my hand a little more and show you more of my motives.

In some ways, it is simple: I am convinced that greater attention to the imagination can be a vital part of the church's work for liberation. I frame it this way because I do a lot of work with the scholarship of Paulo Freire, a Brazilian educator whose writing and teaching on education served as one of the catalysts for Latin American liberation theologies. One of the things that Freire was clear about is that social transformation requires a set of double imaginative actions. Change comes about due to the "dialectical relationship between denouncing the present and announcing the future. To anticipate tomorrow by dreaming today."[1] Any complaining (denouncing) without speaking of a vision for what else might be possible (announcing) is insufficient. Likewise, it is hollow to voice hope without plans for removing the obstacles to get there. For Freire, dreaming is necessary as it is how the present mingles with the possible, seeding in the dreamer a desire that demands tilling by material response. I want there to be more dreaming and more demands. I want to cultivate a critical hope that grapples with the truth of carried pain *and* the future of our faith. We need one hand in the soil of history and the other calling down tomorrow's rain.

1. Freire and Shor, *Pedagogy for Liberation*, 187.

This, of course, is *not* so simple.

Bernard Lonergan has a great line that I think about a lot: "before we look for answers we want them."[2] Part of what a sanctified or liberation-focused imagination can do is bring to consciousness visions of flourishing possibilities that do not yet exist. Once we've imagined a better world, there is a hunger placed in us for the dream of tomorrow. Part of the reason I wrote this book is that more attention to imagination within the church might help us find more of that hunger and the recipes we need to feel fed. I read and write a lot, but underneath it all the reason I bother to do any of it is because I care about the flourishing of the church and those who, in their faith, become the body of Christ. I think that more discussion and practices that are explicitly attentive to imagination can help that body be more receptive to God's invitations to what more might come.

Christianity in the United States is at a precarious moment. Consider a few data points that I think help to bolster that claim. It is 2022, and just last week, the Supreme Court reversed long-standing decisions on both gun rights and abortion, making firearms more accessible and a woman's right to bodily autonomy less so. Some Christians were thrilled with the news on both counts. Others were horrified. Eighteen months ago, there was an attempted insurrection at the US Capitol and many of the folks who invaded the grounds carried Christian flags and crosses, feeling compelled to rebel because of their mingled understandings of faith and freedom.[3] It is also the case that today more than 25,000 Christians have signed a statement endorsing the importance of "Christians Against Christian Nationalism."[4] What Christianity means to people is being contested from within the tradition at the same time as those who have left the church look on with either wide eyes or unsurprised shakes of the head. Perhaps the church is always on the cusp of transformation, but if not, it certainly seems to me that now is time to consider one. How can those of us that are Christians stay close to Christ's gospel of care for the least of these and find a way forward? What stories, symbols, hopes, and values do we share? What world do we imagine we live in? What might tomorrow bring for us all?

When a group decides to rebuild a building, it is crucial to ask how it was built in the first place. What did it look like? Who wanted it to look that way? What purpose did it serve? How well did it serve that purpose? Who actively cared about that purpose? These are important facets to know so

2. Lonergan, *Topics in Education*, 83.

3. Duke Kwon's curation in "Jan. 6 Had 'Nothing' To Do With Christianity: A Photo Essay" is a startling and valuable resource.

4. See https://www.christiansagainstchristiannationalism.org/signers.

that we can ask ourselves what we want the new structure to look like. Are we trying to rebuild in the sense of recreating what was? Or do we want something that meets needs that were not addressed before? Likewise, when we say we want to reinvent something—say . . . the model of theological education or the role of a church in community building—a good parallel question is how it was invented in the first place. Who designed it? For what? Do we want to innovate on that design? Begin again? How will we be able to see something new when many of the decision-makers have already been formed in a system that predates them? When we decide to reimagine a program, a ministry, or an organization, all these questions also apply. To consider what is possible in what is to come requires a robust and adaptive imagination.

Ricœur has a line that, at first glance, seems rather silly, but that I think is actually quite important. In his Chicago lectures on imagination, he said, "we tend to call reality what we know already as reality, what has been agreed on as reality."[5] Well of course, Paul. We call a tree a tree because it *is* a tree. Right? Well . . . not quite. We call a "tree" a tree because we've been told that is the word for it and our experience suggests that when we use that word with other people our meaning comes across. We know that other folks have different words for the thing, but we know that whether we say *árvore, árbol, arbre, Baum,* or *mti* we are still talking about a tree. Except . . . some trees are more than trees.

The Fishlake National Forest in Utah has a 106-acre area covered by quaking aspen trees, each of which can grow to about eighty feet tall with trunks three feet wide and a top spread of up to thirty feet. Estimates put the number of trees in the area at above forty thousand. Except there aren't actually forty thousand trees there. There is one single, massive tree. The entirety of the aspen forest at that spot is all part of a tree that has been estimated to have been growing there for fourteen thousand years.[6] In 1992 a team of scientists confirmed that all the "trees" were actually branches of a single sprawling organism, and named it *"Pando,"* the Latin word for "I spread."[7] When I look at one of those aspen trunks and think "tree" I'm not entirely wrong, but neither am I capturing the fullness of what is the case.

5. Ricœur, "Imagination Lectures," 17:15, as cited in Taylor, "Ricoeur's Philosophy of Imagination," 93.

6. DeWoody et al., "'Pando' Lives," 493–97.

7. Grant, "Trembling Giant," 82–89.

Figure 10.1: Photo of the Aspen forest "Pando"
(United States Department of Agriculture; public domain).

To some degree, the point I'm after here can be seen as a language problem, but I think there is more to it than that. When Ricœur says, "we tend to call reality . . . what has been agreed on as reality," he reminds us that agreement is part of the process. There are limits, of course. I can't say Pando is actually made of tigers and have it be sensible, but the fact is that even something as clear, concrete, and simple as "tree" can unfold into whole new ways of thinking and perceiving. If I walk into the heart of Pando, I will be surrounded by tree. Looking around, my eyes will tell me "trees" in the plural. So will any physical contact with any of the forty thousand branches. But there, under the surface of the earth, there is a single root system connected to a single organism. One tree. How long would it take, I wonder, before I could learn to perceive *tree* and not *trees*? Could I ever? What kind of work would it take—what practices?—before I could have my *experience* feel like "tree" and match what I *know* to be tree?

Proverbs 29:18 is often cited in the context of leadership, especially in the King James translation of "where there is no vision, the people perish." Vision in this use is often understood as something like a strategic plan or organizational road map for what comes next. I agree that those things are usually helpful, but it is also the case that the "vision" here is the same word in Hebrew (*chazon*/חָזוֹן) used in 1 Sam 3:1. "The word of the Lord was rare in those days; visions were not widespread." This vision is a dream and a revelation. What the people need to flourish is vision as prophecy, seeing what might yet come to be, getting some sense of what is possible. Will everything imagined be prophecy? Not even close. That is why discernment, community, and prayer are so necessary: we need to be good at sifting through what we have seen and tasted to determine what is life-giving and God-given.

When I consider anticipating tomorrow by dreaming today, I sometimes get stuck thinking I'm just talking about the renewal of systems and social structures. It does mean that for sure, but we're also talking about a kind of relearning of perception. Dreaming today and valuing the imagination is a decision to orient ourselves in a way that makes space for the emergence of some feeling of tomorrow's possible in today's present. With its operation so intimately tied to perception, interpretation, and possibility, imagination feels like a good thing to turn to as we continue to learn and relearn so that the people do not perish. I hope this book has helped you to feel the same.

An Imagination Bibliography Timeline

700 to 400 BCE—Book of Proverbs

592 to 570 BCE—Book of Ezekiel

375 BCE—Plato's *The Republic*

350 BCE—Aristotle's *De Anima*

335 BCE—Aristotle's *Poetics*

70 to 90 CE—Book of Acts

70 to 218 CE—Book of Esdras

415—Augustine's *De Genesi ad Litteram*

1748—David Hume's *An Enquiry Concerning Human Understanding*

1790—Immanuel Kant's *Critique of Judgment*

1805—Friedrich Schelling's *The Philosophy of Art*

1807—Samuel Taylor Coleridge's *Biographia Literaria*

1867—George MacDonald's "The Imagination: Its Functions and Its Culture" in *A Dish of Orts*

1881—Horace Bushnell's "Our Gospel: A Gift to The Imagination"

1901—E. H. Johnson's *The Religious Use of Imagination*

1954—William Lynch's "Theology and The Imagination" series in *Thought: Fordham University Quarterly*

1968—Ray Hart's *Unfinished Man and the Imagination: Toward an Ontology and a Rhetoric of Revelation*

1972—Rubem Alves's *Tomorrow's Child: Imagination, Creativity, and the Rebirth of Culture*

1972—Gordon Kaufman's *God: The Problem*

1975—Paul Ricœur's Chicago "Lectures on Imagination"

1975—Gordon Kaufman's *An Essay on Theological Method*

1975—Cornelius Castoriadis's *The Imaginary Institution of Society* (in English)

1976—Amos Wilder's *Theopoetic: Theology and the Religious Imagination*

1976—Mary Warnock's *Imagination*

1978—Walter Brueggemann's *The Prophetic Imagination*

1981—Gordon Kaufman's *The Theological Imagination: Constructing the Concept of God*

1981—David Tracy's *The Analogical Imagination: Christian Theology and the Culture of Pluralism*

1982—Sallie McFague's *Metaphorical Theology*

1982—Marlene Halpin's *Imagine That! Using Phantasy in Spiritual Direction*

1987—John McIntyre's *Faith, Theology, and Imagination*

1987—Sallie McFague's *Models of God*

1987—Mark Johnson's *The Body in the Mind: The Bodily Basis of Meaning, Imagination, and Reason*

1987—Maria Harris's *Teaching and Religious Imagination: An Essay in the Theology of Teaching*

1988—Paul Scott Wilson's *Imagination of the Heart: New Understandings in Preaching*

1989—Garrett Green's *Imagining God: Theology and the Religious Imagination*

1989—David J. Bryant's *Faith and the Play of Imagination: On the Role of Imagination in Religion*

1990—Thomas Troeger's *Imagining a Sermon*

1991—John Thiel's *Imagination and Authority: Theological Authorship in the Modern Tradition*

1991—Eva Brann's *The World of the Imagination: Sum and Substance*

1991—Sandra Schneiders's *The Revelatory Text: Interpreting the New Testament as Sacred Scripture*

1995—Jerome Berryman's *Godly Play: An Imaginative Approach to Religious Education*

1998—Richard Kearney's *Poetics of Imagining: Modern to Post-modern*

1999—Garrett Green's *Theology, Hermeneutics, and Imagination*

1999—David Brown's *Tradition and Imagination: Revelation and Change*

2003—Charles Taylor's *Modern Social Imaginaries*

2004—Gordon Kaufman's *In the Beginning . . . Creativity*

2005—Kwok Pui-lan's *Postcolonial Imagination and Feminist Theology*

2006—Gordon Kaufman's *Jesus and Creativity*

2006—Emilie Townes's *Womanist Ethics and the Cultural Production of Evil*

2007—Mark Johnson's *The Meaning of the Body: Aesthetics of Human Understanding*

2008—Sandra Levy's *Imagination and the Journey of Faith*

2010—Willie James Jennings's *The Christian Imagination: Theology and the Origins of Race*

2013—Trevor Hart's *Between the Image and the Word: Theological Engagements with Imagination, Language and Literature*

2015—Kathleen Lennon's *Imagination and the Imaginary*

2015—Kate Bruce's *Igniting the Heart: Preaching and Imagination*

2020—Garrett Green's *Imagining Theology: Encounters with God in Scripture*

2020—Patrick R. Manning's *Converting the Imagination: Teaching to Recover Jesus' Vision for Fullness of Life*

2020—Annie Lockhart-Gilroy's *Nurturing the Sanctified Imagination of Urban Youth*

2022—Jason Goroncy and Rod Pattenden's (eds.) *Imagination in an Age of Crisis: Soundings from the Arts and Theology.*

2022—George Taylor et al.'s (eds.) *Paul Ricœur's Lectures on Imagination*

Bibliography

Abram, David. *The Spell of the Sensuous: Perception and Language in a More-Than-Human World*. New York: Pantheon, 1996.

Achtemeier, Elizabeth. *Creative Preaching: Finding the Words*. Nashville: Abingdon, 1980.

Adams, Suzi. *Cornelius Castoriadis: Key Concepts*. London: Bloomsbury Academic, 2014.

Aleshire, Daniel O. *Beyond Profession: The Next Future of Theological Education*. Grand Rapids: Eerdmans, 2021.

Alves, Rubem A. "Theopoetics: Longing and Liberation." In *Struggles for Solidarity: Liberation Theologies in Tension*, edited by Lorine M. Getz and Ruy O. Costa, 159–71. Minneapolis: Fortress, 1992.

———. *Tomorrow's Child: Imagination, Creativity, and the Rebirth of Culture*. New York: Harper & Row, 1972.

Aponte, Edwin D. "Friedrich Schleiermacher." In *Beyond the Pale: Reading Theology from the Margins*, edited by Miguel A. De La Torre and Stacey M. Floyd-Thomas, 105–14. Louisville: Westminster John Knox, 2011.

Aquinas. *De Veritate*. Translated by Robert W. Mulligan. 1952. https://isidore.co/aquinas/QDdeVer.htm.

Athanasius. *On the Incarnation*. https://ccel.org/ccel/athanasius/incarnation/incarnation.

Augustine. *De Trinitatae*. https://www.newadvent.org/fathers/130101.htm

Avis, Paul. *God and the Creative Imagination: Metaphor, Symbol, and Myth in Religion and Theology*. London: Routledge, 1999.

Bailey, Justin Ariel. *Reimagining Apologetics: The Beauty of Faith in a Secular Age*. Downers Grove, IL: IVP Academic, 2020.

———. "The Theodramatic Imagination: Spirit and Imagination in the Work of Kevin Vanhoozer." *International Journal of Public Theology* 12 (2018) 455–70.

Baldelomar, César. *Fragmented Theological Imaginings*. Miami, FL: Convivium, forthcoming.

Barry, William A., and William J. Connolly. *The Practice of Spiritual Direction*. San Francisco: HarperOne, 2009.

Barth, J. Robert. "Theological Implications of Coleridge's Theory of Imagination." *Studies in the Literary Imagination* 19 (1986) 23–45.

———. *Romanticism and Transcendence: Wordsworth, Coleridge, and the Religious Imagination*. Columbia: University of Missouri Press, 2003.

Barth, Karl. *Church Dogmatics*. Edinburgh: T. & T. Clark, 1961.

———. *Letters, 1961–1968*. Grand Rapids: Eerdmans, 1981.

Beck, Richard. *Unclean: Meditations on Purity, Hospitality, and Mortality*. Cambridge, UK: Lutterworth, 2012.

Bednar, Gerald J. *Faith as Imagination: The Contribution of William Lynch, S.J.* New York: Sheed & Ward, 1996.

Berendsen, Desiree. "Imagination and Art in the Christian Faith: On Imagination and Art in the Church." In *Crossroad Discourses Between Christianity and Culture*, edited by Jerald D. Gort et al., 215–32. Currents of Encounter 38. Amsterdam: Rodopi, 2010.

Berryman, Jerome. *The Complete Guide to Godly Play, Volume 1*. Denver: Living the Good News, 2002.

———. *Godly Play: An Imaginative Approach to Religious Education*. Minneapolis: Augsburg, 1995.

———. "Playful Orthodoxy: Reconnecting Religion and Creativity by Education." *Sewanee Theological Review* 48 (2005) 436–56.

Boys, Mary. *Educating in Faith*. San Francisco: Harper & Row, 1989.

Brackley, Dean. *The Call to Discernment in Troubled Times: New Perspectives on the Transformative Wisdom of Ignatius Loyola*. New York: Crossroad, 2004.

Braithwaite, William C. *The Beginnings of Quakerism*. Cambridge: Cambridge University Press, 1955.

Brann, Eva. *The World of the Imagination: Sum and Substance*. Savage, MD: Rowman & Littlefield, 1991.

Brown, David. *Tradition and Imagination: Revelation and Change*. New York: Oxford University Press, 1999.

Browning, Don S. *A Fundamental Practical Theology: Descriptive and Strategic Proposals*. 1st ed. Minneapolis: Fortress, 1996.

———. "Ricœur and Practical Theology." In *Paul Ricœur and Contemporary Moral Thought*, edited by John Wall et al., 251–63. New York: Routledge, 2002.

Bruce, Kate. *Igniting the Heart: Preaching and Imagination*. London: SCM, 2015.

———. "Praying with a Pen in Hand: An Exploration of the Effects of Creative Writing on People's Images of God." *Anvil* 24 (2007) 183–96.

Brueggemann, Walter. *Finally Comes the Poet: Daring Speech for Proclamation*. Minneapolis: Fortress, 1989.

———. *The Prophetic Imagination 40th Anniversary Edition*. Baltimore: Project Muse, 2018.

———. *Texts Under Negotiation: The Bible and Postmodern Imagination*. Minneapolis: Fortress, 1993.

Bryant, David J. *Faith and the Play of Imagination: On the Role of Imagination in Religion*. Macon, GA: Mercer University Press, 1989.

———. "Imago Dei, Imagination, and Ecological Responsibility." *Theology Today* 57 (2000) 35–50.

Buber, Martin. *Between Man and Man*. Translated by Ronald Gregor Smith. London: Kegan Paul, 1947.

Bullock, Jeffery, et al. "Preaching as the Creation of an Experience: The Not-So-Rational Revolution of the New Homiletic." *The Journal of Communication and Religion* 21 (1998) 1–9.

Castoriadis, Cornelius. *The Imaginary Institution of Society.* Cambridge: MIT Press, 1998.

———. "Radical Imagination and the Social Instituting Imaginary." In *Rethinking Imagination: Culture and Creativity,* edited by Gillian Robinson and John Rundell, 136–54. New York: Routledge, 1994.

———. "Socialism and Autonomous Society." In *Cornelius Castoriadis, Political and Social Writings, Volume 3, 1961–1979: Recommencing the Revolution: From Socialism to the Autonomous Society,* edited and translated by David Ames Curtis, 314–31. Minneapolis: University of Minnesota Press, 1993.

———. *World in Fragments: Writings on Politics, Society, Psychoanalysis, and the Imagination.* Stanford, CA: Stanford University Press, 1997.

Chauncy, Charles. "Enthusiasms Described and Caution'd Against." In *The Great Awakening: Documents Illustrating the Crisis and Its Consequences,* edited by Alan Heimert and Perry Miller, 231. Indianapolis: Bobbs-Merrill, 1967.

Chittick, William C. *The Sufi Path of Knowledge: Ibn al-Arabi's Metaphysics of Imagination.* Albany, NY: State University of New York, 1989.

Cloud, David. *Contemplative Mysticism: A Powerful Ecumenical Bond.* Port Huron, MI: Way of Life Literature, 2008.

Coleridge, Samuel Taylor. *Biographia Literaria, Chapters I–IV, XIV–XXII: Wordsworth, Prefaces and Essays on Poetry, 1800–1815.* Edited by George Sampson. Cambridge: Cambridge University Press, 1920.

Conniff, Richard. "When Continental Drift Was Considered Pseudoscience." *Smithsonian Magazine,* June 2012. https://www.smithsonianmag.com/science-nature/when-continental-drift-was-considered-pseudoscience-90353214/.

Daily, Eileen. "Theological Education at the Art Museum." *Journal of Adult Theological Education* 6 (2009) 116–29.

Daly, Mary. *Beyond God the Father: Toward a Philosophy of Women's Liberation.* Boston: Houghton Mifflin, 1973.

Dawney, Leila. "Social Imaginaries and Therapeutic Self-Work: The Ethics of the Embodied Imagination." *The Sociological Review* 59 (2011) 535–52.

Dearborn, Kerry. *Drinking from the Wells of New Creation: The Holy Spirit and the Imagination in Reconciliation.* Eugene, OR: Cascade, 2014.

DeRoo, Neal. "Richard Kearney's Relevance for Psychology: A Review Essay." *Journal of Phenomenological Psychology* 51 (2020) 207–25.

DeWoody, Jennifer, et al. "'Pando' Lives: Molecular Genetic Evidence of a Giant Aspen Clone in Central Utah." *Western North American Naturalist* 68 (2008) 493–97.

Djuth, Marianne. "Veiled and Unveiled Beauty: The Role of the Imagination in Augustine's Esthetics." *Theological Studies* 68 (2007) 77–91.

Duque, João Manuel. "Para uma Teologia do futuro como futuro da Teologia." *Carthaginensia* 35 (2019) 343–76.

Edward, Farley. *The Fragility of Knowledge: Theological Education in the Church and the University.* Philadelphia: Fortress, 1988.

Eisenhauer, David C. "Up in the Air: Informing and Imagining Climate Adaptation along the New Jersey Shore." PhD diss., Rutgers, 2019.

Engmann, Joyce. "Imagination and Truth in Aristotle." *Journal of the History of Philosophy* 14 (1976) 259–65.

Eslinger, Richard L. *A New Hearing: Living Options in Homiletic Method.* Nashville: Abingdon, 1987.

Falcetano, Michelle J. "Confession as Narrative Contemplation: The Role of the Imagination in Saint Augustine's Religious Epistemology." PhD diss., Villanova University, 2018.

Fettes, Mark. "Senses and Sensibilities: Educating the Somatic Imagination." *Journal of Curriculum Theorizing* 27 (2011) 114–29.

Feuerbach, Ludwig. *The Essence of Christianity.* Translated by Marian Evans. New York: Blanchard, 1855.

———. *The Essence of Faith According to Luther.* Translated by M. Cherno. New York: Harper & Row, 1967.

Fischer, Kathleen. *The Inner Rainbow: The Imagination in Christian Life.* Ramsey, NJ: Paulist, 1983.

Fleming, David L. *What Is Ignatian Spirituality?* Chicago: Loyola, 2008.

Foster, Richard J. *Celebration of Discipline: The Path to Spiritual Growth.* San Francisco: Harper & Row, 1978.

———. "What Is Spiritual Direction?" *Christianity Today* 53 (2009) 30.

Fowler, James. "Future Christians and Church Education." In *Hope for the Church: Moltmann in Dialogue with Practical Theology*, edited Theodore Runyon, 93–111. Nashville: Abingdon, 1979.

Freire, Paulo, and Ira Shor. *A Pedagogy for Liberation: Dialogues on Transforming Education.* Westport: Bergin & Garvey, 1987.

Frost, Gloria. "Medieval Aristotelians on Congenital Disabilities and Their Early Modern Critics." In *Disability in Medieval Christian Philosophy and Theology*, by Scott M. Williams, 51–79. Milton: Routledge, 2020.

Gafney, Wilda C. *Womanish Midrash: A Reintroduction to the Women of the Torah and the Throne.* Louisville: Westminster John Knox, 2017.

Gaonkar, Dilip Parameshwar. "Toward New Imaginaries: An Introduction." *Public Culture* 14 (2002) 1–19.

García-Rivera, Alejandro. *The Community of the Beautiful: A Theological Aesthetics.* Collegeville, MN: Liturgical, 1999.

———. "Sacraments: Enter the World of God's Imagination." *U.S. Catholic* 59 (1994) 6–12.

Gardner, Sebastian, ed. *Philosophy Guidebook to Kant and the Critique of Pure Reason.* London: Routledge, 1999.

Gare, Arran. "From Kant to Schelling to Process Metaphysics: On the Way to Ecological Civilization." *Cosmos and History: The Journal of Natural and Social Philosophy* 7 (2011) 26–69.

Gaudin, Sharon. "50 Years of Star Trek: Boldly Inspiring Generations of Scientists." *Computerworld*, September 8, 2016. https://www.computerworld.com/article/3118059/50-years-of-i-star-trek-i-boldy-inspiring-generations-of-scientists.html.

Geniusas, Saulius. "Between Phenomenology and Hermeneutics: Paul Ricœur's Philosophy of Imagination." *Human Studies* 38 (2015) 223–41.

Getty Museum Collection. "Claude Monet." http://www.getty.edu/art/collection/artists/257/claude-monetfrench-1840-1926/.

González, Justo L. *The History of Theological Education.* Nashville: Abingdon, 2015.

González-Andrieu, Cecilia. *Bridge to Wonder: Art as a Gospel of Beauty.* Waco, TX: Baylor University Press, 2012.

Goto, Courtney T. *The Grace of Playing: Pedagogies for Leaning into God's New Creation.* Eugene, OR: Pickwick, 2016.

Graber, Evan. "The Shape of Imagination in the Theology of John McIntyre." PhD diss., University of Edinburgh, 2020.

Grant, Michael C. "The Trembling Giant." *Discover* 14 (1993) 82–89.

Grau, Marion. *Refiguring Theological Hermeneutics: Hermes, Trickster, Fool.* New York: Palgrave Macmillan, 2014.

Green, Garrett. *Imagining God: Theology and the Religious Imagination.* Grand Rapids: Eerdmans, 1998.

———. *Imagining Theology: Encounters with God in Scripture, Interpretation, and Aesthetics.* Grand Rapids: Baker Academic, 2020.

———. Review of *The Analogical Imagination,* by David Tracy. *Zygon* 17 (1982) 419–21.

———. Review of *The Theological Imagination: Constructing the Concept of God,* by Gordon D. Kaufman. *Religious Studies Review* 9 (1983) 219–22.

———. *Theology, Hermeneutics, and Imagination: The Crisis of Interpretation at the End of Modernity.* New York: Cambridge University Press, 2000.

Greene, Maxine. "Imagination and the Healing Arts." https://maxinegreene.org/uploads/library/imagination_ha.pdf.

Haerpfer, C., et al, eds. "World Values Survey: Round Seven—Country-Pooled Datafile Version 4.0." Madrid, Spain: JD Systems Institute & WVSA Secretariat, 2022. doi: 10.14281/18241.18.

Halpin, Marlene. *Imagine That! Using Phantasy in Spiritual Direction.* Dubuque, IA: Religious Education Division, W. C. Brown, 1982.

Haney Lopez, Ian F. "The Social Construction of Race: Some Observations on Illusion, Fabrication, and Choice." *Harvard Civil Rights-Civil Liberties Law Review* 29 (1994) 1–62.

Happel, Stephen, and James Walters. *Conversion and Discipleship: A Christian Foundation for Ethics and Doctrine.* Philadelphia: Fortress, 1986.

Harper, Douglas. "Apocalypse (n.)." https://www.etymonline.com/word/apocalypse#etymonline_v_15471.

———. "Hermeneutic (adj.)." https://www.etymonline.com/word/hermeneutic#etymonline_v_9189.

Harris, Maria. *Teaching and Religious Imagination.* San Francisco: Harper & Row, 1987.

Hart, Ray L. *Unfinished Man and the Imagination: Toward an Ontology and a Rhetoric of Revelation.* New York: Herder & Herder, 1968.

Hart, Trevor. *Between the Image and the Word: Theological Engagements with Imagination, Language and Literature.* Burlington: Ashgate, 2013.

———. "Eschatology." In *The Oxford Handbook of Evangelical Theology,* edited by Gerald R. McDermott, 262–75. New York: Oxford University Press, 2010. https://doi.org/10.1093/oxfordhb/9780195369441.003.0018.

———. "Imagination for the Kingdom of God? Hope, Promise, and the Transformative Power of an Imagined Future." In *God Will Be All In All: The Eschatology of Jürgen Moltmann,* edited by Richard Bauckham, 49–76. Edinburgh: T. & T. Clark, 1999.

———. "An Interview with Professor Trevor Hart." https://www.transpositions.co.uk/an-interview-with-professor-trevor-hart/.

———. "Why Imagination Matters." In *Imagination in an Age of Crisis: Soundings from the Arts and Theology,* edited by Jason Goroncy and Rod Pattenden, 48–67. Eugene, OR: Cascade, 2022.

Hartman, Geoffrey H. "On the Jewish Imagination." *Prooftexts* 5 (1985) 201–20.

Hays, Richard. "The Conversion of the Imagination: Scripture and Eschatology in 1 Corinthians." *New Testament Studies* 45 (1999) 391–412.

Hefner, Phillip. *The Human Factor: Evolution, Culture, Religion*. Minneapolis: Fortress, 1993.

———. *Technology and Human Becoming*. Minneapolis: Fortress, 2003.

Henry, Peter. "Shared Imaginings: The Understanding and Role of Imagination in Contemporary Homiletics." PhD diss., Princeton Theological Seminary, 2009.

Hobbes, Thomas. *The Elements of Law Natural and Politic*. https://library.um.edu.mo/ebooks/b13602317.pdf.

———. *Leviathan*. https://www.gutenberg.org/files/3207/3207-h/3207-h.htm.

hooks, bell. *Teaching Critical Thinking: Practical Wisdom*. New York: Routledge, 2010.

Horstmann, Rolf-Peter. *Kant's Power of Imagination*. Cambridge: Cambridge University Press, 2018.

Hume, David. *An Enquiry Concerning Human Understanding*. https://www.gutenberg.org/files/9662/9662-h/9662-h.htm.

Ignatius of Loyola. *The Autobiography of St. Ignatius*. https://www.gutenberg.org/files/24534/24534-h/24534-h.htm.

———. *Spiritual Exercises of St. Igatius*. Translated and edited by Louis J. Puhl. Eastford, CT: Martino Fine Books, 2010.

Imbelli, Robert P. *Rekindling the Christic Imagination: Theological Meditations for the New Evangelization*. Collegeville, MN: Liturgical, 2014.

Isasi-Díaz, Ada Maria. "Burlando Al Opresor: Mocking/Tricking the Oppressor: Dreams and Hopes of Hispanas/ Latinas and Mujeristas." *Theological Studies* 65 (2004) 340–62.

———. "Lo Cotidiano: A Key Element of Mujerista Theology." *Journal of Hispanic/ Latino Theology* 10 (2002) 5–17.

———. *Mujerista Theology: Theology for the Twenty-First Century*. Maryknoll, NY: Orbis, 1996.

James, William. *The Principles of Psychology*. https://www.gutenberg.org/files/57628/57628-h/57628-h.htm.

Jennings, Willie James. *The Christian Imagination: Theology and the Origins of Race*. New Haven: Yale University Press, 2010.

John Paul II, Pope. *To Artists*. Boston: Pauline, 1999.

"Johnson & Graham's Lessee v. McIntosh." https://www.oyez.org/cases/1789-1850/21us543.

Johnson, E. H. *The Religious Use of Imagination*. New York: Silver & Burdett, 1901.

Johnson, Mark. *The Body in the Mind: The Bodily Basis of Meaning: Imagination and Reason*. Chicago: The University of Chicago, 1987.

Jones, Serene. "Feminist Theology and the Global Imagination." In *The Oxford Handbook of Feminist Theology*, edited by Sheila Briggs and Mary McClintock Fulkerson, 24–42. Oxford: Oxford University Press, 2012.

Justiano, Silouian. "Imagination, Expression, Icon: Reclaiming the Internal Prototype." *Orthodox Arts Journal*, October 10, 2017. https://orthodoxartsjournal.org/imagination-expression-icon-reclaiming-internal-prototype/.

Kamalaśīla. *Buddhist Meditation: Tranquillity, Imagination and Insight*. Cambridge: Windhorse, 2012.

Kant, Immanuel. *Critique of the Power of Judgment*. Translated by Werner Pluhar. Indianapolis, IN: Hackett, 1987.

————. *Critique of Pure Reason.* Translated by Paul Gyer and Allen W. Wood. New York: Cambridge University Press, 1998.

Kaufman, Gordon. *An Essay on Theological Method.* Missoula, MT: Scholars, 1975.

————. *God—Mystery—Diversity.* Minneapolis: Fortress, 1996.

————. *God the Problem.* Cambridge: Harvard University Press, 1972.

————. *In Face of Mystery.* Cambridge: Harvard University Press, 1993.

————. *In the Beginning . . . Creativity.* Minneapolis: Fortress, 2004.

————. *Jesus and Creativity.* Minneapolis: Fortress, 2006.

————. "On Thinking of God as Serendipitous Creativity." *Journal of the American Academy of Religion* 69 (2001) 409–26.

————. *The Theological Imagination: Constructing the Concept of God.* Philadelphia: Westminster, 1981.

Kearney, Richard. *Modern Movements in European Philosophy: Phenomenology, Critical Theory, Structuralism.* Indianapolis: Indiana University Press, 1995.

————. *Poetics of Imagining: Modern to Post-Modern.* New York: Fordham University Press, 1998.

————. *The Wake of Imagination: Toward a Postmodern Culture.* Minneapolis: University of Minnesota, 1988.

Keefe-Perry, L. Callid. "Schooling the Imagination: A Practical Theology of Public Education." PhD diss., Boston University, 2020.

————. *Way to Water: A Theopoetics Primer.* Eugene, OR: Cascade, 2014.

Kegan, Robert. *In Over Our Heads: The Mental Demands of Modern Life.* Cambridge: Harvard University Press, 1994.

Kenneson, Phillip. "Gathering: Worship, Imagination, and Formation." In *The Blackwell Companion to Christian Ethics,* edited by Stanley Hauerwas and Samuel Wells, 53–69. Malden, MA: Blackwell, 2006.

Kim, Kyung Hee. "The Creativity Crisis: The Decrease in Creative Thinking Scores on the Torrance Tests of Creative Thinking." *Creativity Research Journal* 23 (2011) 285–95. https://doi.org/10.1080/10400419.2011.627805.

Kind, Amy. "Introduction." In *The Routledge Handbook of Philosophy of Imagination,* 1–12. London: Routledge, 2016.

King, Martin Luther, Jr. "I Have a Dream." Speech presented at the March on Washington for Jobs and Freedom, Washington, DC, August 28, 1963. Special Collections, March on Washington, Part 17. https://openvault.wgbh.org/catalog/A_76C3B93 B557D4976A032C27C72ACED18#at_89.00_s.

Kuhn, Thomas S. *The Structure of Scientific Revolutions.* Chicago: University of Chicago Press, 1962.

Kwok, Pui-lan. *Postcolonial Imagination and Feminist Theology.* Louisville: Westminster John Knox, 2005.

Kwon, Duke. "Jan. 6 Had 'Nothing' To Do With Christianity: A Photo Essay." https://twitter.com/dukekwondc/status/1479303622697500678.

Lakeland, Paul. *The Wounded Angel: Fiction and the Religious Imagination.* Collegeville, MN: Liturgical, 2017.

Langan, Janine. "The Christian Imagination." In *The Christian Imagination: The Practice of Faith in Literature and Writing,* edited by Leland Ryken, 63–80. Colorado Springs: Shaw, 2002.

L'Engle, Madeleine. *A Circle of Quiet.* New York: Farrar, Straus & Giroux, 1972.

Lennon, Kathleen. *Imagination and the Imaginary.* Oxfordshire: Routledge, 2015.

Levy, Sandra M. *Imagination and the Journey of Faith*. Grand Rapids: Eerdmans, 2008.

Lewis, C. S. *The Last Battle*. San Francisco: HarperCollins, 1990.

Linhares, Bruno. "Nevertheless I Am Continually with You." PhD diss., Princeton Theological Seminary, 2008.

Lockhart-Gilroy, Annie. *Nurturing the Sanctified Imagination of Urban Youth*. Skyforest, CA: Urban Loft, 2020.

Lonergan, Bernard. *Topics in Education: The Cincinnati Lectures of 1959 on the Philosophy of Education*. Toronto: University of Toronto Press, 1988.

Loomis, David. "Imagination and Faith Development." *Religious Education* 83 (1988) 251–63.

Lucas, Thomas. "Grandeur of God." *Company* 13 (1995) 17–18.

MacDonald, George. *A Dish of Orts: Chiefly Papers On the Imagination, and On Shakespeare*. London: Low and Marston, 1895.

Mackinac Center for Public Policy. "The Overton Window." https://www.mackinac.org/OvertonWindow.

Manning, Patrick R. *Converting the Imagination: Teaching to Recover Jesus' Vision for Fullness of Life*. Eugene, OR: Pickwick, 2020.

———. "SEE Process." https://blogs.shu.edu/patrickmanning/see-process/.

Martin, Douglas. "Madeleine L'Engle, Author of the Classic 'A Wrinkle in Time,' Is Dead at 88." *New York Times*, September 8, 2007. https://www.nytimes.com/2007/09/08/books/08lengle.html.

Matherne, Samantha. "Kant's Theory of the Imagination." In *The Routledge Handbook of Philosophy of Imagination*, 55–68. Routledge Handbooks in Philosophy. London: Routledge, 2016.

McFague, Sallie. "Imaginary Gardens with Real Toads: Realism in Fiction and Theology." *Semeia* 13 (1978) 241–61.

———. *Metaphorical Theology: Models of God in Religious Language*. Philadelphia: Fortress, 1982.

———. *Models of God: Theology for an Ecological, Nuclear Age*. Philadelphia: Fortress, 1987.

McIntyre, John. *Faith, Theology, and Imagination*. Edinburgh: The Handsel, 1987.

Merton, Thomas. "Lectio Divina." *Cistercian Studies Quarterly* 50 (2015) 5–37.

Middleton, J. Richard. *The Liberating Image: The Imago Dei in Genesis 1*. Grand Rapids: Brazos, 2005.

Mills, C. Wright. *The Sociological Imagination*. New York: Penguin, 1959.

Mills, Kevin. *Approaching Apocalypse: Unveiling Revelation in Victorian Writing*. Lewisburg: Bucknell University Press, 2007.

Montessori, Maria. *The Absorbent Mind*. New York: Holt, 1967.

Moore, Mary Elizabeth. *Educating for Continuity and Change: A New Model for Christian Religious Education*. Nashville: Abingdon, 1983.

———. "Imagination at the Center: Identity on the Margins." *Process Studies* 34 (2005) 192–210.

———. "Youth Navigating Identities: Charting the Waters through Narrative." In *Complex Identities in a Shifting World: Practical Theological Perspectives*, edited by Pamela Couture et al., 65–76. Zürich: Lit Verlag, 2015.

Murphy, Michael P. *A Theology of Criticism: Balthasar, Postmodernism, and the Catholic Imagination*. Oxford: Oxford University Press, 2008.

Newman, John Henry. *Discussions and Arguments on Various Subjects.* 4th ed. London: Pickering, 1882.

O'Gorman, Robert T. "Imagination Embodied: The Sacraments Reappropriated." *Religious Education* 111 (2016) 430–46. https://doi.org/10.1080/00344087.2016.1185768.

O'Malley, John W. "Jesuit Schools and the Humanities Yesterday and Today." *Studies in the Spirituality of Jesuits* 47 (2015) 28–29.

Pearson, Jacqueline. *Women's Reading in Britain, 1750–1835.* Cambridge: Cambridge University Press, 1999.

Phan, Peter C. *Being Religious Interreligiously: Asian Perspectives on Interfaith Dialogue.* Maryknoll, NY: Orbis, 2004.

———. "Betwixt and Between: Doing Theology with Memory and Imagination." In *Journeys at the Margin: Toward an Autobiographical Theology in American-Asian Perspective*, edited by Peter Phan and Jung Young Lee, 113–34. Collegeville, MN: Liturgical, 1999.

Phillips, Julie. "'The Fantastic Ursula K. Le Guin." *The New Yorker Magazine*, October 10, 2016. https://www.newyorker.com/magazine/2016/10/17/the-fantastic-ursula-k-le-guin.

The Philokalia. Translated by Phillip Sherrard and Kallistos Ware. London: Faber & Faber, 1984.

Planck, Max. *Year Million: Science at the Far Edge of Knowledge.* Edited by Damien Broderick. New York: Atlas, 2008.

Pramuk, Christopher. *Sophia: The Hidden Christ of Thomas Merton.* Collegeville, MN: Liturgical, 2009.

Rausch, Thomas P. *Eschatology, Liturgy, and Christology: Toward Recovering an Eschatological Imagination.* Collegeville, MN: Liturgical, 2012.

Reinders, Hans S. *Receiving the Gift of Friendship: Profound Disability, Theological Anthropology, and Ethics.* Grand Rapids: Eerdmans, 2008.

Reklis, Kathryn. "Imagination and Hermeneutics." In *The Oxford Handbook of Jonathan Edwards*, edited by Douglas A. Sweeney and Jan Stievermann, 309–23. London: Oxford, 2021.

Resnick, Irven M. *Marks of Distinction: Christian Perceptions of Jews in the High Middle Ages.* Washington, DC: Catholic University of America Press, 2012.

Ricœur, Paul. *Freud and Philosophy: An Essay on Interpretation.* Translated by Dennis Savage. London: Yale University Press, 1970.

———. *Hermeneutics and the Human Sciences.* New York: Cambridge University Press, 1981.

———. *Interpretation Theory: Discourse and the Surplus of Meaning.* Fort Worth, TX: Texas Christian University Press, 1976.

———. "The Model of the Text: Meaningful Action Considered as Text." *Social Research* 38 (1971) 529–55.

———. "Poetry and Possibility: An Interview." In *A Ricœur Reader: Reflection and Imagination*, edited by Mario Valdés, 6–21. Toronto: University of Toronto Press, 1991.

———. *Time and Narrative.* Translated by Kathleen McLaughlin and David Pellauer. Chicago: University of Chicago Press, 1984.

Rivera, Mayra. "Thinking Bodies: The Spirit of a Latina Incarnational Imagination." In *Decolonizing Epistemologies: Latina/o Theology and Philosophy*, edited by Ada María Isasi-Díaz and Eduardo Mendieta, 207–25. New York: Fordham University Press, 2011.

Romocea, Cristian. *Church and State: Religious Nationalism and State Identification in Post-Communist Romania*. London: Bloomsbury, 2012.

Rorty, Richard. *Contingency, Irony, and Solidarity*. Cambridge: Cambridge University Press, 1989.

Rose, Seraphim. *Letters from Father Seraphim*. Houston: Nikodemos Orthodox Publication Society, 2008.

Rush, Ormond. *Still Interpreting Vatican II: Some Hermeneutical Principles*. Mahwah, NJ: Paulist, 2004.

Saiving, Valerie. "The Human Situation: A Feminine View." *The Journal of Religion* 40 (1960) 110–24.

Sartre, Jean-Paul. "The Psychology of Imagination." In *Jean-Paul Sartre: Basic Writings*, edited by Stephen Priest, 89–105. New York: Routledge, 2001.

Schneiders, Sandra M. "The Paschal Imagination: Objectivity and Subjectivity in New Testament Interpretation." *Theological Studies* 43 (1982) 52–68.

———. *The Revelatory Text : Interpreting the New Testament As Sacred Scripture*. 2nd ed. Collegeville, MN: Liturgical, 1999.

———. "Women Religious in a Renewing Church: Development or Demise?" In *God Has Begun a Great Work in Us*, edited by Jason King and Shannon Schrein, 3–27. Maryknoll, NY: Orbis, 2015.

Sellars, Jeff T. *Reasoning Beyond Reason: Imagination as a Theological Source in the Work of C. S. Lewis*. Eugene, OR: Pickwick, 2011.

Sewell, Elizabeth. "The Death of the Imagination." *Logos: A Journal of Catholic Thought and Culture* 1 (1997) 154–92.

Shedinger, Robert F. "Kuhnian Paradigms and Biblical Scholarship: Is Biblical Studies a Science?" *Journal of Biblical Literature* 119 (2000) 453–71.

Shields, Christopher. "Aristotle's Psychology." *The Stanford Encyclopedia of Philosophy*, edited by Edward N. Zalta. https://plato.stanford.edu/archives/win2020/entries/aristotle-psychology/.

Shields, John M. *An Eschatological Imagination: A Revisionist Christian Eschatology in the Light of David Tracy's Theological Project*. New York: Lang, 2008.

Smith, James K. A. *Desiring the Kingdom: Worship, Worldview, and Cultural Formation*. Grand Rapids: Baker Academic, 2009.

———. *Imagining the Kingdom: How Worship Works*. Grand Rapids: Baker Academic, 2013.

Smith, Justin E. H. *The Problem of Animal Generation in Early Modern Philosophy*. Cambridge: Cambridge University Press, 2006.

Stevenson, Leslie. "Twelve Conceptions of Imagination." *The British Journal of Aesthetics* 43 (2003) 238–59.

Stockitt, Robin. *Imagination and the Playfulness of God: The Theological Implications of Samuel Taylor Coleridge's Definition of the Human Imagination*. Eugene, OR: Pickwick, 2011.

Studzinski, Raymond. "Tutoring the Religious Imagination: Art and Theology as Pedagogues." *Horizons* 14 (1987) 24–38.

Summerell, Orrin F. "The Theory of the Imagination in Schelling's Philosophy of Identity." *Idealistic Studies* 34 (2004) 85–98.

Sveshnikov, Sergei. *Imagine That: Mental Imagery in Eastern Orthodox and Roman Catholic Private Devotion through the Writings of Great Saints.* San Francisco: Kyrill, 2015.

Tattersall, Ian Y. *Becoming Human: Evolution and Human Uniqueness.* London: Harcourt, 1998.

Taylor, Charles. *Modern Social Imaginaries.* London: Duke University Press, 2007.

Taylor, George H. "Ricœur's Philosophy of Imagination." *Journal of French and Francophone Philosophy* 16 (2006) 93–104.

Thayer, H. S. "Plato on the Morality of Imagination." *The Review of Metaphysics* 30 (1977) 594–618.

Thiel, John. *Imagination and Authority: Theological Authorship in the Modern Tradition.* Minneapolis: Fortress, 1991.

Thompson, J. B. "Hermeneutics." In *The Social Science Encyclopedia*, edited by Adam Kuper and Jessica Kuper, 360–61. Routledge World Reference. New York: Routledge, 1996.

Thompson, Leonard. "A Sociological Analysis of Tribulation in the Apocalypse of John." *Semeia* 36 (1986) 147–74.

Timalsina, Sthaneshwar. "Imagining Reality: Image and Visualization in Classical Hinduism." *Southeast Review of Asian Studies* 35 (2013) 50–69.

Tovar-Restrepo, Marcela. *Castoriadis, Foucault, and Autonomy: New Approaches to Subjectivity, Society, and Social Change.* London: Continuum, 2012.

Townes, Emilie Maureen. *Womanist Ethics and the Cultural Production of Evil.* New York: Palgrave Macmillan, 2006.

Tracy, David. *The Analogical Imagination: Christian Theology and the Culture of Pluralism.* New York: Crossroad, 1981.

Tracy, David, and John B. Cobb. *Talking About God: Doing Theology in the Context of Modern Pluralism.* New York: Seabury, 1983.

Ursic, Elizabeth. "Imagination, Art, and Feminist Theology." *Feminist Theology* 25 (2017) 310–26.

Vanhoozer, Kevin J. *Is There a Meaning in This Text? The Bible, the Reader, and the Morality of Literary Knowledge.* Grand Rapids: Zondervan, 2009.

Viladesau, Richard. *Theological Aesthetics: God in Imagination, Beauty, and Art.* New York: Oxford University Press, 1999.

Warnock, Mary. *Dishonest to God.* London: Continuum, 2010.

———. *Imagination.* London: Faber & Faber, 1976.

———. *Imagination and Time.* Cambridge: Blackwell, 1994.

———. "Religious Imagination." In *Religious Imagination*, edited by James P. Mackey, 142–57. Edinburgh: Edinburgh University Press, 1986.

Warrior, Robert Allen. "Canaanites, Cowboys, and Indians." *Christianity and Crisis* 49 (1989) 261–65.

Watson, Gerard. "Imagination: The Greek Background." *Irish Theological Quarterly* 52 (1986) 54–65.

Wilder, Amos N. *Early Christian Rhetoric: The Language of the Gospel.* Cambridge: Harvard University Press, 1971.

———. "The Relation of Eschatology to Ethics." PhD diss., Yale, 1933.

Williams, Raymond. *Marxism and Literature.* New York: Oxford University Press, 1977.

Wilson, Ken. *Mystically Wired: Exploring New Realms in Prayer.* Nashville: Nelson, 2012.

Wilson, Paul Scott. *Imagination of the Heart: New Understandings in Preaching.* Nashville: Abingdon, 1988.

Woolf, Michael. "What Reparations Is Costing My Church." *Sojourners*, February 23, 2022. https://sojo.net/articles/what-reparations-costing-my-church.

Yale Youth Ministry Institute. "Imagination – Dr. Rodger Nishioka." *YouTube*, 2013. https://www.youtube.com/watch?v=s9_EXaFj2lc.

Zeitz, Joshua. "Does the White Working Class Really Vote against Its Own Interests?" *Politico*, December 31, 2017. https://www.politico.com/magazine/story/2017/12/31/trump-white-working-class-history-216200.

Zygulski, Piotr. "Catholic Eschatological Imagination and the Mystics of Fire: Possible Perspectives for a Muslim-Christian Dialogue." *Religions* 13 (2022) 219–42.

Index

sensory, xiii, 8, 11, 15–16, 25, 53, 154,
182–83
sermon, 4, 50, 179–81, 183, 224
Sewell, Elizabeth, 58, 236
Shedinger, Robert F., 45–47, 236
Shields, Christopher, 12, 236
Shields, John M., 137, 236
Shor, Ira, 217, 230
simulacrum, 57–58
sin, 6, 57–58, 64–66, 85, 116, 131, 139
Sinai, 152
smell, 26, 53, 173, 181
Smith, James K. A. , 170, 185, 191, 236
Smith, Justin E. H. , 131, 185–91, 228,
236
Smithsonian, 229
solidarity, xiv, 66, 101, 132, 227, 236
soteriology, 117
soul, 12–14, 57–59, 83, 110, 117, 130,
149, 158, 175, 213
sound, 26, 83, 93, 118, 127, 179
spirit, 12, 33–34, 46, 59–60, 67, 89, 91,
93, 116–17, 123–30, 140–41,
163, 172–75, 179, 181–83, 185,
190, 197–98
spirituality, xxiii, 4, 25, 172–73, 175,
191, 230, 235
Stevenson, Leslie, 23–24, 236
Stockitt, Robin, 18–19, 236
storytelling, 159, 195–97
structuralism, 233
student, xix–xx, 88, 122, 210, 212
Studzinski, Raymond, 123, 236
subject, 20, 23, 91, 111, 116, 120, 150,
152, 155, 162, 168, 195
subjectivity, 17–18, 57, 154
suffering, 93, 135, 164–65, 175, 201
Sufi, xxiii, 229
Summa Theologica, 13, 26, 130. See
also Aquinas
Summerell, Orrin F. , 18, 237
Sveshnikov, Sergei, 175, 237
symbolic, 9, 43, 132, 150, 171, 174, 212
symbolism, 75, 94, 201

taste, 15, 56, 138, 173, 181
Tattersall, Ian Y. , 132, 237

Taylor, Charles, xxi–xxii, xxvii, 152, 169,
201, 225
technology, 133, 137, 232
Thayer, H. S., 10, 237
theodramatic, 127–28, 227
theopoetic, 118–19, 141, 224, 227, 233
therapeutic, 154, 229
Thiel, John, 99, 114, 126, 224, 237
Thompson, Leonard, 43, 237
Thompson, J.B., 36, 43, 237
totalism, 178
Tovar-Restrepo, Marcela, 155, 237
Townes, Emilie, xxi, xxvii, 157–60, 163,
168–69, 225, 237
Tracy, David, xxi, 95–96, 105, 110, 224,
231, 236–37
tradition, xiii–xiv, xxii–xxiii, xxvi, 4–5,
21, 50, 52, 74, 76, 81–83, 91,
96–98, 100–103, 105–7, 109,
111–15, 126, 135, 137–38, 147,
150–51, 155, 165, 170, 174–75,
179, 181, 183, 185–87, 189, 193–
94, 200–202, 204, 207, 214, 218
traditionalism, 83, 90
transcendence, 9, 16–17, 58, 82, 100,
106, 117, 121, 123–24, 133, 140,
174, 178–79, 183, 206, 215
translation, 6–7, 220
transmission, 83
Trump, Donald, 79, 238
trust, 6, 83–85, 104, 122
truth, xv, 6, 8–11, 16, 26, 33, 42, 52–55,
58, 61–62, 64–65, 69–70, 81,
86–89, 96–97, 103–6, 111–12,
117–18, 122, 126, 135, 145, 157,
160, 184, 201, 217, 229
Twitter, 115, 233

universalization, 27, 39, 43, 63–64, 91,
110
Ursic, Elizabeth, 133, 237
utopia, 49, 91–92, 137

Van Gogh, Vincent, 39
Vanhoozer, Kevin J, 38, 51, 227, 237
Vatican, 47, 110, 125–26, 236
Viladesau, Richard, 28, 237